SOCIAL COGNITION

Social Cognition

How Individuals Construct
Social Reality

Herbert Bless
University of Mannheim, Germany

Klaus Fiedler
University of Heidelberg, Germany

Fritz Strack
University of Würzburg, Germany

Psychology Press
Taylor & Francis Group

HOVE AND NEW YORK

First published 2004 by Psychology Press
27 Church Road, Hove, East Sussex, BN3 2FA, UK

www.psypress.co.uk

Simultaneously published in the USA and Canada
by Taylor & Francis Inc.,
270 Madison Avenue, New York, NY 10016

Reprinted 2005

Psychology Press is part of the Taylor & Francis Group

British Library Cataloguing in Publication Data
A catalogue record for this book is available from the British Library

Library of Congress Cataloging-in-Publication Data
Bless, Herbert.
  Social cognition : how individuals construct social reality / Herbert
Bless, Klaus Fiedler, Fritz Strack.
      p. cm. – (Social psychology, ISSN 1368-4574)
Includes bibliographical references and index.
  ISBN 0-86377-828-3 (hardcover) – ISBN 0-86377-829-1 (pbk.)
  1. Social perception. I. Fiedler, Klaus, 1951–. II. Strack, Fritz,
1950–. III. Title. IV. Series: Social psychology (Philadelphia, Pa.)
  BF323.S63B55 2003
  302–dc21
                                                                    2003001508

  ISBN 0-86377-828-3 (hbk)
  ISBN 0-86377-829-1 (pbk)

Cover design by Joyce Chester
Painting by Vasily Kandinsky, *Composition VIII*, July 1923, oil on
canvas, 140×201 cm. Copyright © ADAGP, Paris and DACS,
London, 2004.
Cover artwork: Copyright © Solomon R. Guggenheim Foundation,
New York
Typeset in Palatino by Mayhew Typesetting, Rhayader, Powys
Printed and bound in the UK by TJ International Ltd, Padstow, Cornwall

Contents

Series preface

Social Psychology: A Modular Course, edited by Miles Hewstone, aims to provide undergraduates with stimulating, readable, affordable, and brief texts by leading experts committed to presenting a fair and accurate view of the work in each field, sharing their enthusiasm with students, and presenting their work in an approachable way. Together with three other modular series, these texts will cover all the major topics studied at undergraduate level in psychology. The companion series are: *Clinical Psychology*, edited by Chris R. Brewin; *Developmental Psychology*, edited by Peter Bryant; and *Cognitive Psychology*, edited by Gerry Altmann and Susan E. Gathercole. The series will appeal to those who want to go deeper into the subject than the traditional textbook will allow, and base their examination answers, research projects, assignments, or practical decisions on a clearer and more rounded appreciation of the research evidence.

Also available in this series:

Attitudes and Attitude Change
By Gerd Bohner and Michaela Wänke

Attribution: An Introduction to Theories, Research, and Applications
By Friedrich Försterling

Prosocial Behaviour
By Hans-Werner Bierhoff

The Social Psychology of Aggression
By Barbara Krahé

For more information about this series please visit the *Social Psychology: A Modular Course* web page at http://www.psypress.co.uk/socialmodular

Preface

How do people think about the world? How do individuals make sense of their complex social environment? What are the underlying mechanisms that determine our understanding of the social world? Researchers in social cognition focus primarily on the investigation of the mental processes that mediate between the input from a stimulus and a person's behaviour. Historically, investigating mental processes has not always been a popular enterprise in the various subfields of psychology. However, unlike other disciplines within psychology, social psychology traditionally has placed a strong emphasis on how individuals internally represent their environment. Social cognition research, drawing on these historical roots and borrowing concepts from cognitive psychology, deals with the specific cognitive processes that are involved when individuals think about the social world. The social cognition perspective holds that an understanding of how individuals behave in the social world essentially requires an understanding of their mental processes. Researchers in social cognition therefore investigate how social information is encoded, how the information is stored and retrieved from memory, how social knowledge is structured and represented, and what processes are involved when individuals form judgments and make decisions. Over the last two decades, social cognition research has become a central part of social psychology and has exerted a strong influence on virtually every field within social psychology, including attitude change, person perception, and prosocial and antisocial behaviour.

The primary goal of the present book is to provide an introduction to the realm of social cognition by examining the main concepts and how they interrelate. What we hope to present to the reader is an insight into the whole social cognition framework. We have tried to do this, first, by discussing the key concepts from different perspectives, stating and re-stating the core assumptions and seeking to emphasize how the various aspects of social cognition are related to each other; and second, by deliberately choosing not to be exhaustive in our coverage of research findings. While we believe that this selectiveness makes it easier to grasp the broader picture, the unavoidable consequence is that some important aspects will not be discussed. Similarly, it was not our goal to include all the latest developments and research findings. In writing an introductory textbook, our goal has been to strike a balance between a clear organization of the material and sufficient attention to qualifications, controversies, and the latest developments. This selectiveness is also made possible because the book is part of a larger series. Because other volumes will cover important material (for example, volumes on attribution processes, on person perception and stereotyping, on attitude and attitude change, etc.) the present book does not need to cover aspects addressed in these volumes.

Our attempt to provide a solid overview of social cognition research is reflected not only in the selective content of the book but also in its structure. The different aspects of social cognition—how information is perceived, encoded, stored and retrieved from memory, and how judgments are formed—are all interdependent. Ideally, one would like to examine them simultaneously. However, the linear structure of a book imposes a sequential presentation. To keep readers from getting lost in the details before they have a grasp of the overall pattern, we have opted for a *step-by-step approach*. The first two chapters provide a general overview of the sequence of information processing and outline general principles. Here we address the core concepts and themes of social cognition research. Subsequent chapters will pick up the issues raised in the first two chapters and provide a more in-depth discussion. Because the same principles will be discussed from different perspectives and on different levels, some redundancy is unavoidable. We felt that this was a small price to pay, and this redundancy may in fact help the reader to review and reinforce the key concepts. It is our hope that readers will come to share our view that social cognition addresses a highly fascinating field within social psychology, and that the present book will encourage them to pursue this field in greater depth beyond this introduction.

Acknowledgements

In writing this book, we were provided with very supportive ideas, comments, and help from numerous persons. We would especially like to thank Miles Hewstone and all the people from Psychology Press for their support, encouragement, and patience. We also received very valuable insights from reviewers who commented on a prior version. We are very grateful for their input. In particular we would like to thank the students in our classes for providing us with comments from their perspective.

Introduction: What is social cognition research about? 1

Making sense: Constructing social reality

What determines how we think and feel about our social environment? How do we form impressions about other people? What determines our social behaviour? For the most part, the social environment of individuals is very complex and dynamic, with no two situations ever entirely the same. But individuals need to "understand" each and every situation in order to interact successfully with others. And while making sense of social situations often seems easy and simple on the surface, in actuality it poses an enormous challenge. As a consequence, individuals need a highly differentiated system of "tools" to accomplish this essential task.

To get a sense of the magnitude of this challenge, think of some very simple examples. Imagine yourself at a lively party, similar to

Credit: Art Directors and TRIP.

the one shown in the picture. A lot of people are standing around in groups, carrying on lively conversations; others are dancing. Some of the guests you have known for a long time; others you have never seen or met before. Chatting with some guests, you hear about a person who helped a friend cheat on an exam. Walking through the room you overhear another person exclaiming, "Any time I start a new project, I know I will succeed." In another corner of the room two friends of yours are engaged in a loud argument, but you have no idea what it is about. Finally, the next day, on your way to class, you see a new acquaintance from the party standing in a group of people, but she does not greet you.

What would be your impressions about the different persons in all these situations? How would you feel? What would you do if you had to interact with these persons? One common response to these questions is "It depends." Among other things, it depends on how the perceiver interprets the specific behaviour he or she witnessed. For example, if you assumed that your new acquaintance simply did not see you, you would feel quite differently than if you assumed that she saw you and intentionally avoided greeting you. Depending on your interpretation, you would presumably respond very differently to this person the next time you met her. The notion that the same objective input can be interpreted in very different ways is similarly reflected in the other examples. You might consider the person who helped a friend on the exam dishonest because he was cheating, or helpful because he supported his friend. Similarly, someone who claimed that he was successful on every new project could be perceived as haughty and arrogant—or as self-confident.

As these examples illustrate, the same stimulus input may result in different interpretations of a given situation. Individuals construct their own subjective social reality based on their perception of the input. It is this construction of social reality, rather than the objective input, that determines behaviour in a complex social world. For example, if you believe that your new acquaintance intentionally avoided greeting you, it is this subjective interpretation that guides your behaviour—even if objectively your acquaintance simply did not see you. If you ever had an argument with a friend over some misunderstanding, you will remember how two persons experiencing the same situation may construct very different subjective realities, depending on their own perspectives. Sometimes the differences in interpretations are so glaring it is hard to believe that the two individuals actually experienced the same situation.

The assumption that individuals construct their subjective social reality and that this construction provides the basis for social behaviour leads us to the very heart of social cognition research: How is an "objective" situation transferred into subjective reality? How do individuals construct social reality? What processes mediate between a specific input situation and behaviour? Why does the same input often result in different interpretations? How is the interpretation influenced by prior social experiences and knowledge? These are precisely the kinds of questions that social cognition addresses. Social cognition research is thus concerned with the study of social knowledge and the cognitive processes that are involved when individuals construct their subjective reality.

Different perspectives on the social thinker

Not surprisingly, individuals may have different general motives when they construct their own social reality—and the history of social cognition research reflects these different motives. One perspective maintains that individuals try to perceive the world just as they believe it is. In more general terms, individuals act as *consistency seekers* (Fiske & Taylor, 1991) who strive for consistency between their prior beliefs about the world and their interpretation of a specific new situation. Imagine someone who believes he is smart and has just learned that he did poorly on an exam. In order to create some consistency between his self-image as smart and the poor performance on the exam, he could, for example, discount the diagnostic value of the exam and argue that it tested unimportant peripheral abilities. This interpretation allows him to maintain his prior belief. Research has shown that the need for consistency is a major influence on the way individuals construct social reality. It is incorporated into many theoretical approaches, most prominently in Festinger's dissonance theory (1957; see also the volume on *Attitudes and Attitude Change* by Bohner & Wänke, 2002, in *Social Psychology: A Modular Course*). The basic assumption in Festinger's theory, as in many other consistency theories (for an overview see Abelson, Aronson, McGuire, Newcomb, Rosenberg, & Tannenbaum, 1968), is that inconsistencies in social thinking (for example, "I am a smart person" and "I failed an important exam") can create a negative, aversive feeling. This aversive state in turn motivates individuals to reduce the inconsistency, for example by changing one element of it ("After all, the exam wasn't really that important"), or by adding additional elements ("I would have performed better if I had not been partying all night prior to the exam"); for more recent theorizing on this motivated social thinking see Kunda (1990).

Fortunately, or unfortunately, the social world is not always consistent, which means that new information is not always consistent with a person's prior social knowledge. It is easy to see how individuals who strive only for consistency sometimes create rather inaccurate constructions of social reality. However, since a person needs a reasonably accurate perception of the world in order to act successfully in a complex social world, these inaccurate constructions may turn out to be quite maladaptive for social interactions, if not in all, at least in many situations. A second perspective on the social thinker captures this need to perceive the world accurately. It suggests that individuals gather all relevant information

unselectively and construct social reality in an unbiased manner. The interpretation of the world is barely influenced by any form of wishful thinking, and conclusions are drawn in an almost logical, scientific manner. This perspective regards the human thinker as a *naive or lay scientist*, and in particular it is articulated in attribution theories. Attribution theories address how people explain behaviour and events (e.g., Jones & Davis, 1965; H. H. Kelley, 1972; see also the volume on *Attribution* by Försterling, 2001, in *Social Psychology: A Modular Course*). For example, to find an explanation for why you failed the exam, you might consider other students' performance on this exam, your performance on other exams, and particular situational circumstances that might have caused the failure. The naive scientist perspective holds that we would elaborate on the available information and process it in an unbiased manner in order to find out the cause of the event.

In many situations, individuals are overwhelmed with information. They simply cannot perceive and use all information and consequently have to use strategies that may simplify and short cut information processing. Credit: Art Directors and TRIP.

Research has shown that individuals can act like lay scientists under certain conditions. In many situations, however, individuals are not sufficiently able or motivated to engage in systematic, elaborative thinking. For example, in social situations individuals must respond within a reasonable period of time and often have to make their judgments very quickly. Moreover, even in simple social interactions there is so much information to be processed that individuals are not always willing or able to act as a naive scientist. Instead, individuals have developed mental short cuts that allow them to simplify their processing. This is captured in the third perspective, that of the social thinker as *cognitive miser* (Fiske & Taylor, 1991). It maintains that individuals, especially when they are under time pressure or confronted with an unusually complex situation, strive to simplify the cognitive processes. Like the naive scientist, the cognitive miser is aiming for high accuracy—however, under the constraint of strategies that are faster and require less effort. For example, when watching the numerous advertising spots on television, we are unlikely to process the provided information extensively. Instead, we may often rely on simplifications (e.g., well, if this celebrity is in favour of the product, it must be good). Although cognitive misers may sometimes come up with different conclusions to those implied by a quasi-normative lay scientist perspective, the evolved mental short cuts often serve very well in everyday life.

It is also possible that individuals are quite flexible in their strategy when constructing subjective social reality. Sometimes they act as consistency seekers, sometimes as naive scientists, and sometimes as cognitive misers. This flexibility is captured in the fourth perspective, that of the social thinker as *motivated tactician* (Fiske & Taylor, 1991). This model holds that individuals may have multiple strategies, which can be applied depending on the situational constraints. For example, when individuals perceive a situation as highly relevant to them personally, they are more likely to engage in elaborative processing than act as cognitive misers. Conversely, when faced with strong time pressure, individuals are less likely to consider all relevant information as a lay scientist and more likely to rely on available and applicable short cuts (e.g., Petty & Cacioppo, 1986).

These different perspectives have received different emphasis at various times in the course of social cognition research (see Fiske & Taylor, 1991). But regardless of their underlying assumptions about the nature of the social thinker, over the years social cognition researchers have become increasingly interested in the specific *cognitive processes* of the construction of *social* reality. How is social knowledge stored in memory? How do individuals deal with the enormous amount of incoming information? How do they relate new information to their prior social knowledge? In the last two decades, the primary focus in social cognition has rested on the investigation of how social information is encoded, how the information is stored and retrieved from memory, how social knowledge is structured and represented, and what processes are involved when individuals compute judgments and make decisions. As already expressed by the term "social cognition," social cognition research combines *social* and *cognitive* elements. In the next two sections, we will briefly address the importance of the these two components, the cognitive and social elements of social cognition.

The cognitive component of social cognition

Social cognition researchers investigate how individuals mentally construct social reality because they believe that social behaviour, rather than being directly determined by the external stimulus of a situation, is mediated by the internal mental representation of that situation. Understanding social behaviour essentially requires an understanding of these internal mediating processes. Although the investigation of mediating processes seems rather straightforward from such a perspective, psychologists have not always been interested in the hidden link between external stimuli and overt behavioural responses. In particular, behaviourists have proposed that (social) behaviour can be explained better in terms of reinforcement contingencies (reward and punishment; e.g., Skinner, 1938), or in terms of contiguity (e.g., Watson, 1930) rather than in terms of mediating cognitive processes. Of course, these researchers did not deny the existence of mental processes. They argued, however, that unlike external stimuli and overt behaviour, cognitive processes cannot be observed objectively. Consequently they suggested treating internal processes as *black box* phenomena beyond the realm of psychological science.

By contrast, social cognition researchers argue that scientific theorizing about mental processes is a fruitful enterprise and that testable hypotheses can be derived from these theories. This general assumption is deeply grounded in the work of Gestalt theorists. The latter (e.g., Koffka, 1935; Wertheimer, 1945) always emphasized that it is not the stimulus per se that influences our behaviour but our perception of it; in other words, the way in which we mentally construct and represent reality. They suggested that a person's response to a particular stimulus depends on the context in which it is embedded. As a result, the whole is more than the mere sum of all the parts. In very general terms, the context in which a particular stimulus is interpreted

THE CAT

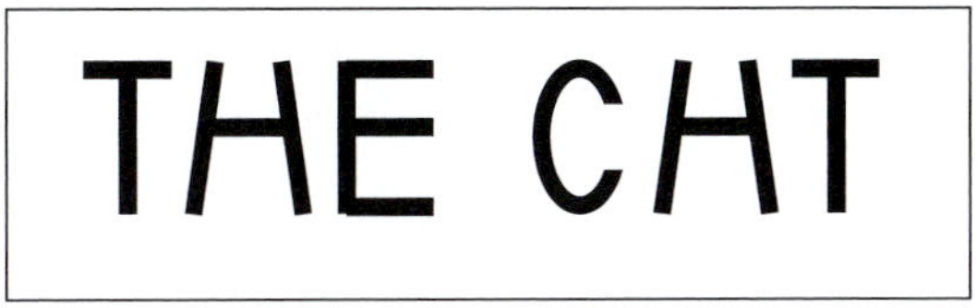

Figure 1.1.

The influence of context information on letter perception. In the example, the same identical feature is interpreted differently, in the first word as an "H" and in the second word as an "A" (after Selfridge, 1955).

may take two different forms: The context may vary as a function of other stimuli that are present in the same situation, or it may vary as a function of the prior (social) knowledge that is used to interpret the target stimulus. Both cases can be illustrated with fairly simple tasks. For example, most people have no problem reading the words depicted in Figure 1.1. Although objectively identical, the two middle "letters" in Figure 1.1 are interpreted differently, either as "H" in THE or as "A" in CAT (Selfridge, 1955).

In the "THE CAT" example, the interpretation of the same stimulus is altered depending on which other stimuli are present in the situation. As another possibility, prior social knowledge that is brought to the situation may constitute different contexts and may similarly alter the interpretation of a given stimulus. Figure 1.2a is a rather ambiguous stimulus. It can be seen either as a young woman or an old woman. Prior exposure to another situation can influence how individuals interpret the same input. When individuals are first presented with Figure 1.2b they are more likely to see the young woman in Figure 1.2a. In contrast, when first presented with 1.2c, individuals are more likely to see the old woman. Due to the prior exposure, individuals process the same stimulus (1.2a) in the context of different prior knowledge. Depending on which prior knowledge is used, a young or an old woman is reflected in a person's subjective reality.

The context dependency of social judgment is a highly fascinating phenomenon, and there are numerous examples of how the same stimulus is perceived and evaluated differently depending on the situational context. For example, in one situation individuals may interpret "helping to cheat in an exam" as "dishonest" and in another situation as "helpful." One may argue that this context sensitivity is a flaw of social judgment. As the "THE CAT" example illustrates, however, context dependency is by no means a flaw of social judgment. On the contrary: Context sensitivity in constructing social reality has a highly important function for adaptive behaviour in a complex world. To quote Henri Tajfel (1969), one of the most prominent European social psychologists: "[T]he greatest adaptive advantage of man is his capacity to modify his behaviour as a function of

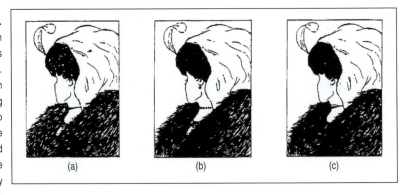

(a)   (b)   (c)

the way in which he perceives and understands a situation" (p. 81). Ignoring the cognitive link that causes this context sensitivity would result in a highly impoverished perspective of human behaviour. Excluding this link altogether would restrict human behaviour to rigid biological routines. Because human behaviour is far beyond biological routines, social behaviour can hardly be explained without theorizing about the cognitive processes that mediate between an observable input and an observable response.

What is social about social cognition?

Given its emphasis on mediating processes, it comes as no surprise that social cognition research has borrowed heavily from cognitive psychology. Numerous concepts have been taken over and applied to the domain of social perception. Looking at some of the brief illustrations used above, for example the "THE CAT" figure, one might wonder how social cognition is different from cognition about inanimate objects. While there is substantial overlap, two important differences set social cognition apart from cognitive psychology: the *nature of the stimulus* and the *nature of the processing*. Although both aspects are highly intertwined, we will briefly discuss them separately.

On the most obvious level, social cognition research is specific because of the *social nature of the stimulus* and its relation to the perceiver. As Fiske and Taylor (1991) have pointed out, there are quite a number of aspects in which the target of social perception is different from the target of nonsocial perception. After all, estimating the height of a building is quite different from judging the trustworthiness of a new acquaintance. Unlike buildings and other inanimate objects, people may influence their environment. For example, they may try to appear trustworthier than they are, whereas a building rarely tries to appear taller than it actually is. People may change rapidly, and individuals therefore need to adapt their judgments. For example, at the beginning of a conversation a new acquaintance may seem rather shy, but after a while she appears quite extraverted. Moreover, people, unlike inanimate objects, change when they are aware that they are being observed.

These factors all contribute to an increased complexity of social judgment. But perhaps the most pronounced and important difference between social and physical targets rests on still another aspect. Individuals are able to "observe" the stimulus attributes of their physical environment. They can "see" colour or size, they can "hear" pitch, they can "smell" scent, and they can "feel" whether something is hot or cold, for example. In social cognition, however, individuals need to know about numerous attributes that cannot be perceived directly or assessed objectively. In social cognition, the perceiver is interested in attributes such as intelligence, trustworthiness, love, aggressiveness, or humour. Individuals have no sensory receptors for these attributes, which refer to distal entities that have to be inferred or construed from more proximal cues, and sometimes have no objective existence at all. For example, we cannot directly observe the "aggressiveness" of a particular person. We can observe whether the person is hitting someone, and we may use this observation to infer aggressiveness. Because these kinds of attributes cannot be directly observed, their assessment requires far more constructive processing than the assessment of size or colour. To make social judgments, individuals must go beyond the information given (Bruner, 1957a) far more than when judging inanimate objects. One may argue that even basic perceptions such as colour and size require a considerable degree of inference. However, in most cases, it is the social judgments that require far more inferential processes, and it is precisely this large proportion of constructive processes that makes social cognition a specific and unique process.

Two other aspects are directly related to the nonobservability of the attributes in social cognition. First, because these attributes have to be inferred from distal cues, the accuracy of social judgment is difficult to check. Second, the attributes themselves are often quite illdefined. For example, there might be very different ideas about the implications of "trustworthiness," depending on the perceiver's prior experiences and on the situational context. Given this lack of accurate

Differing targets—different amounts of constructive processes: First, estimate the size of the squares. Which one is larger? Next, judge the trustworthiness of each speaker. The difference in size between the squares can be observed directly. Size refers to a well-defined attribute, and the accuracy of our judgment is easy to verify. By contrast, not only are we unable to observe trustworthiness directly, as a concept it is also more vague and controversial than size. Credit: Art Directors and TRIP.

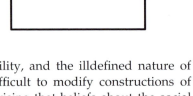

feedback, the absence of verificability, and the illdefined nature of many concepts, it can be very difficult to modify constructions of social reality. Hence it is not surprising that beliefs about the social world, for example stereotypes, are often more difficult to change than beliefs about the nonsocial world.

The social aspect, however, is not restricted to the social nature of the stimulus. Just as a young child could hardly learn her first language from a radio, the processing of social information is a *genuinely social process*. Most obviously, constructing social reality is a highly mutual process. This mutuality emerges in different forms. An individual's construction of social reality is strongly influenced by the constructions of others. Individuals perceive the behaviour of others and make inferences about the other's subjective reality. Conversely, an individual's constructions colour the social perception of other people. Although different persons in the same situation may construct quite different social realities, there is a strong mutual relationship between the construction of these social realities.

There is a strong link between the way most people think about their social world and their self-conception. Their construction of reality has strong implications for how they feel and think about themselves. At least two aspects of self-involvement are worth considering. First, when a person's self is involved and the situation is highly important, individuals are more likely to process incoming information extensively. Because the situation is so important to the self, people have a greater need for accuracy or, conversely, a greater fear of invalidity (Kruglanski, 1989a). Personal relevance and importance usually increase the *amount* of processing, a central variable in the processing of information. Second, under certain conditions, self-involvement influences not only the amount of processing, but also its direction. At times an "accurate" construction of social reality can be quite self-threatening. For example, an accurate interpretation of a failed exam could imply that we are not as smart and successful as we had thought. As a consequence, the processing individuals engage in can be biased or motivated in one direction or another in order to maintain a particular position. For instance, under certain conditions individuals may prefer to search for and attend to information that is consistent with their prior beliefs (Festinger, 1957; Kunda, 1990).

The specific nature of social cognition is also reflected in its strong time constraints. In most social situations individuals have a fairly limited time to respond. For example, when you are at a party and meet someone for the first time, you need to respond instantaneously. You can hardly stand there and wonder for a long time whether the other person's initial statement had a friendly or an aggressive tone. In any case, your interpretation will influence your response, which in turn influences the other person's subsequent behaviour, and so forth. Time constraints demand that the amount of processing be reduced to a sufficient level—yet, even under these constraints, individuals' constructions of social reality need to be reasonably adequate for them to act successfully in social situations. As a result, social cognition needs to be highly adaptive and sensitive to the requirements of a situation.

Two examples may further illustrate the importance of the social component in cognitive processes. In a study on statistical reasoning, Schaller (1992) presented students with statistical tables indicating that female performance was inferior to male performance. Students failed to consider the spurious nature of such a correlation—they did not detect that the apparent relationship between gender and performance was due to some third variable (e.g., women have to work under less favourable conditions). Supporting the importance of the social aspect, Schaller observed that statistical reasoning was markedly improved when individuals were socially or emotionally involved, as when feminist participants were motivated to defend the gender group to which they belong.

Research on the Wason selection task (Wason, 1966), which assesses logical reasoning abilities, similarly emphasizes the social component. In order to solve this selection task, individuals must find out which information is needed to test an "if-then" rule (see Box 1.1). Extensive research has led to the conclusion that individuals are quite poor at solving this kind of task: Reasoning errors persisted even when the rule referred to familiar and meaningful content. Basing her work on an evolutionary approach to logical reasoning, Cosmides (1989; see also Gigerenzer & Hug, 1991) demonstrated that embedding the very same rules into the form of social contracts (e.g., "If someone wants to use public transportation, then he must have a valid ticket") resulted in an enormous increase in correct solutions (see also the volume on *Reasoning and Thinking* by Manktelow, 1999, in *Cognitive Psychology: A Modular Course*). Findings of this kind suggest that the social context has a very pronounced impact on individuals' processing. They also imply that detaching the cognitive tasks from the social context may alter the quality of the underlying process. Detaching the cognitive processes from the social context will thus often result in seemingly poor performance and errors—as in the nonsocial presentation of the Wason selection task. However, within a social context these errors are not necessarily observable in the form of real mistakes (see Funder, 1987, for the difference between errors and mistakes).

In sum, social cognition is unique in several ways. Most importantly, unlike other judgments, social judgments usually refer to very complex and nonobservable attributes. As a consequence, the constructive aspect plays a particularly important role. In combination with time constraints, motivational aspects, and self-involvement, this "going beyond the information given" (Bruner, 1957a) renders social cognition a unique and fascinating topic.

Overview: The structure of this book

As outlined above, social cognition research investigates how information is encoded, stored, and retrieved from memory, how social

BOX 1.1.

How introducing a social context may change the mediating processes in logical reasoning

In this task, participants have to check whether a given set of stimuli conforms with a specific rule. In general, the rule has an 'if p then q' structure. In the original paradigm introduced by Wason (1966), participants were presented with four cards. They were informed that on one side of each card was a letter, on the other side a number. The visible symbols were 4, A, L, and 7. The participants had to check whether the following statement was true or false: If there is a vowel on one side of the card, then there is an even number on the other side of the card. Which card would you need to turn, in order to check this rule?

The correct solution holds that you would have to turn A and 7 (which is p and non-q in the "if p then q" structure). If on the other side of the 7 was a vowel, the rule would be disconfirmed. Similarly, if on the other side of the A was an odd number, the rule would be disconfirmed. Reversely, turning the 4 and the L would make no sense, because the rule says nothing about the relation between consonants and numbers—so both, an odd or an even number on the back side of the L would have no implication for the rule. Similarly, turning the 4 would not be diagnostic, because a consonant would not be inconsistent with the rule. Participants usually fail to turn the two logically correct cards (most often they turn the A and the 4).

Even explaining the task extensively and embedding it in a more familiar context does not improve performance. However, simply adding the social aspects strongly changes participants' responses. Cosmides (1989) suggested that people have no problems with this kind of task if it is embedded in a context of social exchange (see also Gigerenzer & Hug, 1991). For example, such an exchange rule could hold "if a person uses public transportation, he must have a valid ticket." Note that this rule has the same "if p then q" structure as the letter/number example above.

Person has a valid ticket	Person uses public transportation	Person does not use public transportation	Person has no valid ticket

In this scenario, participants check whether the person who uses public transportation has a valid ticket (which is equivalent to turning A in the task above) and they check whether the person who has no valid ticket uses public transportation (which is equivalent to turning the seven in the example above). Although the task has the same "if p then q" structure, participants are far better in the second task at coming up with the logically correct solutions. In other words, embedding the task in a social context (here social exchange context) changed the underlying cognitive processes. Our key point here is not the improved performance but that introducing the social context changes the mediating processes. Whereas in the present example, this change improved performance, the change may sometimes also impair performance.

knowledge is structured and represented, and what processes are involved when individuals compute judgments and make decisions. Not surprisingly, these different processes are highly intertwined, even for simple tasks, and they can hardly be seen in isolation from each other. Before disentangling the various aspects, we will therefore begin with a general overview of the sequence of information processing and an outline of general principles (Chapter 2). Next we look at how social knowledge is represented, stored, and retrieved (Chapter 3). The subsequent two chapters focus on judgmental processes, in particular: Chapter 4 examines judgmental heuristics, or rules of thumb, that allow individuals to simplify complex social judgments; Chapter 5 takes another look at judgmental processes, now with an emphasis on how individuals use and combine the information that is provided, and on the fact that social judgments are most often comparative in nature. Chapter 6 emphasizes the role of the "data" and its relation to individuals' construction. In particular, we discuss how individuals test whether their constructions match with the data in their environment. The final Chapter 7 highlights that looking at the construction of social reality from the perspective of an "information processing paradigm" does not neglect individuals' feelings at all. The chapter addresses how affective states influence social cognition and social judgment.

Chapter summary

(1) Social cognition research is concerned with the study of social knowledge and the cognitive processes that are involved when individuals construct their subjective reality. Researchers in social cognition therefore investigate how social information is encoded, stored in, and retrieved from memory, how social knowledge is structured and represented, and what processes are involved when individuals form judgments and make decisions.

(2) Different perspectives of the social thinker have been proposed: The consistency seeker striving for consistency between their various beliefs about the world, the lay scientist gathering information unselectively and constructing social reality in an unbiased manner, or the cognitive miser striving to simplify cognitive processes, particularly when under time pressure or in

complex situations. The motivated tactician applies multiple strategies depending on the situational constraints.

(3) The cognitive component of social cognition emphasizes the role of cognitive processes that mediate between a stimulus and a behavioural response. This mediation is particularly obvious when the objectively same stimulus results in different responses. The cognitive component allows individuals to modify their behaviour as a function of their subjective interpretation of the situation.

(4) The social component of social cognition emphasizes the specific aspects of the mediating cognitive processes in thinking about the social world. First, these aspects result from the nature of the social stimulus. Most importantly, the attributes of interests are usually nonobservable and require a considerable amount of constructive processes. Second, the processes are highly sensitive to the constraints of the social situation.

Discussion questions

(1) What is meant by the phrase "constructing social reality"? In this respect, what is meant by "going beyond the information given"?

(2) Describe an example from everyday life in which the same objective input results in different subjective realities as a function of the social context.

(3) What different goals might individuals have when they construct social reality? Describe an example in which the different goals will result in different constructions.

(4) Present Figure 2b to some of your friends, and Figure 2c to some other friends. Then show Figure 2a. Examine how prior exposure may alter the interpretation of 2a.

(5) What advantage lies in the cognitive link between stimulus and response?

(6) Describe how judging a person is different from judging an inanimate object.

Recommendations for further reading

Fiske, S. T., & Taylor, S. E. (1991). *Social cognition*. New York: McGraw-Hill.

This book provides an extensive coverage of social cognition research, more suitable for advanced students.

Kruglanski, A. W. (1989a). *Lay epistemics and human knowledge. Cognitive and motivational biases*. New York: Plenum Press.

This book discusses different motives for ways in which individuals construct their social reality.

A first look at social cognition: General framework and basic assumptions

2

This chapter provides a general overview of the social cognition framework. We will begin with a look at the main ingredients that are essential for the way in which individuals construct reality, and with a brief survey of the steps in the sequence in which information is processed. The second section offers a discussion of four general themes underlying the social cognition perspective. In the third section we return to the information processing sequence in more detail, explaining the various steps and discussing how they relate to the four general themes.

Overview: Main ingredients and steps in information processing

How does a person go about constructing social reality? On a very general level we can distinguish three different elements that enter into the process: (1) input from a given situation; (2) input in the form of the prior knowledge that individuals bring to a situation; and (3) the processes that operate on the input.

First, and most obviously, there are the stimuli of the situation itself. These stimuli are one form of input that influences the interpretation of the situation. For example, the straightforward information that someone "helped a friend cheat on an exam" could be considered this kind of input or raw data. Second, as has become evident in the introductory chapter, the stimuli from a situation determine its interpretation only in part, since the fate of a particular stimulus input depends on the prior knowledge that the perceiver brings to the situation. This prior knowledge may take very different forms. It may comprise, for example, general knowledge in the form of stereotypes about the group the target person belongs to, or general knowledge about honesty and trustworthiness. It may also comprise specific episodes, for example a person's own prior experiences with cheating. Third, we must give due attention to the processes that operate on the direct stimuli and prior knowledge. For example, individuals could consider the different implications of the "data" input in light of their prior knowledge and combine these implications into a judgment of how likeable the target person was.

Most importantly, even if the pattern of stimuli in a given situation is constant, there is a potentially high variance in the prior knowledge individuals bring to that situation, and a potentially high variance in the processes that are applied. For example, instead of drawing on prior knowledge about honesty, a person could use his or her knowledge about friendship. Similarly, individuals can process the information very quickly and rather superficially, or they can mull it over for quite a while. It needs to be emphasized that the three aspects we have identified (stimuli, prior knowledge, and processes) are not nearly as distinct and easily distinguished as this preliminary overview might suggest. In fact, further discussion will show that they are highly intertwined and separable only in an idealized presentation. With these three aspects in mind, we can now take a brief look at what the task of constructing social reality entails.

The task of interpreting a social situation, of making sense of and responding to one's social environment, comprises a variety of highly interconnected subtasks. These different subtasks can be seen as steps that link the observable input to a person's overt behaviour. Following the paradigm of cognitive psychology, we can organize the sequence of cognitive processes into the different stages depicted in Figure 2.1. To begin with, individuals have to *perceive* the stimulus events. For example, while talking to someone at the party you recognize that this person is hardly looking at you. Next, the perceiver needs to *encode* and interpret this perception, i.e., give it some meaning. For example, you interpret the fact the other person is not looking at you as a lack of interest or, alternatively, as shyness. This encoding relies heavily on prior knowledge stored in memory. Thus, in order to support the encoding processes, the prior knowledge stored in memory must first be *retrieved*. For example, we may retrieve prior knowledge about social interactions where one person was hardly looking at her communication partner. Finally, the encoded perception will be *stored* in memory and will potentially affect the assessment of future events. Both the newly encoded input

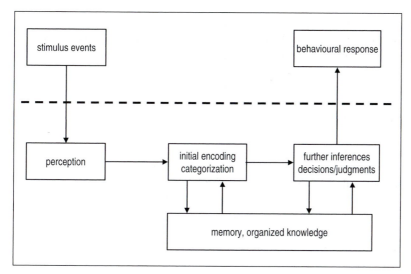

Figure 2.1.
Sequence of
information processing.

and the old knowledge stored in memory will then provide the basis for further processing, leading to *inferences, judgments, and decisions.* For example, you may infer that the other person is not interested in your detailed description of the latest sport event. These inferences and judgments are again stored in memory. Sometimes, but not always, the final outcome of this cognitive process is manifested in an overt *behavioural response.* For example, you might decide to change the topic of your conversation.

As will become evident in the remainder of this chapter, the different processing stages of the idealized sequence depicted in Figure 2.1 are interdependent and are characterized by various feedback loops. Before elaborating on the various steps in more detail, we will point out some general themes in social cognition theory that affect virtually every element of this sequence.

General themes underlying the construction of social reality

Given the complex nature of how social reality is constructed, it is not surprising that theoretical and empirical research has addressed numerous aspects of human information processing. This section will look at four general themes: (1) the interplay of stimulus information and prior knowledge; (2) the limitations of processing capacity;

(3) the amount of processing; and (4) the interplay of automatic and controlled processes. As we shall see, different facets of these issues re-emerge throughout the book.

Theme 1: Top-down and bottom-up processing

We have already noted that the way in which individuals interpret and judge social situations is influenced by the stimuli from a given situation and by prior knowledge. Both aspects are essential ingredients in the process and cannot be seen in isolation. The interplay of situational stimuli and prior knowledge occurs in almost every cognitive process in the sequence depicted in Figure 2.1. With respect to the encoding of a particular stimulus, imagine someone at the party saying "I am a librarian." This brief sentence makes sense only if the perceiver can link the word "librarian" to some prior knowledge. The listener has prior conceptions what this means, for example, that the person works in a library, checks out books, buys new books for public use, and so on. A specific stimulus will not have been understood if it cannot be linked to prior knowledge. For example, if a person were to say "I am a *heudoi*," most people would have no idea what this means. They would be unable to make sense of this statement, that is, they could not *encode* the statement.

The interplay of these two aspects is similarly present in the subsequent processing that individuals engage in. Let us assume that you are supposed to judge how introvert or extravert the person is who made the statement about being a librarian. You could base your *judgment* on what you have observed at the party, for example, that the person has been conversing animatedly with many people. Of course the encoding of this observation is once again influenced by prior knowledge. In addition, prior knowledge can have a direct impact on the judgment process. You may, for example, base your judgment at least partly on your stereotype, your prior knowledge that librarians are usually rather introvert. When *storing* the information in memory, new input is related to prior knowledge and thus alters the prior knowledge that individuals bring to the next situation. For example, the observation that this librarian was engaged in lively conversation with many people may change the prior knowledge that librarians are usually rather introvert. Finally, the interplay of situational stimuli and prior knowledge also affects *retrieval* processes. A particular stimulus input, for example someone saying "I am a librarian," will retrieve information from memory that is associated with this concept. Note that this is the same example we have used for the encoding process, thus illustrating that retrieval processes are essential to any encoding process.

The notion that the interplay of new stimuli and prior knowledge is manifested in virtually every cognitive process does not imply that the relative impact of the two aspects is balanced or constant across situations. On the contrary: Sometimes human information processing is guided primarily by prior knowledge and the expectations individuals bring to a situation. In this case the processing is called *concept-driven* or *top-down processing*. At other times human information processing is influenced primarily by the stimuli from a given situation. In this case the processing is called *data-driven* or *bottom-up processing*. We can illustrate these two ideal types of processing with an example taken from the realm of person perception. In top-down processing, impressions and judgments about a specific target person are based predominantly on prior beliefs about the group to which the target person is assigned (e.g., librarians). Prior knowledge in the form of the stereotype colours the evaluation of a new input (for examples see Bodenhausen, Macrae, & Sherman, 1999; Brewer, 1988; Fiske & Neuberg, 1990; Hamilton & Sherman, 1994). In bottom-up processing, judgments about the target person are based predominantly on the implications of the behaviour that is observed. The resulting judgment can be inconsistent with our prior beliefs and the new input may contribute—under certain conditions—to a change of the stereotype (Bless, Schwarz, Bodenhausen, & Thiel, 2001; Hewstone, 1994; Kunda & Oleson, 1995; Weber & Crocker, 1983).

The idea that human thinking is sometimes best characterized by top-down processes and sometimes by bottom-up processes gives rise to two types of research questions that are addressed in many facets in the remainder of this book: (1) What are the differential effects of top-down versus bottom-up processing on encoding, judgment, storage, and retrieval processes? (2) What conditions increase and decrease the likelihood of top-down versus bottom-up processing?

Theme 2: The limitation of human processing capacity requires simplifications and short cuts

As discussed in Box 2.1, human information processing is sometimes compared to the operations of a computer. One of the most important aspects determining the quality of a computer is the size of its working memory, which is where the actual processing is performed.

BOX 2.1.

Understanding the basics of social cognition: Thinking about your computer might help

Since social cognition has borrowed many concepts from computer science, it might be helpful to think about how a computer works and see how this can be related to social cognition. A computer has various sources of input: the keyboard, the CD-ROM drive, the floppy drive, information from other computers via the Internet, and so on. Your computer can make sense of this input only when it has access to programs that allow for the encoding of data, for example in the form of various software programs that are stored on the hard disk (see Theme 1). Even if you download this software from some external sources, the computer needs some basic prior information, such as the initial default set-up, for example.

One of the key features to watch for when buying a computer is the size of the working memory. The working memory determines how much information can be handled, how fast some information is processed, and how many programs can be run simultaneously. Notwithstanding the impressive ability of the computer industry to provide computers with ever more working memory, there is an upper limit (see Theme 2). Note that the available programs, the "procedural knowledge," differ with respect to how much they tax the processing resources. Some programs require more working memory than others. Some programs may require too many resources to be run at all, while some may take far too much time (see Theme 3). Finally, depending on the set-up of the computer, some programs are launched and run automatically when you start up your computer whereas other programs need to be started intentionally with extra effort (see Theme 4).

It is possible that several different software programs are installed on your computer. Which program, that is, which prior knowledge will be used when a new input is processed? Answer: The program that has been started and loaded into the working memory, in other words, the information that has been activated. In addition to processing the current input, the computer can store information. There is some structure underlying the storage processes so that things belonging together are stored into one file. On a somewhat higher level, different files are sorted into directories, again reflecting some structure. This structure should enable later retrieval. Besides storing information, the computer can provide some observable output, for example by printing data or by displaying something on the screen.

The analogy between social cognition and the way a computer operates also emerges with respect to some of the problems we encounter with computers. For example, sometimes we are unable to find a particular file even though we are certain that we have stored it somewhere. We may have received a file from some external source but are unable to open the file because the computer lacks the necessary software. Sometimes we receive the message "out of working memory"—reflecting that something has gone wrong and that the computer has allocated too many resources to allow further processing.

Having said all this, it is important to emphasize that we are NOT arguing that human cognition is identical to the mechanisms that operate a computer. The point of the analogy is merely to indicate that many concepts and mechanisms that are used in social cognition can perhaps be understood more easily in the context of our knowledge about computers. In fact, the core of human cognition—our subjective experiences, self-awareness, our feelings resulting from our perception of the world—is absent in computers. Moreover, we believe that the human mind is far more capable and adaptive than even the latest computer designs. For an illustration, imagine the seemingly simple task of speech recognition. Although there have been substantial advances in computer science, the mere semantic understanding of an utterance provides enormous problems for computers. And the semantic meaning is only a very first step in how individuals interpret an utterance. For example, computers are still far from "understanding" irony.

For example, before you can work with a software program or a file it must be loaded into working memory. The size of the working memory determines whether programs and processes can be executed at all, and if so, how much time it takes for a specific operation. Similar conceptual assumptions have been made about human information processing. One key assumption of social cognition holds that a person's processing capacity is limited. This limitation implies that individuals cannot process all information that is potentially relevant for the interpretation of a specific situation, and especially not within a reasonable time frame that allows them to respond successfully to the needs of the situation.

Much like top-down versus bottom-up processing, the limitations on capacity affect all stages of information processing. Imagine a party situation with different groups of people. Individuals are not able to listen to and encode all statements that are made. When encoding a particular statement, individuals are not able to consider all possible interpretations of it. When asked at the end of the party for an impression about a particular guest, individuals are not able to retrieve all of the guest's statements, how he or she reacted to other people, his or her bodily and facial expressions, and so on. Even if it were possible to do all of these things, considering, weighing, and integrating this information into a judgment would constitute a highly complex and presumably unmanageable task.

The combination of limitations on human processing capacity, on the one hand, and time constraints, on the other, has highly important consequences for cognitive processing. Most obviously, individuals need to simplify their processing in order to cope with these constraints. Mere simplification, however, is not enough. The simplification has to be highly efficient so that the resulting construction of social reality still provides an adequate basis for a person's responses to the social environment. Simplifications that systematically result in wrong interpretations in the real world may have severe consequences.

As we shall see, individuals have developed highly adaptive mechanisms that allow for very efficient processing. First, instead of considering all relevant information, individuals may rely on less information, they may not attend to all situational stimuli, they may not consider all of their prior knowledge for encoding a stimulus, and they may not store all encoded information. In any case, a selection of the information is required. This selection of information to be processed is far from random. In fact, the nature of the situation influences the selection, which makes possible a highly context-dependent and thus highly adaptive construction of social reality. Research questions resulting from this assumption address the precise mechanism of these selection processes: What determines which stimulus individuals attend to? What determines which concept is used for interpreting a given stimulus?

Reducing the amount of information that is processed simplifies processing and is consequently one possible way of dealing with capacity constraints. A second possible way is more directly related to the very process that operates on the given situation. Cognitive processes differ with respect to the load they impose on processing capacity. Instead of relying on elaborative processes, individuals often rely on mental short cuts and heuristics. A *heuristic* is a cognitive device that enables the social individual to make judgments by rules-of-thumb which require little effort but yield valid results most of the time. For example, when asked to estimate whether there were more male or female persons at a party the previous week, individuals may base their judgment on the ease with which male or female guests can be retrieved from memory (Tversky & Kahneman, 1973). These kinds of heuristics are more extensively discussed in Chapter 4. Another form of short cut rests on an increased reliance on top-down processes (see Theme 1). Top-down processes usually require fewer processing resources than bottom-up processes. For example, judgments based primarily on stereotypes require fewer resources than judgments based primarily on the data at hand (cf. Bodenhausen et al., 1999; Fiske & Neuberg, 1990). Thus, individuals may reduce their processing load by applying their prior knowledge about their social environment.

The different forms of simplifications of cognitive processes are a central issue in social cognition research and will reappear throughout this book (see, in particular, Chapter 4). It is important to emphasize that these simplifications yield valid results most of the time. However, the price of economy is systematically biased judgments under certain conditions. When looking at social cognition research, the reader can get the impression that this price is fairly high and that human judgment is full of flaws and biases. This impression stems partly from the fact that researchers tend to focus on deviations and biases. Researchers argue that investigating these deviations, that is, investigating the conditions under which judgments are systematically biased, provides better access to human information processing than merely focusing on conditions in which biases do not occur. This research emphasis does not imply, however, that human information processing is generally flawed.

Theme 3: Amount of processing: Processing capacity and processing motivation

In the discussion of Theme 2 we outlined how the need to simplify cognitive processes results from the limitation of human processing resources. Simplifying processes is important and essential, but the way in which individuals short cut cognitive processes can vary as a function of the situation. Individuals can allocate more or fewer processing resources depending on the requirements of the situation. Imagine a person at a party doing several things simultaneously: listening to someone else in the group, thinking about what to say next, tasting some food, and noticing a new guest entering through the door. All these activities will tax the individual's resources. From a functionalist perspective, it would be highly adaptive if individuals did not simplify all their processes all the time. Presumably, individuals would be better off if they could process the information in either a simplified heuristic manner or a more elaborative and systematic manner depending on the demands of the situation. And, indeed, we find that human information processing has an adaptive quality. In fact, the amount of processing can vary enormously. This being the case, the requirement to simplify processing due to the limitation of human processing resources (Theme 2) is qualified by a person's ability to allocate more resources to a particular task.

This gives rise to the next question: What determines the amount of processing? Or, to put it differently: What variables influence whether individuals tend to simplify their task or not? First, the amount of processing allocated to a particular task depends on the amount of free resources. How much of the resources is occupied by other tasks—in other words, how much *processing capacity* is available? The smaller the number of other taxing activities, the greater the likelihood that more elaborative processes will occur. In addition to capacity, it is *processing motivation* that determines the amount of processing that takes place. Not surprisingly, individuals have a strong processing motivation if the target of their cognitive processes is perceived as interesting or important, particularly when the target has a high personal relevance. In these cases, individuals will allocate more processing resources to the task. If the cognitive system is already working at its limits, this assumption directly implies that resources will be withdrawn from other tasks. In our example, if the new guest entering the room is of high personal relevance, more resources are allocated to watching this person. This in turn potentially implies that resources devoted to other activities are cut back, for example, the person will be listening less carefully to what is said in the group.

Many models in social cognition treat processing capacity and processing motivation as key factors influencing cognitive processes. Perhaps most prominently, processing motivation and capacity are conceptualized as central variables in theories on attitude change (for examples see Eagly & Chaiken, 1993; Petty & Cacioppo, 1986) and person perception (Fiske & Neuberg, 1990; see also Chaiken & Trope, 1999). Although most of these models treat processing capacity and processing motivation as disjunct aspects on a theoretical level, empirically the two aspects may often be hard to separate. For example, individuals will allocate fewer resources to a particular task (e.g., listening to the lecture) when they simultaneously engage in an second task (e.g., talking to other students). One might argue that the second task is reducing the processing capacity that is available for the first task. However, one might also argue that the student is less motivated to listen to the lecture. The general question of the amount of processing will emerge throughout this book in different facets pertaining to different cognitive processes.

Theme 4: Automatic and controlled processes

Cognitive processes can differ with respect to their automaticity and controllability (Shiffrin & Schneider, 1984). For example, when a new guest appears at the party, individuals can actively call to mind some particular content from their memory, such as where they saw the person previously. However, information may also come to mind automatically. For example, by assigning the new guest to a group (e.g., fraternity member, business major, etc.) the perceiver's general expectations about that group may pop up automatically, unin-tended, and uncontrolled (Devine, 1989; Fiske & Neuberg, 1990; Lepore & Brown, 1997).

Several dimensions have been applied to distinguish cognitive processes on the continuum from automaticity at one end to con-trollability at the other. Ideally, *automatic processes* are unintentional, require very little cognitive resources, cannot and need not to be controlled, and lie outside of an individual's awareness. The initiation and the running of automatic processes thus requires no conscious regulation (see Bargh, 1999; see also Fiske & Taylor, 1991, for a concise discussion). Imagine, for example, someone driving home from the office. All the necessary turns and stops are highly automa-tized, requiring no intentional control. Automatic processes may differ with respect to how much they match the ideal criteria listed above (see Fiske & Taylor, 1991, for a discussion of different facets of automaticity such as subliminal perception, post-consciousness, and goal-dependence).

Controlled processes, on the other hand, require considerable resources, their initiation and running requires conscious regulation, and they are potentially within the scope of an individual's awareness. In particular, deviations from a specific automatized sequence of processes, for example, taking a detour on the way home to pick up something at the grocery store, require more controlled and intentional processing. Because automatic processes require few resources, and controlled processes require considerable resources (see Theme 2 on the limitation of processing resources and Theme 3 on the flexibility of the amount of processing), they operate best under different situational conditions. Controlled processes are particularly likely to fail when other tasks are taxing a person's resources. For example, despite the driver's need to pick something up at the grocery store, he or she arrives home having taken the usual route and forgotten to stop. The person obviously did not allocate the mental resources for the controlled processes that were required to deviate from the usual routine.

In some cases, controlling one's own processes seems pretty easy. For example, it is easy to recall any situation you want, say the last party you attended. But the attempt to control cognitive processes is not always successful. In particular, avoiding particular thoughts is no simple task. In fact, some intrusive thoughts arise even though a person is intentionally trying to avoid them. Sometimes it seems that the more a person tries to avoid these thoughts, the more they persist and intrude on their awareness (Wegner, 1994). For example, people who are worried about a particular problem often cannot stop thinking about it, even though they would like to (Martin & Tesser, 1996). These examples suggest that there are two aspects to the question of control: Control pertains to a person's ability to bring a particular content to awareness, as well as the ability to suppress a particular content. Research and everyday experience suggest that the former kind of control is far more successful than the latter.

As is the case with automaticity, there are different types of controlled processes that match the ideal criteria to varying degrees. It is therefore not surprising that the distinction between automatic and controlled processes is sometimes less sharp than one might expect. This fluid differentiation between automaticity and control is not only an aspect of different processes, but can also be observed within the same process. Mental activities can start out as controlled processes and eventually shift towards highly automatized processes, especially as a result of long practice (Smith, 1989). For example, driving a car in an unknown city requires a considerable amount of controlled processes—where to turn, what to watch out for, etc. With more practice and a growing familiarity with the new city, the same processes become more and more automatized, require fewer and fewer resources and less awareness.

The general message from this example is that the more familiar individuals are with a particular stimulus situation, the more likely it is that automatic processes have a pronounced impact. Controlled processes are more likely to come into play in unfamiliar stimulus situations. This again points to the adaptive and highly efficient nature of human information processing. Because automatic processes require fewer processing resources, they save resources that can be allocated to other tasks. The cognitive system is designed in such a clever way that this saving of resources by automatic processes is most likely in highly familiar situations. When the situation becomes unfamiliar, the system shifts towards the more controlled processing. Note that this aspect, the fact that the required resources are highly context-dependent, directly relates to the limitations of processing capacity (Theme 2) and the amount of processing (Theme 3). Automaticity and controllability have become an important aspect in understanding human information processing. Several different facets of this distinction will be touched on explicitly and implicitly in the remaining chapters.

A moment for reflection

This is a good time to pause briefly for a look back and a look ahead. So far we have outlined three major ingredients of human information processing: the stimulus situation (the "data"), prior knowledge, and the processes operating on the input. After a brief look at the sequence of information processing, we have discussed four highly interrelated themes that have a bearing on virtually every cognitive process. These themes pertain to the interplay of new social stimuli and prior knowledge, to the limitation of processing resources, to the variability in the amount of processing allocated to a particular task, and to the distinction between automatic and controlled processes. In discussing these themes we have emphasized the highly adaptive nature of human information processing.

Keeping this in mind, we will now return to the sequence of information processing (see Figure 2.1). In the remainder of this chapter we will provide a more extended discussion of the various steps, the goal of which is to provide a preliminary understanding of how these steps are linked and intertwined. At this stage we will not address all the complexities and qualifications. We will return to the core components in a second round, when the three major ingredients of social cognition, prior knowledge, and judgmental processes, and the nature of the stimuli, are discussed in separate chapters (Chapters 3 to 6).

The sequence of information processing

Perception and attention

Let us return to the example of the party situation. Imagine yourself at this party with many people in the same room. Different groups have formed, all carrying on lively conversations. In this situation there is an almost infinite number of stimuli your senses could register. You could attend to what all the different people are saying, the verbal and nonverbal reactions of their partners, the sound of the music, the smell of the different foods, the taste of your wine, and much more. In addition to these external stimuli, you also register internal stimuli. For example, you may feel aroused, happy, sad, or angry; you may feel pain or the contraction of muscles.

In order to act in a such a setting, individuals need to construct an internal representation of the situation, ideally using all the different stimuli. However, as discussed in Theme 2, the capacity of human information processing is limited. We cannot process all stimuli that reach our sensory system—not even by relying on highly simplified processes. As a consequence, individuals need to select which stimuli will enter into further processing. To deal with this essential requirement, individuals have the ability to direct their attention to some aspects of the situation and exclude other aspects from being processed further and thereby taxing resources.

The well-known cocktail-party effect illustrates this important skill. Suppose you were later asked what the group in the other corner of the room had been discussing. You would probably have no idea. Obviously, the entire conversation of this other group would be lost although it had reached your senses. Imagine, however, you had overheard someone in that distant group mentioning your name.

Even if you continued to converse in your own group, you would probably direct some of your attention toward that other conversation, and later you would be able to recall parts of it.

This example illustrates that individuals have the ability to direct their attention to various aspects of a given situation. This ability is an important mechanism for dealing with the limitations of human information processing (Broadbent, 1958). It is obviously directly linked to Theme 4, the controllability of information processing. The attentional processes allow individuals to process only a small and manageable subset of the immense number of stimuli that reach their senses. It is this subset that gets processed further in the next steps. The important function of attentional processes in the very early stages gives rise to the next questions: What are the antecedents of attentional processes? What are the consequences of these processes? We will look at these questions in turn.

What attracts an individual's attention?

Which stimuli are likely to be further processed, and which stimuli are likely to be ignored? Our attention is generally attracted by stimuli that stand out, in other words by stimuli that are *distinct* or *salient* in the context of other stimuli. Note that the salience of a stimulus is not a property of the stimulus itself—it is its relationship to the context that creates salience. For example, the only woman in a group of men attracts more attention and, conversely, the only male person in a group of female persons captures the first attention.

A particular stimulus can be distinctive in various ways. First, as suggested by the above example, a stimulus can be distinctive in relation to other stimuli in the situational context. Second, a stimulus can be salient with respect to an individual's prior knowledge and the expectations that person brings to the situation. Third, salience can result from the relationship between the stimulus and a person's current goals that guide processing (cf. Fiske & Taylor, 1991). Let us take a closer look at these different facets of salience.

A good deal of research suggests that a stimulus attracts more attention if it has a solo status in relation to other stimuli in a given situation. For example, the only female (male) in a group of otherwise all males (females) will attract special attention. This impact of standing out has been demonstrated with respect to a number of variables, such as race or age (see Fiske & Taylor, 1991). You can test this aspect of salience by wearing some unusual clothes the next time you go to class. For example, wearing a shirt and jeans all in red with yellow dots will attract the attention of your fellow students. If you do

perform this test, you might realize that attracting the attention of others does not necessarily imply their approval. Note that this attraction will diminish if other persons start wearing the same type of clothes; a fact underscoring that it is not the stimulus per se but its relation to the situational context that creates salience.

Salience of stimuli as a function of the context. Credit: Art Directors and TRIP.

There are other ways in which a stimulus can acquire salience by standing out: for example, the target is moving in the context of a fixed environment, or, conversely, the target is fixed and the other contextual stimuli are moving (McArthur & Post, 1977). Similarly, "highlighting" the target in an otherwise dark context creates salience (McArthur & Ginsberg, 1981).

In order to make sense of a current situation, individuals need to relate the situational stimuli to their prior knowledge, as emphasized in Theme 1. Usually, a particular stimulus that does not match prior knowledge and expectations appears as more distinctive and captures more attention than a stimulus that matches perfectly with a person's prior social knowledge. For example, if you go out for dinner and the waiter is dressed up as Santa Claus on roller skates, he will receive more attention than if he had dressed up in a more standard and expected costume. From this perspective it seems clear why it has been argued that infrequent stimuli can attract more attention than frequent and expected stimuli, or that individuals attend especially to extreme and unanticipated behaviours (Hamilton & Gifford, 1976). In general, this mechanism of attention attraction is highly adaptive because it directs a person's focus to those aspects of the situation that are not already incorporated into his or her prior social knowledge. As with most mechanisms that are very adaptive overall, this attention attraction process may have unwanted side effects. For example, a driver's attention can be attracted by an unusually severe accident on the other side of the freeway. With less attention devoted to his own driving, the risk of causing an accident himself increases. Similarly, it is no surprise that individuals often gaze at other people who look different from the norm and the expectations the perceiver brings to the situation—for example because the target is physically handicapped, unusually small, tall, large, and so on (e.g., Langer, Fiske, & Taylor, 1976).

Attention to a particular stimulus does not necessarily require a discrepancy with other stimuli or with prior knowledge and expectations. Attention may also arise from the relation between the stimulus and the perceiver's current goals (see Gollwitzer & Moskowitz, 1996, for a discussion on how goals affect cognition and behaviour). For example, if you are very hungry when you come to a party, the food will attract your special attention (Bruner, 1957b). Similarly, if your goal pertains to finding a new date, your attention will be directed at party guests who could potentially match your preferences. Because goals can be very diverse, almost any stimulus may receive particular attention from individuals (for examples see Berscheid, Graziano, & Monson, 1976; Erber & Fiske, 1984). In Theme 3 we discussed that the amount of processing is influenced by the personal relevance of stimuli. With respect to attention, this implies that targets which are personally relevant attract more attention than others (Neuberg & Fiske, 1987; Ruscher & Fiske, 1990). This is also the case with attentional effects that are due to external instruction: Individuals can be instructed to attend to a particular stimulus in a situation, for example, by teachers or coaches. In the absence of other conflicting goals, instructions can focus an individual's attention on a subset of the potentially observable stimuli (Taylor & Fiske, 1975).

The ability to attract a person's attention is particularly important in a social world that is characterized by a tremendous density of incoming information. Not surprisingly, in everyday life we are exposed not only to a virtually infinite number of social stimuli, but also to numerous attempts designed to attract our attention. For example, many advertisers assume that it is an essential step to attract the potential customer's attention before successfully providing further information about a particular product (McGuire, 1985; see Shavitt & Wänke, 2000, for applying the social cognition paradigm to consumer psychology).

In sum, attention may arise for different reasons. On the one hand, attention may result almost automatically from the discrepancy between a stimulus and the immediate context or the perceiver's prior knowledge. On the other hand, individuals may actively and intentionally direct their attention towards specific stimuli because they are relevant for their current goals. Note that the issue of automaticity versus controllability (Theme 4) is related to the different causes of salience. In any case, attention regulation is an essential process with important consequences and ramifications. Indeed, it has been argued that the selection of information itself can sometimes be more consequential than the inferences based on the selection (McArthur & Baron, 1983). Besides being very consequential, attention regulation is a highly adaptive process in the very first stage of information processing. Although in some cases the salience of a stimulus is irrelevant to its importance, most often a person's construction of social reality, based on the "selected" salient stimuli, reflects to a high degree his or her current needs and the most important features of a given situation.

What are the consequences of salience?

The salience of a specific stimulus in a very early stage of information processing has important consequences on subsequent processes. Generally, salience increases the amount of processing (see Theme 3) related to the stimulus information. The following discussion will examine how the increased amount of processing allocated to a particular stimulus affects (1) social judgments and (2) recall performance.

An increased amount of processing usually increases the impact of the stimulus information on *social judgments* relative to the impact of other stimuli. For example, considerable research has demonstrated that more causality is attributed to individuals who are salient due to their clothes, gender, race, or prominence in the visual field of the perceiver. Salient persons are seen as more influential and as more responsible for group actions (McArthur, 1981; Taylor & Fiske, 1978; see Fiske & Taylor, 1991, for a concise review).

Whereas the size of a stimulus impact on social judgments usually increases with its salience, the direction of the judgment is more difficult to predict. A considerable amount of research suggests that increasing the salience of a stimulus exaggerates an already existing judgmental tendency (Fiske, Kenny, & Taylor, 1991). For example, imagine two party guests, one you moderately like and one you moderately dislike. Keeping everything constant while increasing the salience of the two persons will accentuate what was initially a minor difference in the way they were evaluated. The assumption that an increased amount of processing can emphasize initial tendencies has also been supported by studies in which individuals were explicitly instructed to engage in more or less extensive processing. Judgments became more extreme when individuals simply thought more about an issue or target ("mere thought," Millar & Tesser, 1986; Tesser, 1978).

Of course, salience effects are also due to the fact that a person will give less attention to other potentially relevant stimuli. Allocating more resources to a particular stimulus will reduce the resources that can be allocated to other stimuli (see Theme 2). Conditions that reduce a person's ability to consider the nonsalient stimulus information should therefore elicit more pronounced salience effects. In line with this assumption it is reasonable to assume that salience effects are more likely if the nonsalient information is processed superficially due to time pressure or other processing constraints (Strack, Erber, & Wicklund, 1982).

Salience effects on social judgments do not necessarily reflect the direction of the initial implication of the stimulus. On the one hand, salience increases the likelihood that stimulus information enters into subsequent processes. On the other hand, salience may make individuals aware of this potentially strong influence. Awareness of a potential influence, however, can elicit processes that counteract it if the influence is perceived as unwanted. In many cases this can result in effects in the opposite direction (Lombardi, Higgins, & Bargh, 1987; Petty & Wegener, 1993; Strack, Schwarz, Bless, Kübler, & Wänke, 1993). For example, assigning a person to a social category (e.g., fraternity member, business major, ethnic group, etc.) can automatically bring to mind the general expectations about that group (Devine, 1989; Fiske & Neuberg, 1990). If a perceiver, for example a judge in a court, wants to provide a fair evaluation, he or she could try to control for the unwanted influence of the stereotype information (Devine, 1989; Lepore & Brown, 1997). Increasing the salience of the features that constitute group membership should increase the perceiver's awareness of the influence and thus attempts to counteract it. Of course, whether or not counteracting processes are elicited depends on how much the perceiver believes that the general expectations apply to the specific target. Chapter 5 will discuss in greater detail that on the one hand salience increases the likelihood that corresponding prior knowledge will come to mind, and, on the other hand, that salience may influence how the information brought to mind is used.

In addition to affecting judgments, salience should also influence the *recall* of the information in a later situation. This assumption seems straightforward: After all, if salience elicits more processing, more processing should in turn facilitate later recall. For example, the greater the amount of processing allocated to studying a text for an exam, the greater the likelihood that the presented ideas will be recalled later (Palmere, Benton, Glover, & Roning, 1983). However, the general pattern of research findings is somewhat mixed with respect to whether salience necessarily increases recall performance (see McArthur, 1981; Taylor & Fiske, 1978). The mixed pattern can be due to several partly interdependent reasons. First, salience may attract a person's attention, eliciting more subsequent processing on the particular stimulus. However, because of other constraints, individuals are sometimes unable to allocate additional processing. In such cases, improvement of recall is unlikely. We will return to this issue in Chapter 3, when we discuss the question of whether information that is consistent or inconsistent with an individual's prior knowledge has a recall advantage (cf. Stangor & McMillan, 1992). Second, additional processing is particularly likely to improve recall performance if the encoding and the retrieval conditions are compatible (Craik & Lockhart, 1972). When the encoding conditions differ from the retrieval conditions, recall improvement due to salience is unlikely. Third, it has been suggested that salience does not necessarily influence the amount of recall but rather the ease with which the information can be retrieved from memory (see Pryor & Kriss, 1977; Rholes & Pryor, 1982). Thus, while individuals may be equally likely to recall salient and nonsalient information, the salient information can be retrieved more easily, without a strenuous search in memory. The ease of retrieval has important consequences and will be addressed below, as well as more extensively in Chapter 4. Fourth, and finally, we need to specify what the recall measure pertains to. For example, imagine an ad with a scantily clad spokesperson providing arguments in favour of a particular product. The spokesperson would presumably be fairly salient and attract attention. Although viewers will later recall the spokesperson, this does not necessarily imply that they will also have a good recall of the arguments that were presented (see also Chapter 3).

In summary, at a very early stage in the information processing sequence individuals can direct their attention to a subset of the potentially available stimuli in a given situation. The attention regulation mechanism has highly adaptive functions and provides an important tool to bridge the gap between limited processing resources and the enormous amount of stimuli. Individuals allocate their attention to salient stimuli in particular. Stimulus salience results from stimuli standing out, either in relation to other situational stimuli or in contrast to prior expectations. Moreover, a stimulus can be salient because it is relevant for the individual's current goals. As a consequence of salience, initial judgment tendencies are often exaggerated.

Encoding and interpretation

After an individual has perceived a stimulus and allocated sufficient attention to it, the next step in the information processing sequence requires the perceiver to *encode* and *interpret* this perception, that is to say, give meaning to the stimulus input. Encoding comprises various processes that are involved when an external stimulus is transformed into an internal representation. Although the boundaries between perception and encoding are fuzzy, encoding usually relies more heavily on prior knowledge. Individuals accomplish the encoding task by relating the new stimulus to prior knowledge, i.e., information they already know about (Theme 1). The target stimulus is categorized into a meaningful category. The term *category* denotes an elementary knowledge structure, corresponding to a singular concept or class of objects (for a more extended discussion of different types of knowledge structures see Chapter 3). Identifying a perceived target as belonging to a category allows the perceiver to infer more information than is actually given.

Imagine, for example, that your attention is directed towards an object moving quickly down the road. Based on your prior knowledge, you are able to relate this stimulus input to a meaningful knowledge structure, in this case the category "car." As a consequence, the perception is enriched with stimulus-independent knowledge, and this knowledge information helps to interpret the meaning of the input. You can infer that the car has an engine, runs on gas, has brakes, and that it will stop when the traffic light turns red. Note that you can see none of these attributes when the object is moving down the road. By adding the information from their prior knowledge, individuals are "going beyond the information given" (Bruner, 1957a). This is an essential process inherent in any encoding task.

Applying this principle to person perception allows individuals to assign a target to a social category; for example, male or female, elderly, student, professor, an ethnic group, skinhead, police officer, etc. Having categorized a target, individuals can use their knowledge of the social category—their stereotype—for subsequent interpretations and inferences. The perceiver could infer personality characteristics or likely behaviours, although—like the engine in the car example—these are not observable. For example, it could be inferred that the target is slow, aggressive, smart, helpful, and so on, depending on which prior knowledge is associated with the category to which the target is assigned.

Individuals need to categorize behaviours much as they do objects and persons. How do individuals interpret the behaviour of someone who "helped a friend cheat on an exam"? The behaviour is assigned to pre-existing knowledge, for example, to the category "dishonest." The implications of this prior knowledge will influence further storage, retrieval, and inferential and judgmental processes. Note that some trait categories, such as dishonest, friendly, aggressive, outgoing, etc. are part of stereotypes. This information may serve two different purposes. First, it can be used directly for further processes such as judgments and inferences (see below). For example, it could be inferred that a target categorized as elderly is slow, although no direct observation was made. Second, the information can be used to encode behaviours of the target. For example, if assigning a target person to a particular category has brought to mind the trait "aggressive," this information can be used in interpreting observed behaviours. Ambiguous behaviour will therefore be interpreted as less favourable if the perceiver holds a negative rather than a positive stereotype about the group to which the target is assigned (cf. Fiske & Neuberg, 1990).

In many cases a particular input can be assigned not just to one but to several categories, and these different categories may hold very different implications. As a result, the same input can be interpreted very differently. The example "helped a friend cheat on an exam" illustrates these different interpretations. Instead of classifying the behaviour as "dishonest," a perceiver could classify it as "helpful." The question now is which category is more likely to be used. In order for a stimulus to be assigned to a category, the category must be applicable and accessible (Higgins, 1996; Wyer & Srull, 1989). *Applicability* refers to whether the category can potentially be used to give meaning to the specific stimulus in the first place. For example, whereas prior knowledge about "dishonest" or "helpful" is applicable to the above example, knowledge about "athletic" or "humorous" is hardly applicable in trying to make sense of the behaviour. *Accessibility* refers to the ease with which prior knowledge can be retrieved from memory. Some information comes to mind quickly; other information takes longer and requires more processing. Note that accessibility is logically independent of applicability. It is entirely possible that the less applicable category is more accessible and is therefore more likely to be used for encoding than the more applicable category.

What determines the accessibility of prior knowledge? Two general principles govern the ease of retrieval: *recency* and *frequency*. First, information that has been recently used is more likely to be retrieved again than information that has been used much longer ago. If an individual recently thought about "dishonesty versus honesty," the statement that someone "helped a friend cheat on an exam" is more likely to be interpreted as dishonest behaviour. Second, information that is used frequently is more accessible than information that is used infrequently. If the "dishonest versus honest" category is used often, the behaviour in question is more likely to be interpreted as dishonest.

The recency principle is nicely demonstrated in so-called *priming* experiments, in which recently activated categories have been shown to possess enhanced accessibility. Priming can be referred to as information activation—rendering it more likely to be used in further processing. Perhaps the most prominent study addressing the accessibility and applicability of prior knowledge on the interpretation of data is provided by Higgins, Rholes, and Jones (1977). Participants were asked to judge a target person, Donald, based on a rather ambiguous description of his habits and interests. Prior to this task, participants were presented with a list of words. The words were subtly embedded in an unrelated verbal-learning experiment in which participants were asked to name the colour of presented slides and to utter words they were supposed to remember while the slide was being presented. Some of these words were applicable to interpreting the meaning of the behaviour descriptions about Donald. These applicable trait categories offered either positive interpretations (independent, persistent, self-confident, adventurous) or negative interpretations (aloof, stubborn, conceited, reckless) of the same behaviours. Participants were not aware of the connection between the two allegedly unrelated experiments, and they did not notice any influence that the preceding verbal learning task could have on later judgments. Nevertheless, they provided more favourable judgments of Donald when the primed trait categories had been positive than when the primed traits had been negative. Importantly, when the primed words, positive and negative, were not applicable to the target behaviours, judgments by participants showed no differences.

One fundamental assumption underlying the influence of priming holds that individuals do not search for all potential categories that could be relevant for the encoding of a given stimulus input. Because of capacity constraints (Theme 2), individuals are not able to check all potentially applicable categories and consequently need to *truncate the search process*. The search process is truncated when a category that comes to mind has a sufficient degree of applicability. If the search process were not truncated, all potentially relevant concepts would be brought to mind, and the most applicable concept would be used; in that case, priming effects would become less likely. Note that the truncation of the search process is not constant. Sometimes individuals engage in more and sometimes in less extensive search processes, depending on their processing capacity and their processing motivation (see Theme 3).

Note the adaptive component of these principles. As described above, it may well be that inadequate categories are more easily accessible than adequate categories, resulting in suboptimal interpretations of the stimulus information. In the large majority of cases, however, the recency and frequency principles will bring to mind the information that is most likely to be relevant: either the information has been recently used and is therefore potentially still relevant (recency principle), or it is used very frequently and therefore it is potentially of general importance to the individual (frequency principle). Again, individuals rely on cognitive mechanisms that (1) allow for a simplification of the required processes, and (2) possess a high degree of efficiency and adaptation.

To summarize, what we should take away from our discussion of information activation is that recently or frequently activated information is more likely to be used for further processing. To guide the encoding process, the activated information has to be applicable to the stimulus input. In Chapter 3 we will discuss more extensively the underlying mechanism of *how and why* recency and frequency impact accessibility. We will then also discuss other aspects of information activation, for example different forms of priming, subconscious priming, the direct priming of behaviour, or consequences of the perceiver's awareness of the priming procedure (see Chapter 5).

Storage and retrieval

When a stimulus has received sufficient attention and has been encoded, it may enter into further cognitive processes. One aspect of these further processes involves the storage of the information in memory. After all, individuals might use the information as a basis for their behaviour not only in the immediate circumstances, but also in later situations. For example, at the party you make a number of new acquaintances. A couple of days later you meet one of them in the cafeteria, and most probably your behaviour will be guided by what you can recall. Researchers usually investigate the storage process in conjunction with the retrieval process. In most cases, we can infer whether and how some information is stored only by assessing whether and how it is retrieved.

What information do individuals store? First, the more an individual thinks about a piece of information, the more likely it is to be stored in memory. Thus, attention-grabbing information (see above) is more likely to be stored and later retrieved than other information. Second, individuals frequently do not store the "raw data" of the factual stimulus input, but rather their encoding of the stimulus input. This offers an obvious advantage, since it allows individuals to simplify their processing (Theme 2) by focusing on the encoded information rather than on the raw stimulus data. This advantage, however, is accompanied by a disadvantage. When individuals rely on the stored information for further processing, the initial basis for the judgment is no longer taken into account. If the initial encoding was influenced by situational constraints, the effects of these constraints will extend to later situations, even though they may be quite different. Box 2.2 provides a nice illustration of how initial judgments rather than the original input itself may influence subsequent judgments in later situations.

Information should be stored in such a way that it can be recalled easily if needed in a later situation. Like the way in which information is stored in a filing cabinet, individuals require an efficient organization that allows fast retrieval of information when needed. Not surprisingly, the storage of information depends on a person's *processing goals* and the *prior knowledge* that guides the encoding and storage processes. Investigating the impact of processing goals, Hamilton, Katz, and Leirer (1980) provided their participants with a large set of behaviour descriptions. These descriptions pertained to four different topics (sports, intellectual interests, interpersonal relations, religious interests). Half of the participants were explicitly instructed to memorize the descriptions (memory set), while the other half was merely instructed to form an impression about the target person performing these behaviours (impression set). In a later recall task, participants who received the impression set instructions showed better performance than participants who were explicitly instructed to memorize the information. Presumably, forming an impression had led participants to create a high degree of inter-item links and a coherent memory representation, which facilitated later recall.

Although these results will depend on the effectiveness and memorability of the presented information, the pattern of these findings illustrates that under some conditions incidental learning may have an advantage over intentional learning. Because a coherent representation implies a good "understanding" of the material—of how everything fits together—these findings also suggest that when studying for an exam, attempts to understand the material are often more effective for recall performance than attempts to memorize single items.

Individuals need not always "create" a coherent knowledge structure. In many cases, they can rely on their prior knowledge to provide them with an already existing structure. Not surprisingly, this existing structure has a pronounced impact on storage and retrieval processes. If the incoming information is consistent with the prior knowledge, it is sufficient to store a link to the prior knowledge structure rather than storing the new information again. For example, when one of the party guests talks about having gone out for dinner, the listener does not need to store that the guest made reservations, that the waitress escorted them to the table, that she brought the menu, etc. All this information is already part of the person's general knowledge about "going out for dinner." As a consequence, it is sufficient to store a link to this existing general knowledge structure.

When retrieving the information at some later time, individuals simply need to recall "going out for dinner," and can then reconstruct that a waitress brought the menu. As a result, *consistent information* can be recalled easily—or better, more precisely—and can be easily reconstructed. This advantage comes at the cost of *intrusion errors*: Individuals may also reconstruct information that is part of their general knowledge but was not part of the actual information given. For example, a person might reconstruct the waitress bringing dessert even though this information was never supplied (Graesser, Gordon, & Sawyer, 1979; Snyder & Uranowitz, 1978).

Inconsistent information, by contrast, cannot be reconstructed on the basis of prior knowledge. However, this does not imply that inconsistent information, for example, that the waitress was wearing in-line skates, will be lost. Inconsistent information usually draws more attention (see above) and individuals allocate more processing resources to deal with the discrepancy between the implications of the stimulus and their prior knowledge. Not surprisingly, the more individuals think about something, the more likely they are to recall the event. Individuals will therefore be able to recall the inconsistent information later, provided they allocated sufficient processing resources during encoding and storing. Thus, both consistent and inconsistent information may have recall advantages, albeit for very different reasons. Once again the themes outlined in the beginning of this chapter re-emerge. Obviously, storage and retrieval depends strongly on prior knowledge structures (Theme 1) and on the amount of processing (Theme 3). Moreover, the adaptive nature of human cognition becomes obvious. Whenever possible, individuals simplify their processing (in the case of consistent information), and allocate more processing if necessary (in the case of inconsistent information). Chapter 3 will provide a more detailed discussion of how social information is organized in human memory. In addition to a further discussion of the storage of consistent versus inconsistent information, we will also address different forms of recall (implicit versus explicit) and why information related to the self has a recall advantage. In Chapter 4 we will see how individuals make use not only of the content they recall, but also of the ease with which they can recall information.

Further processes, inferences, judgments, and decisions

Drawing on encoded information and on information retrieved from memory, individuals need to engage in further processing in order to respond to the requirements of the social world. They need to make further inferences, form judgments, and make decisions. The distinction between inferences, judgments, and decisions is fuzzy and often seems quite arbitrary. One characteristic shared by all of these processes is their constructive quality. Although the constructive nature of human cognition is also inherent in encoding, storage, and retrieval processes, the "going beyond the information given" is particularly pronounced in inferences, judgments, and decisions.

One important form of inference that has received considerable attention is how individuals infer general dispositions or traits on the basis of specific behaviours (observed directly or indirectly). For example, at the party you may be watching a person who is talking to another guest. You encode his behaviour as nervous. Would you conclude that he is an anxious person in general? You could, but you could also take into account potential situational influences. For example, if the person is new in this group and does not know anybody at the party, you would perhaps be less likely to infer that he is generally anxious. Observers often seem to underestimate situational constraints and are more likely to attribute an observed behaviour to the actor's disposition ("He is behaving nervously because he is an anxious person in general") rather than to situational influences ("He is behaving nervously because he is in an unfamiliar situation"). The tendency to attribute the behaviours of others to dispositions rather than to situational influence is called the fundamental attribution error (Jones & Harris, 1967; Ross, 1977). Research suggests that taking into account the situational constraints—which would often result in fewer dispositional attributions—requires additional resources, which individuals are often unable or unwilling to allocate (Gilbert, Pelham, & Krull, 1988; see Theme 3). These attributional inferences constitute a very important facet of the way in which individuals process social information. The discussion of these inferences is partly covered in the remaining chapters, as well as in a separate module of *Social Psychology: A Modular Course* (see Försterling, 2001).

In general, inferences can also be seen as judgments, which are often considered the end product of the sequence of information processing. Grading an exam, evaluating a product presented in a commercial, evaluating the trustworthiness of a politician, judging the likeability of a person, judging a philosophical idea, evaluating the food at the party—any concrete stimulus or abstract concept can be a judgmental target. Judgments are hardly distinguishable from decisions, and many researchers refrain from making a distinction.

One potential difference is that judgments usually reflect the fact that the individual is locating the judgmental target along a particular continuum or dimension: a politician is judged to be more or less trustworthy, a product is evaluated more or less favourably, etc. Decisions, on the other hand, often entail that individuals select one of at least two options. These options do not necessarily have anything in common (e.g., if you had the choice, what would you do: go to a movie, eat a bowl of soup, surf the web, or study for the next exam?). This potential difference is reduced, however, if we assume that judgments can be considered a selection of different alternatives along the underlying dimension. For example, "very trustworthy" and "not trustworthy" constitute two alternatives when judging a politician. In any case, the difference is fuzzy, and depending on the researcher different lines are drawn between inferences, judgments, and decisions. In the following discussion, we go along with those researchers who do not explicitly differentiate between the different forms of further processes.

How do individuals arrive at a particular judgment? How do they make decisions? In the following section we briefly address two aspects that are highly intertwined but will be examined separately for ease of presentation. First we discuss how individuals select, weigh, and integrate information into a judgment. Second, we look at the specific procedures that enable individuals to short cut the formation of judgments.

Selecting, weighing, and integrating information

The argument that individuals base their judgments and decisions on activated information seems straightforward enough. Thus, an individual's judgments reflect the content of the information that comes to mind when the judgment is formed. On the one hand, this information comprises prior knowledge that is retrieved from memory; on the other hand, it comprises the encoded stimulus input of the situation, which is, of course, already heavily influenced by prior knowledge (see Theme 1). The judgmental processes are again heavily affected by an individual's processing constraints (Theme 2). Imagine, for example, the seemingly simple judgment in response to the question "How satisfied are you with your life in general?". You may retrieve an endless number of aspects and information from memory that are potentially relevant for forming this judgment. Because of capacity constraints, individuals will not be able to consider or even retrieve all the potentially relevant information. Instead, they can rely on a subset of information (Wyer & Srull, 1989) by truncating the search for relevant information. Similar to the way in which applicable categories are selected at the encoding stage (see above), the recency and frequency principles govern which information is used. If you have just recently thought about health or if you are presently suffering from a toothache, health-related information will come to mind very easily compared to a situation in which you have thought about the financial aspect of your life. Again, individuals can engage in more or less processing (Theme 3): The more relevant the judgment and the greater the available processing capacity, the greater the likelihood that individuals will consider more, and a broader range of, information.

Note that individuals' prior knowledge may often allow for more simplified judgmental processes than attending to the implications of the specific information provided by the situation. For example, when forming judgments about other persons, individuals can rely primarily on individuating information, that is, on information that is specific to the target person, or they can base their judgments primarily on their stereotype about the group the target is assigned to. Motivational deficits and capacity constraints have been demonstrated to increase the impact of stereotypes on individuals' impressions about other persons (e.g., Bodenhausen et al., 1999; Fiske & Neuberg, 1990). Similarly, in the domain of attitude change (see *Attitudes and Attitude Change* in *Social Psychology: A Modular Course*) individuals can base their attitude judgment on an extensive elaboration of the content of a persuasive message. Alternatively, if processing constraints do not allow for careful consideration of the content, they can rely on peripheral cues, such as the attractiveness of a communicator (Eagly & Chaiken, 1993; Petty & Cacioppo, 1996).

After selecting which information provides the basis for their judgment, individuals need to combine and integrate the various pieces of information into a final judgment and decision (N. H. Anderson, 1981). Since not all information favours a particular position, individuals need to weigh the pro and cons. Moreover, not all information is equally important; again, individuals need to weigh the less important relative to the more important information (for an example see Box 2.3 for the differential importance of positive and negative information). In Chapter 5 we will discuss in greater detail how individuals select and combine information.

Heuristics as judgmental short cuts

In many cases, selecting, weighing, and integrating information into a final judgment is a very complex task, even if individuals simplify the

BOX 2.3.

The differential diagnosticity of positive vs. negative information for morality vs. ability judgments

John Skowronski and Donal Carlston (1987) investigated how individuals weigh a particular piece of information when forming an evaluative judgment about other persons. In their research, participants were provided with information about targets performing different behaviours. These behaviours were either morality-relevant (e.g., pertaining to honesty) or ability-relevant (e.g., pertaining to intelligence). The behaviours were either of positive or of negative valences. Examples:

- stole money from his roommate's wallet (*morality-related negative*)
- returned a lost wallet intact (*morality-related positive*)
- graduated in the bottom 10% of his high school class (*ability-related negative*)
- understood the equations presented in the calculus class (*ability-related positive*)

Participants then evaluated the target on morality and ability dimensions. The results show that negative but not positive information had a pronounced impact on morality judgments (negativity bias). Conversely, positive information had a more pronounced impact on ability judgments (positivity bias) than negative information. In other words, a single piece of negative information received more weight than positive information when judging the morality (e.g., the honesty) of a target. However, when judging someone's ability, a single piece of positive information received more weight than negative information.

process by truncating the search for relevant information. In order to deal with this complexity, individuals have developed additional strategies that allow them to simplify the judgmental task by relying on rules of thumb. As briefly noted above, these cognitive devices are called *heuristics*. These rules of thumb require little cognitive effort but still yield valid results most of the time. Not surprisingly, heuristics capture a wide spectrum of simplifying devices. For example, they also comprise the reliance on general knowledge structures that simplify the processing of a specific input (see above). Other forms of heuristics pertain to general procedural knowledge that is applicable to specific judgmental tasks.

The most prominent of these heuristics pertaining to procedural knowledge were introduced by Tversky and Kahneman (1973). One of them is the *availability heuristic*. According to the availability heuristic, individuals can base frequency and probability judgments not only on the content of activated information, but also on the ease with which this information comes to mind. The assumption underlying this heuristic holds that if exemplars of a category come to mind easily, there must be many of them. For example, if you can easily retrieve the names of many persons who play soccer, then there must be many people who play soccer; conversely, if it is difficult to retrieve the names of persons who play soccer, then there are probably not too many of them. While this heuristic generally provides solid results, it can also bias judgments if factors unrelated to the recalled number influence the retrieval processes. For example, if you are a member of a soccer club it is easy to think of many people who play soccer, whereas if you have no connection to the sport you will have greater difficulty recalling exemplars. As a result, you would come up with different judgments about the percentage of people who play soccer.

In addition to the availability heuristic, Kahneman and Tversky (1973) have suggested other heuristics that support and simplify judgment processes, such as the representative heuristic or the anchoring and adjustment heuristic. Chapter 4 will provide a review of these different heuristics.

The selection of a behavioural response

One general notion of social cognition holds that individuals' behaviours are based on their internal representation of the social world— on their inferences, their judgments, and decisions. The behavioural response can take very different forms. First, individuals can directly communicate their judgment to other persons. For example, you can tell a friend your impressions of the other guests. The communication about how one perceives and interprets the social world plays a very important role. Obviously, it can facilitate the interaction with other individuals. If we know how the other person thinks, we can guide our behaviour accordingly. For example, if the other person told us that she did not like a particular guest, we would hesitate to invite the two persons for dinner at the same time. Moreover, by communicating their interpretation of the situation, individuals are provided with feedback about how others see it. Individuals have a strong motivation to compare their world views—not least to receive support for their own view, or to change their view according to other interpretations (Festinger, 1954). From this perspective it is not surprising that on a daily basis we learn about surveys of virtually any possible issue: A whole business is concerned with assessing individuals' perception of the world. Second, internal judgments and decisions provide the basis for the whole spectrum of behaviours. Depending on their internal representation of the situation, individuals will engage in different activities: Individuals approach or avoid other persons, they help other persons in need, they react aggressively, they ignore others, they purchase certain products, they buy or sell stocks, they vote for a political candidate, etc.—all behaviours which are based on individuals' internal representations.

It is important to note that communicated judgments, as well as behaviours, do not always correspond with the internally generated representation of the judgmental target. For example, if the guest you don't like is a good friend of the person you are talking to, you will be more hesitant about expressing your negative impression. Similarly, individuals may sometimes seem to interact in a very friendly way with another person although they do not like them. Obviously, the judgment about the likeability of the person is not the only basis for individuals' behaviours. In addition to their interpretation of the target (the other person, a specific product, etc.), individuals will take into account other aspects of the situation. Most obviously, individuals' behaviour is also guided by social norms—which may have different implications for the behaviour than the interpretation about the target. For example, we may not express a particular attitude or opinion (and perform the corresponding behaviour) because this opinion is politically not correct in the current context. The interplay of attitudes and social norms in guiding social behaviour is captured in Fishbein and Ajzen's theory of reasoned action (1974; Ajzen & Fishbein, 1980). Attitudes are assumed to influence behaviour, but it is argued that social norms may override this impact. For example, if the social norm holds that you say nice things to the host of the party, you are likely to talk about how exciting the party was, although in fact you thought it was quite boring. In the absence of strong social norms, individuals' behaviour will reflect those attitudes that are most accessible (see above) at the time (see Fazio & Towles-Schwen, 1999; for a general discussion of the attitude–behaviour link see Eagly & Chaiken, 1993, Chapter 4).

Chapter summary

(1) In order to understand how individuals construct their social reality, we have to take into account three different elements: (a) the input from a given situation; (b) the input in the form of the prior knowledge that individuals bring to that situation; and (c) the processes that operate on the input.

(2) In this chapter, four general themes of social cognition were outlined. These themes pertain to (a) the interplay of stimulus

information and prior knowledge; (b) the limitations of processing capacity; (c) the amount of processing depending on processing motivation and processing capacity; and (d) the interplay of automatic and controlled processes.

(3) In an idealized fashion, the sequence of cognitive processes can be separated into different stages. Individuals first *perceive* a stimulus event, they then *encode* and interpret this perception. Encoded information will be *stored* in memory so that it can be *retrieved* when required in later situations. Newly encoded input and retrieved prior knowledge provide the basis for further processing, leading to *inferences, judgments, and decisions.* Sometimes, but not always, the final outcome of this cognitive process is manifested in an overt *behavioural response.*

(4) Individuals do not have the processing capacity to attend to all stimuli of a given situation. To deal with this shortcoming, individuals have the ability to direct their *attention* to some aspects of the situation and exclude other aspects from being processed.

(5) The encoding of a stimulus is heavily influenced by prior knowledge. Which prior knowledge is applied depends on its *accessibility* and *applicability.* Accessibility is affected by the recency and the frequency with which prior knowledge has been used.

(6) Encoded information is stored in relation to prior knowledge. Different processes underlie the storage of new information that is consistent versus inconsistent with prior knowledge.

(7) Individuals can rely on different processes when forming judgments and inferences. Depending on the situational constraints, they may select, weigh, and integrate as much relevant information as possible, or they may short cut the processes by applying heuristic processing strategies.

Discussion questions

(1) What are the main ingredients for individuals' construction of social reality? Apply these ingredients to a specific example.

(2) What is usually meant by the terms "top-down" and "bottom-up" processing? Give some examples from everyday life.

(3) Discuss some of the introduced concepts (e.g., impact of accessibility, automatic versus controlled processes, attention processes) with respect to how social cognition reflects a high level of adaption towards the requirements of the social world.

(4) Select a specific step from the information processing sequence (e.g., encoding, retrieval) and apply it to a specific example. Then relate the four major themes to this example.

(5) What could an advertiser do to increase the chances that viewers attend to a particular commercial? Derive some specific examples from the considerations about attentional processes. Discuss potential advantages and disadvantages of the strategies.

Recommendations for further reading

The further chapters of this book will provide a more in-depth coverage of the issues raised in this overview chapter. Additional coverage for more advanced readers can be found in:

Higgins, E. T. (1996). Knowledge activation: Accessibility, applicability, and salience. In E. T. Higgins & A. W. Kruglanski (Eds.), *Social psychology: Handbook of basic principles*. New York: Guilford Press.

With the present chapter in mind it might be worthwhile to see how the social cognition paradigm is applied to different areas. The two chapters listed below provide such an opportunity for the domain of stereotyping and consumer behaviour, respectively.

Hamilton, D. L., & Sherman, J. W. (1994). Stereotypes. In R. S. Wyer & T. K. Srull (Eds.), *Handbook of social cognition* (Vol. 1, 2nd ed., pp. 1–68). Hillsdale, NJ: Lawrence Erlbaum Associates Inc.
Shavitt, S., & Wänke, M. (2000). Consumer cognition, marketing, and advertising. In A. Tesser & N. Schwarz (Eds.), *Handbook of social psychology* (pp. 569–590). Oxford, UK: Blackwell.

Memory organization as a key to understanding social cognition

3

In Chapter 2 we outlined the various steps in the information processing sequence. It has become evident that almost any cognitive process relies on prior knowledge that is stored in memory. For information to be stored effectively in memory and to be retrievable for later judgments, decisions, and action planning, it has to be structured and organized appropriately. Just as a meaningful word is much easier to read and to be held in memory than a random sequence of letters, social information has a stronger impact on individuals and their behaviour if it is organized and embedded in an orderly context. Imposing structure on human memory is similarly important as an efficient and systematic organization of an index card file, a computer directory, or a library. In this chapter we will address memory processes in more detail. We will start out with two questions that are directly linked to each other: *How is information organized in memory?* and *How is information retrieved?* The next section will then focus on how new information is linked to already stored information and how existing cognitive structures can be changed by new information. We will then address how prior stored knowledge impacts social judgment, discuss conditions that can increase or decrease this impact, and examine how individuals may try to control for the sometimes unwanted impact of prior knowledge. The concluding section will address the constructive nature of human memory.

How is information organized in memory?

The key to efficient information processing is a well-organized memory. Just like a library, a computer directory, or any other knowledge store, our memory requires an internal organization that allows for economic storage and efficient memory search and retrieval. The elementary unit of organization in memory is a *category*. Categories capture the common meaning and the distinctive features of entire classes of stimulus objects. Categories may refer to the physical world (e.g., denoting tools such as hammer, pencil, computer) or to the social world (e.g., denoting vocational groups such as salesman, nurse, politician). They can refer to natural kinds (man, woman, seniors) or to artificial products of human intelligence (automobile, software); and categories may be abstract (dignity, intention) versus relatively concrete in meaning (journal, weapon). However, even when referring to very concrete, visible, physically existing stimulus objects, a category (e.g., weapon) abstracts from many subsidiary features of individual stimuli (e.g., hundreds of different weapons), thus providing a highly economical means of grouping and clustering the environment.

Categories render the world predictable. When recognizing a new stimulus object as belonging to a particular category, the individual can infer many properties and uses of the object. Understanding a stimulus as belonging to a category affords an elementary model of the interplay between bottom-up and top-down processes—one of the basic themes introduced in Chapter 2. The bottom-up influence of the stimulus is enriched with top-down inferences derived from the category. For example, recognizing a stimulus as belonging to the category of weapons means that the object is dangerous, that it can serve an aggressive or a defensive function, that it is mobile, and that using the weapon may require certain skills. Likewise, the professional category to which a person belongs (e.g., tennis professional) can be used to predict personality traits, interests, attitudes, and style of living; or ethnic categories can help to predict language, religion, and cultural norms. In many cases, the predictions and inferences derived from categorical knowledge are very helpful. However, as we shall see below, they may not always be correct; they may be the source of severe fallacies, stereotypes, and superstitious beliefs.

All the above examples refer to stable, commonly shared categories of well-known meaning. Thus, the weapons or tennis professionals categories belong to the general world knowledge that we expect to share with all other people. This holds even more so for many biological categories (mother, race, sex) and mundane categories (hand, car, drink, laughing) that are frequently used in everyday encounters. Apart from these long-established categories, we can also learn new concepts that have not been known before but that arise as we deal with new developments, such as bungee jumping, compact disk, or Internet. Moreover, organisms have the capacity to flexibly learn new ad hoc categories that bear little relation to natural world knowledge, if these ad hoc categories help to make predictions and discriminations. For example, we can learn the composition of a newly formed group, what sequence of code is valid in an artificial computer language, or what offside is in football. Indeed, the same categories that adult people consider highly familiar are seen as strange and unfamiliar to 18-month-old children whose task is to learn the meaning of thousands of linguistic concepts.

Types and representation of knowledge structures

Apart from categories as the most elementary unit, social cognition is concerned with a number of other knowledge structures. What characterizes these structures and which technical terms have been established to denote them are summarized in Table 3.1.

The first entry refers to a *category*, which, as has already been mentioned, is an elementary unit of knowledge that offers an abstract representation for a whole class of particular objects. As a stimulus is identified as an exemplar of a *category* (e.g., a fluid as poison), we abstract from other features of the exemplar and we ascribe the attributes of the category to the exemplar.

TABLE 3.1
Terminological conventions to denote different types of knowledge structure

Technical term	Defining features	Example
Category	Classes of objects with similar meaning and function	Concrete categories like hammer and computer, or abstract categories such as dignity and crime
Stereotype	Categories linking attributes to social groups	Attributes of professional (policemen) or ethnic groups (Chinese)
Schema	Knowledge structures linked to adaptive function	Causal schema for making quick causal inferences
Script	Temporally structured behavioural routine	The sequence of behaviours that constitute a visit to the theatre
Cognitive map	Spatial organization of concrete objects in visual modality	Visual imagery of and automatic locomotion in one's university campus
Associative network	Highly interconnected structure involving many different concepts	The self, including all its autobiographic, affective, and semantic aspects

Categories that pertain to social groups or person types are usually referred to as *stereotypes,* which may of course be linked to other categories or knowledge structures. A stereotype entails expectancies about which attributes characterize a particular group and set this group apart from others. For example, the stereotype of a skinhead associates this group label with trait categories like impolite, rude, and dull.

The meaning of a *schema* is also very close to a category; in fact, these terms are often used in an almost synonymous fashion. What the additional meaning of a schema highlights is a procedure or routine in which categorical knowledge is used quasi-automatically. For example, a baby-face schema (Berry & Zebrowitz-McArthur, 1988) not only describes a class of people but also entails some quasi-automatic reaction to baby-face stimuli, such as protection, care, and leniency, treating the baby-faced person like an immature child.

Knowledge structures about standard sequences of events and actions in time are referred to as *scripts,* using a theatre analogy. Examples of very common scripts include checking in at the airport, going to church, or buying a hamburger in a fast-food restaurant. The following box uses the airport check-in episode to illustrate the nature of scripted knowledge.

BOX 3.1.

A script for routinized behaviour, such as checking-in at the airport

A check-in at the airport, for instance, is characterized by the following standard sequence: entering the airport building → looking for a sign leading to the departure hall → searching the counter belonging to a particular carrier → queuing → writing an address label and fixing it to one's luggage while waiting in the queue → holding available one's passport and flight ticket → moving to a free counter → putting one's luggage on a conveyor belt → giving passport and flight ticket to the officer behind the counter → expressing one's seat preference → receiving boarding pass → moving towards indicated gate with hand luggage. The standard sequence not only allows us to check-in automatically (see Theme 4 on automatic processes), without any conscious awareness, while thinking of something completely different, but also to reconstruct the entire episode using scripted knowledge. For instance, if immediately after the check-in we notice that we have lost our telephone card, or sunglasses, we can go back all the way to the starting point and search for the lost article, even though we were not aware of the whole action sequence. Scripted knowledge is not only structured sequentially but also hierarchically. That is, the individual steps, such as giving passport and flight ticket to the person behind the counter, can be further split into even finer steps, like saying hello → passing over the ticket → holding back the passport → waiting for further instructions → establishing eye contact, etc. Of course, we may also make characteristic mistakes when relying on scripted knowledge. We may hold the passport available when it is not required, or we may erroneously remember having fixed an address label when in fact we did not.

When people form spatial representations of a scenario, one could use the term *cognitive maps*. Most of us have acquired a reasonably accurate cognitive map of our home so that we can move around and find objects we are looking for even when it is completely dark. However, the term cognitive map is not restricted to geographical orientation and locomotion functions, but can also be expanded to knowledge that is not literally spatial. We may thus have a cognitive map of the directory of our computer, or a cognitive map of the friendship structure of the company in which we are working.

Complex knowledge structures involving multiple components that are interconnected vertically and horizontally can be referred to as *associative networks*. On the vertical dimension, the nodes of an associative network can be ordered by superordinate and subordinate relations. As illustrated by the network depicted in Figure 3.1, there are various sports disciplines at a basic level of medium abstractness, such as boxing, football, car racing, or track and field athletics. Horizontally, these concepts are organized by similarity; the more similar two sports disciplines are, the smaller the horizontal distance between them in the associative network. On the vertical dimension, all specific disciplines are included within the same superordinate concept, sports, and each discipline includes a number of subordinate subconcepts. For instance, the basic-level concept, track and field athletics, includes at the subordinate level long jump, decathlon, hurdle race, etc. Both the horizontal similarity structure and the vertical inclusion structure render the network organization highly suitable for memorizing and inference making. Once it is recalled that somebody is interested in track and field athletics, one can infer vertically that he or she is presumably quite informed about, and at least slightly interested in, hurdle races, long jump, decathlon, etc. Moreover, horizontally, one can infer that the same person will be interested in other sports disciplines as well, especially those similar disciplines that are associatively very close to track and field athletics in the network (e.g., football rather than car racing).

For various reasons, basic-level categories at the medium level of abstractness are most informative and useful for communication. Very abstract concepts at the superordinate level, like sports, are applicable to a broader range of stimulus events, but they are too general to convey the nature of somebody's interest. In contrast, highly specific concepts at the subordinate level, like long jump, are overly specific, but restricted to a very narrow reference class. Basic-level categories (track and field athletics, football, gymnastics) seem to provide the best compromise. Indeed, several studies have shown

Figure 3.1.
An associative network of knowledge about hobbies and sports. Knowledge is organized vertically by superordinate–subordinate relationships and horizontally by similarity relations.

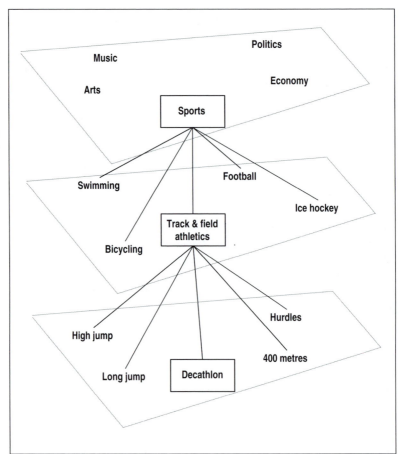

that the basic level is the most preferred and most natural level for representing information in memory (Rosch, Mervis, Gray, Johnson, & Boyes-Braem, 1976). It was also found that in language acquisition, basic-level concepts are learned earlier than superordinate or subordinate concepts. Thus, young children would understand and use the terms "football," "boxing," or "swimming" well before they use the abstract terms "sports," "politics," and "arts," or the subordinate terms "long jump," "hurdle sprint," or "decathlon."

Aside from the terminology for different types of knowledge, an intriguing question is how these structures are represented in memory. The schema or stereotype of disabled people may be represented either in terms of abstracted features (wheelchair, needing help, causing embarrassment) or in terms of particular exemplars (an acquaintance who is disabled). Whether abstract features or exemplars, the memory representation can either use the category's average on relevant attribute values, which is usually called a *proto-type* (Cantor & Michel, 1977), or an extreme value, usually referred to as an ideal type (Barsalou, 1985). For example, the prototype of an athlete can be conceived as the average of all athletes on such dimensions as body-building, dieting, daily hours of training, physical health, etc. An *ideal type*, however, would be an athlete who represents extreme, superlative positions on those dimensions (e.g., maximal body-building, extreme dieting, more than 6 hours of training every day, etc.).

These various formats of mental representations are of theoretical value because they may have different implications for the explanation of psychological phenomena. For example, Judd and Park (1988) assume that out-group knowledge relies mainly on abstract prototypes, whereas cognitive representations of our in-group include many concrete exemplars in addition to prototypical knowledge. This can then explain the phenomenon that people usually perceive more differences and variability in their in-group than in an undifferentiated out-group (Park, Judd, & Ryan, 1991).

Cognitive consistency

The Gestalt notion of consistency has dominated the first two decades of post-World War social psychology. If similar stimuli fall in the same category and dissimilar stimuli belong to different categories, information fits a perfectly consistent pattern. Social perception tends towards consistency because consistent structures are learned more efficiently and inconsistent structures are often falsely reproduced as if they were consistent. Consider the two structures in Figure 3.2. Let the letters represent persons and the solid lines connecting two persons indicate a liking relation; a dotted line between two persons indicates that they dislike each other. It is immediately evident that the left structure is easier to understand and to learn than the right one. On the left, all members of the same group like each other and all relations between groups are of the dislike type. The whole structure can be perfectly reproduced by this single organizing rule. On the right, in contrast, the pattern of liking relationships is much more complex and presumably rather difficult to learn. Given that human processing capacity is limited (see Theme 2 in Chapter 2), consistency provides an extremely valuable tool to reconstruct what cannot be remembered.

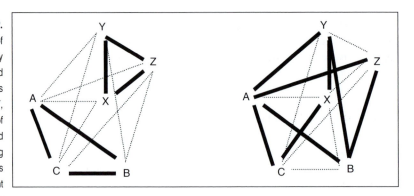

Figure 3.2.
Graphical illustration of
the consistency
principle. Let A, B, and
C represent members
of one group and X, Y,
and Z members of
another group. Solid
lines represent liking
relations whereas
dotted lines represent
disliking. It is easier to
learn and understand
the consistent structure
on the left, in which all
within-group relations
are positive (liking) and
all between-groups
relations are negative
(disliking), than the
inconsistent structure
on the right.

Several studies have confirmed the prediction that cognitive structures tend towards consistency. Heider's balance theory (Heider, 1946) predicts that triadic relations should be easier and more likely to be recalled in memory if the three bilateral relations in a triad (e.g., involving a person P, another person O, and an attitude object X) are balanced. For example, if P likes O and O likes X, balance implies that P should like X as well. Conversely, if P dislikes O but O likes X, P should dislike X. In general, a triad is balanced if either all three connections are positive, or only one connection. Imbalance exists when two connections or no connection are positive (e.g., P likes O, O likes X, P dislikes X). DeSoto (1960) demonstrated that it is easier to remember a network of balanced relations between persons than an imbalanced network, implying that selective forgetting should produce a bias in favour of balanced relations. Consistency, as an organizing principle, imposes a highly efficient and economic code on memory. A considerable part of the information does not have to be encoded directly but can be derived logically from an internally consistent network of positive and negative connections in memory.

As a natural consequence of the consistency advantage in learning, our most important knowledge structures are organized in a highly consistent fashion. The consistency principle in particular can explain that associative networks in semantic memory are organized by similarity, as we have seen earlier (cf. Figure 3.1). Semantically similar concepts (e.g., hobbies or sports disciplines like football – handball; long jump – high jump) that share many features are expected to co-occur within the same persons, whereas dissimilar concepts (e.g., football – boxing) are not. Such a similarity structure creates a high degree of consistency. In addition to the horizontal organization by similarity relations, the vertical organization serves to further enhance the consistency of the cognitive organization;

subordinate concepts, which share the same superordinate concepts, inevitably share all the defining features of the superordinate concepts, thereby increasing the overall consistency of semantic memory.

How is information retrieved?

The more systematically world knowledge is structured in memory—either chronologically, in script-like sequences, or hierarchically and by similarity, as in an associative network—the more effectively information can be retrieved when it is needed for ongoing decisions or actions. The important point here is that in order to understand the process of memory retrieval we have to consider the function that memorized information serves in a larger problem context. When information is retrieved, what information is found in memory, and what stimuli elicit the memory search, depend on this over-arching problem context. On the one hand, the retrieval cues provided by the task context may be rather specific, restricting memory search to a few possible solutions or only one single matching item in memory. Examples for memory tasks with such restrictive retrieval cues include the following: What is the name of the person behind a given face? What is the main language spoken in South Africa? Where did I park my car this morning? The characteristic feature of these convergent search problems, which are common for everyday social behaviour as well as for academic learning, is that very concrete exemplars have to be located in memory (e.g., a name) when given specific retrieval cues (e.g., a face).

On the other hand, however, many divergent problems only provide rather vague retrieval cues that do not greatly restrict the memory search process but allow for many possible outcomes. These less restricted, more creative, and open-ended search processes in memory are particularly interesting, psychologically, because they are open to all kinds of external influences and biases. For instance, consider the problem of finding a suitable birthday present for a friend. The unspecific retrieval cue "birthday present" will hardly be helpful because it allows for hundreds of possible answers. Thinking about the friend's interests and hobbies might lead to further retrieval cues that help to narrow down the search space to a few appropriate alternatives. However, importantly, this process of reducing the search space is susceptible to external influence. Having just passed a sporting goods store, we may be primed for a particular category of

presents, sporting goods. If this category is applicable to our friend—
who is perhaps an enthusiastic athlete—then we might use an
associative network, as in Figure 3.1, to select a present from any
specific sports discipline. If the category is not applicable to our other
knowledge about this friend, we have to search for a new applicable
category. We might, for instance, next pass a bookshop and be
reminded of the fact that our friend is extremely keen on reading
literature. Note that this process of memory search is not exhaustive;
it is typically truncated as soon as a suitable, applicable category or
schema is found to solve the problem at hand. In any case, non-
restrictive, open-ended memory search depends heavily on retrieval
cues that prime the activation of certain structures of memory. Such
priming effects have been a prominent topic of recent experimental
research in social cognition. We will now turn to this important
research paradigm, which we briefly introduced in Chapter 2.

The priming paradigm as a major research tool

We have seen that schemas, scripts, and other knowledge structures
allow for quick short cut inferences, triggered by specific eliciting
events. To the extent that schemas reflect valid world knowledge,
these short cuts will very often lead to correct inferences. However,
they may also lead to premature and unfair inferences, giving rise to
irrational decisions and social prejudice. Psychologically, the dangers
of schema-driven inferences originate in the fact that world knowledge is rich enough to offer several schemas or knowledge structures
for interpreting the same behaviour in different ways. Each target
person belongs to several categories with regard to his race, profession, religion, age, hobbies, and citizenship. Depending on which
of these multiple categories is activated, the same target person's
behaviour will be given quite different interpretations. Social knowledge is so rich and multi-faceted that only a small portion of that
knowledge is activated at any time. Very often, the currently activated information is appropriate to the problem to be solved in a
given context. Sometimes, however, the selectivity of activated world
knowledge makes social judgment susceptible to errors and biases.

Although the terms are often used like synonyms, it is useful to
distinguish between the *availability* of information in memory (i.e.,
whether some representation exists at all) and *accessibility* (i.e.,
whether that representation is ready to be retrieved at the moment).
Availability depends on actual learning experience and what was
really stored in memory. Availability can influence social behaviour,

as when paucity of direct experience with members of a racial group fosters prejudice and superficial inferences. All information that is available in memory can then differ in accessibility at a given moment, dependent on such factors as the frequency and recency of exposure, the degree of elaboration, and the accessibility of competing, incompatible knowledge structures (cf. Higgins, 1996). For instance, having been just exposed to a member of a racial group can render latent stereotypcial knowledge about that group accessible.

Perhaps the most prominent experimental paradigm that was invented to study the selective activation of knowledge structures and its influence on subsequent reactions is the priming paradigm, as already introduced in Chapter 2. Because priming has become such an important research tool, the present section describes this paradigm in some detail. In its broadest sense, priming means that activating one stimulus facilitates the subsequent processing of another, related stimulus. For instance, having just talked about vision at day and night time, the word "light" is likely to be interpreted differently than when the preceding conversation was about weight-lifting.

The classical experimental setting for measuring priming effects is a lexical decision task (Meyer & Schvanefeldt, 1971). A letter string is presented on a tachistoscope or computer screen, and the experimental participant has to decide, as quickly as possible, if the letter string is a word or a nonword (i.e., a meaningless letter string), pressing one of two response keys. A priming effect is defined as the reduction in response latency obtained when a semantically related word has been presented briefly before. Thus, having just read the word "shoes," a subsequent lexical decision about the letter string "boots" is facilitated.

The same experimental procedure suggests itself for measuring the accessibility of knowledge and attitudes in social psychology. Note that priming effects, based on response latencies, usually reflect uncontrolled, automatic processes that are not subject to intentional self-presentation. Implicit priming-based measures should therefore afford more valid evidence on an individual's cognitive structure than explicit introspective measures, which are often contaminated with self-presentation strategies and social desirability. A typical application of the priming paradigm to measuring racial attitude is the procedure developed by Fazio, Jackson, Dunton, and Williams (1995).

After participants were led to believe that the experiment was concerned with the recognition of faces and with the allegedly automatic skill of comprehending word meaning, the actual priming task

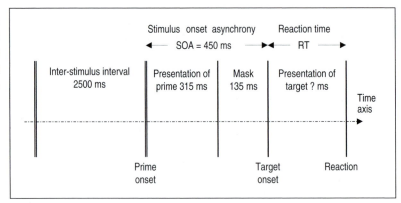

Figure 3.3.
Description of one trial
in a priming
experiment, as in
Fazio et al. (1995).

consisted of a series of trials of the kind depicted in Figure 3.3. Each trial was separated from the end of the preceding trial by a 2.5 s interval. A photograph of a black or white person's face was then presented for 315 ms, followed by a 135 ms interval before the onset of a positive or negative adjective. The entire time from the onset of the prime (face) until the onset of the target adjective is called the stimulus-onset asynchrony (SOA). The participant's task was to decide, as quickly as possible, whether the adjective was positive or negative in valence, using one of two response keys (labelled *good* and *bad*). Analogous to the priming effects on lexical decisions, white participants required less time to judge negative adjectives when preceded by a black face than when preceded by a white face. In contrast, they required more time to recognize the positive valence of adjectives when preceded by a black than a white face. Apparently, an implicit evaluation associated with racial attitudes towards black and white people served to facilitate the subsequent recognition of evaluatively congruent meaning and inhibited the recognition of incongruent meaning.

Types of priming

It is instructive to ask more precisely what aspect of information is being primed. In the above context of attitude measurement, it is obviously the positive versus negative valence of the implicit affective reaction to black or white faces that influences subsequent comprehension of positive and negative words. Only the valence, rather than any other semantic aspects of the black and white category, is relevant to the subsequent task, to discriminate "good" versus "bad" words. Evaluative priming has been shown to be very fast and effective, because the evaluative tone of a stimulus is one of the first aspects of information that is recognized during stimulus perception (Zajonc, 1984).

Evaluative priming is a specific paradigm in which each trial involves two stimuli, the prime and the target, presented in close succession (as specified by the SOA). On consistent trials the prime and the target are of the same valence (i.e., both positive or both negative), whereas on inconsistent trials prime and target are of opposite valence. As a general result, the time required to respond to the target (e.g., to judge whether the target is positive or negative) is shorter on consistent than on inconsistent trials. Evaluative priming works for very short stimulus-onset asynchronies (SOAs; cf. Figure 3.3), well below the 100 ms limit, and even below an absolute awareness threshold (even zero SOAs), making controlled, voluntary responding impossible. That is, an evaluative prime that is presented so briefly that it has no chance of being detected or identified can nevertheless influence the perceiver's subsequent reactions to stimuli of the same and opposite valence. In experiments on evaluative priming (Klauer, Rossnagel & Musch, 1997; Murphy & Zajonc, 1993), the impact of specific stimulus categories is ruled out using primes and targets of variable meaning and contents; the only crucial experimental variable is whether prime and target are of same or different valence.

Priming is even more diffuse and abstracted from specific stimuli in experiments on *mood priming*, in which emotional films or hypnosis are used to induce unspecific positive or negative emotional states in participants (Bower, 1981). Even such a global priming treatment facilitates subsequent reactions of the same valence as the mood prime; people in a good mood tend to judge behaviours more positively than people in a negative mood (Forgas & Bower, 1987); for a more extended discussion, see Chapter 7.

Other experiments have used the priming paradigm to demonstrate the impact of more circumscribed meaning categories. This variant is commonly referred to as *semantic priming*. The priming of specific semantic categories is highlighted in an experiment by Dovidio, Evans, and Tyler (1986), who used prime target pairs like black–musical, white–ambitious (stereotypical) as compared with pairs like white–musical, black–ambitious (counter-stereotypical). The participant's task was to make simple judgments about the target words (viz., whether the target property can ever be true of the prime category). As expected, the mean latencies required to make judgments of traits that matched the stereotypical meaning of the primed category were shorter than the latency required for judging non-matching traits. Note that in this experiment, the crucial comparison is not between the response latencies for positive and negative traits, but between semantically matching versus nonmatching traits.

In the illustrations reported thus far, the priming tool is mainly used for diagnostic purposes, to assess attitudes or to diagnose stereotypical knowledge in memory. However, priming can also function as a causal agent that induces judgment biases and lop-sided decisions. One of the most prominent, almost "classical" studies on priming and social judgment (Higgins, Rholes, & Jones, 1977) has already been presented in Chapter 2. When judging a target person, Donald, based on a rather ambiguous description of his habits and interests, participants were influenced by the semantic meaning and valence of words encountered in an allegedly unrelated preceding experiment on verbal learning. Recall that Donald was judged more positively when positive trait words (adventurous, self-confident, independent, persistent) had been previously primed than when negative traits (reckless, conceited, aloof, and stubborn) had been primed—provided that the trait categories were semantically applicable to the stimulus text in which Donald had been described. Interestingly, the impact of priming on person judgments was not only apparent in subsequent trait ratings, but also in content analyses of free verbal descriptions. This suggests that priming effects are not confined to quantitative reactions on restricted dimensions, such as rating scales with positive and negative scale anchors, but even extend to unconstrained self-determined communication acts.

That priming influences on judgment and decision can involve rather complex, sophisticated knowledge structures was nicely demonstrated in an experiment by Gilovich (1981) on *analogy priming*. A number of subtle context cues were used to prime a historical conception of either the Second World War or the Vietnam War. This manipulation was based, for instance, on the name of the lecture hall where the experiment took place (either "Winston Churchill Hall" or "Dean Rusk Hall") and on subtle cues in the cover story of the experimental task (e.g., whether the current US president came from the state of New York, like Roosevelt, or from Texas, like L. B. Johnson). An international conflict was described in which a hostile nation invaded a small country that belonged to an alliance with the US, and the decisive question was whether the US should intervene and help the allied country. Decisions should depend on which historical analogy is activated—knowledge of the Second World War, where the historical lesson tells American judges that the US ought to have intervened early, or knowledge of the Vietman War, where history says that the US ought not to have intervened. Indeed, a significantly larger proportion of judges decided for military intervention when the priming pointed to the Second World War than when the priming was reminiscent of the Vietnam War.

Note how these priming influences on social judgments differ from the original lexical decision tasks. The dependent measure here is not based on a more or less automatic, reflex-like response on a word recognition task, where the prime is only allowed to affect a single aspect of performance, response latency. Rather than restricting the priming effect to one response dimension, the political problem to be solved in the Gilovich (1981) study leaves considerable freedom for controlled responses. For instance, when historical knowledge of the Vietnam War is primed, the judgment is not yet determined but the judge can still engage in conscious reflection about various ways of translating the historical analogy to an appropriate decision. The outcome of this higher-order cognitive process is not at all determined by the priming treatment, which could be used quite differently. The judge might trust the Vietnam analogy and conclude that the present conflict has to be treated similarly. However, she might equally well conclude that the present case is different and therefore needs different treatment to the Vietnam conflict. In any case, a judgment model is needed, in addition to the associative priming effect, to explain the ultimate outcome of judgments or decisions.

Having seen that priming can impact deliberate descriptions and reflected decisions, it is but one step further to demonstrate direct *action priming*. Bargh, Chen, and Burrows (1996) primed their participants with the category of rudeness versus the category politeness in another condition. This was accomplished by a scrambled-sentence test in which sentences had to be constructed from mixed word sets containing either words related to rudeness (bold, aggressively, intrude, brazen, infringe, etc.) or to politeness (respect, appreciate, cordially, discreetly, etc.). The percentage of participants who later showed rude behaviour (i.e., by interrupting the experimenter) was more than twice as high in the rudeness than in the politeness priming condition. In a similar experiment, Bargh et al. demonstrated that priming the concept of the elderly caused participants to walk more slowly down the hallway after the experiment than participants in a control condition, without such a priming treatment. In a similar vein, Dijksterhuis and Van Knippenberg (1998) demonstrated that actual intellectual performance could be enhanced through priming of intelligent person categories such as "professor." To explain action priming, one has to assume an "ideomotor" tendency, that is, a tendency for primes to directly elicit an open motor response.

Apparently, priming effects can be extended from restricted response modalities like lexical decision tasks, binary decision tasks, and evaluation tasks to free communication and deliberate action. However, the phenomenon can be generalized not only regarding the output or consequences, but also regarding the kind of prime stimuli that can elicit such effects. So far, we have considered mostly experiments in which words or verbal phrases have been used as primes. However, the phenomenon also works, maybe even better so, with pictorial primes (see Fiedler & Schenck, 2001). It is also important to consider the simultaneous effect of priming on different targets; as access to one target is facilitated, access to other targets may be inhibited. The experiment displayed in Box 3.2 illustrates such an inhibitory side effect of priming.

One completely different, and particularly intriguing, variant is *procedural priming*. In this paradigm, what is being primed is not the meaning or valence of concepts, but relations between concepts, or mental procedures applied to preceding tasks. For example, when a student has repeatedly used the same method to solve an arithmetic problem, she is likely to use the same method on subsequent tasks, even when a much simpler task solution is applicable (Luchins, 1942; E. R. Smith & Lerner, 1986).

Last but not least, the prime stimulus may be an internally experienced feeling state for which no word or verbal description exists at all. An illustration of the priming of *experiential feeling states* comes from an investigation of Stepper and Strack (1993). The furniture and equipment of the experimental room forced participants into different body postures while receiving performance feedback. When participants were in an upright position, they felt more pride and provided more positive self-attributions of their performance than when participants had to stand in a somewhat bent-over position. This influence of the participants' experienced body feeling was independent of any conscious thought and inference processes.

To summarize, the present subsection has been concerned with the fact that retrieval processes determine which subset of all information that is represented in memory is accessible at any point in time. Most attention has been devoted to priming effects—the most prominent research tool that is currently in use to investigate the selective accessibility of memorized knowledge. Some well-known priming

Just like any effective treatment, an effective priming treatment involves side effects. Attention given to one stimulus is attention withdrawn from another stimulus. In priming experiments, by analogue, facilitation of access to one category will often come along with inhibition of access to another category. This important insight was nicely illustrated by Macrae, Bodenhausen, and Milne (1995). The rationale underlying their investigation was that all people are members of several different categories at the same time; for instance, somebody may belong at the same time to the category *Chinese* and to the category *women*. Activation of one categorization (Chinese) may inhibit the other categorization (women) and vice versa. For an experimental demonstration, Macrae et al. employed a three-stage paradigm. In the first step, participants were exposed to a completely unconscious priming treatment in an allegedly independent experiment. Their task was to decide, using one of two response keys, whether a rapidly presented flash had appeared on the left or the right side of a computer screen. In fact, the flash contained several extremely brief presentations (75 ms) of either the word *Chinese* or the word *women*. In addition to the short duration, the priming was parafoveal; that is, the words were presented at 2 to 6 degrees of visual angle (relative to a fixation point in the middle of the screen); they were not projected to the fovea (i.e., the retina point that warrants clear vision) but slightly apart.

Then, in the second stage, again under the disguise of an independent experiment, participants saw a videotape of a Chinese woman reading a book. It was expected that priming of one category would facilitate categorization of the stimulus person in that same category and at the same time inhibit categorization in the other, unprimed category. These predictions were tested in the third stage involving a lexical decision task. The time required to decide that a letter string is a word or a nonword was assessed. As predicted, following priming of the Chinese category, lexical decisions for words related to Chinese (trustworthy, considerate, gracious, calm) were facilitated (i.e., required less time) and lexical decisions about words related to women (thoughtful, friendly, emotional, romantic) were inhibited. In contrast, when the women category had been primed, lexical decisions concerning Chinese-related words were inhibited and decisions about women-related words were facilitated. In any case, priming effects involved facilitative main effects but inhibitory side effects at the same time.

studies have been reported and a variety of different priming effects have been distinguished, such as semantic priming, evaluative priming, mood priming, analogy priming, procedural priming, and action priming.

Linking old to new information

All problem solving and learning progress involves the creative interplay of old and new information. On the one hand, one's knowledge structures ought to be updated continuously in the light of new information and changing environments. On the other hand, old knowledge provides a pre-formed framework for embedding and assimilating new information. However, this dialectic interplay is usually not symmetric; the top-down influence of older knowledge on the acquisition of new information is usually stronger than the bottom-up influence of new data on old structures. For several reasons, old knowledge is quite resistant to change and quite flexible in assimilating all kinds of new information. One's values and attitudes are organized in a highly interconnected fashion, with the most central attitudes likely to have the most numerous and most consistent relations to other attitudes. A person whose whole life revolves around one central topic, say, religion, will have many interests, hobbies, and moral and political preferences, will seek a job, and make many friends that all support this central topic of life. Given such a powerful, highly ramified structure of attitudes and related knowledge categories, this person will hardly change her central attitude when confronted with data that cast religion into doubt. Moreover, this person will find it easier than others to learn and memorize new information about religion that can be anchored in the structure of already existing knowledge. Most higher-order learning is of this kind. Efficient learning means to be able to encode and embed, and make sense of, new information in the context of older structures. In this respect, two aspects have received particular attention. First, researchers have investigated how individuals' knowledge affords a powerful encoding structure, and second, researchers have been interested in how individuals deal with information that is inconsistent with their prior knowledge. We will discuss these two aspects in turn.

The self as a powerful knowledge structure

One of the most powerful and elaborated knowledge structures that we all possess is the self, with all its facets of autobiography, appearance, values, goals, attitudes, group membership, family relations, and professional experience. It is no wonder, therefore, that self-referent information has a strong memory advantage. An experimental paradigm for demonstrating this self-reference effect was created by Kuiper and Rogers (1979). A series of trait attributes was presented, and the participants' task was to "Rate whether you feel the trait describes you." In a comparison condition, the same trait words were presented and the encoding task was to rate whether the trait described somebody else. A strong *self-reference effect* was obtained across several experiments of this kind, such that more adjectives could be recalled in a subsequent recall test when stimuli were linked to the self as an organizing structure. This held in particular for those traits that were accepted to be actually descriptive of the self. Apparently, linking stimulus words to the self as powerful memory structures created sufficient associations to result in markedly improved memory.

Klein and Loftus (1988) have pursued the question of whether the memory advantage of self-referent information actually reflects the organizing function of self-knowledge, or the enhanced elaboration or rehearsal of singular self-referent words. The term *organization* refers to inter-item associations (relating an item to other items in memory), whereas the term *elaboration* refers to the creation of intra-item associations (strengthening memory traces of the individual item to be learned). A memory gain through organization can only be expected when the materials to be learned are relatively unrelated. When the relations between stimulus items are already well-organized, an organizing task is of little additional worth. Then a more efficient encoding strategy could be to elaborate on individual items. Using this rationale (cf. Hunt & McDaniel, 1993), Klein and Loftus were able to demonstrate that the self-reference effect is due to both increased inter-item organization and intra-item elaboration. When the words to be learned were unrelated, subsequent recall improved when the learning task required participants to encode the category structure (i.e., to categorize words as belonging to certain categories). Recall of unrelated items decreased when the learning task promoted the cognitive elaboration of individual items (i.e., providing definitions of stimulus words). However, a third self-referent task (linking stimulus words to autobiographical events) was an encoding task equally effective to the organization task. In contrast, when an obvious categorical structure was already imposed on the word list (i.e., several items representing countries, occupations, etc.), an elaboration task (word definitions) led to more improvement than an organization task (sorting words into categories that were evident anyway). However, again, the self-referent task was as effective as the elaboration task. Together, these findings suggest that relating stimuli to the self combines the advantages of both organizational and elaborative encoding.

Self-knowledge is like expert knowledge. We are all experts in our self, and just as an expert (e.g., a stockbroker) can understand and memorize more information in his or her domain (e.g., information on stocks) than a nonexpert, we all are particularly prepared to process self-related knowledge. Inconsistent with the naive view of human memory as a storehouse of fixed capacity (like a sector on a computer file), the ability to include further information does not decrease when much is already stored in memory. Rather, the more we know in an area such as the self, the higher is our capacity to learn even more.

A place for inconsistent information

Once we have acquired highly interconnected, consistently organized knowledge structures, the role of consistency and logical principles has to be refined. If consistency were maximized unboundedly, memory would freeze to include only selective information that fits one's dominant categories and ignore any and all deviant information. Such a memory would be clearly maladaptive, unable to deal with new input and changed environments. Fortunately, the following refined analysis of the relative impact of consistent and inconsistent information yields a much more adaptive picture of the self-regulation of human memory.

As already mentioned, a trait concept that is compared to the self and rejected as inconsistent with one's remaining self-knowledge will nevertheless be encoded effectively and will probably be recalled. In spite of the importance of logical consistency that was emphasized at the beginning of this chapter, the role of consistency is more complicated than depicted thus far. Indeed, there is good evidence showing that memories for observations that are inconsistent and hard to reconcile with existing knowledge may be especially strong.

For an illustration, imagine that your neighbour is a member of Greenpeace. Consistent with this orientation, you observe this person riding a bike, saving energy, eating organic food, liking nature, walking in forests, and avoiding UV light. Then you observe the same person torturing animals in a manner that is hardly compatible with Greenpeace. Such an inconsistent piece of information is very unlikely to be overlooked and forgotten, and it will presumably be remembered much better than most other, expected observations. In the same vein, many other observations that are inconsistent with common knowledge will hardly be forgotten, such as a priest involved in a criminal offence, a politician who turns out to be illiterate, or a horse solving a mathematical calculation.

An often-cited experiment was conducted by Hastie and Kumar (1979). In each of 6 person memory trials, a target person was first characterized by a trait (e.g., intelligent), followed by 20 behaviours

that were either consistent with the trait ("won the chess tourna-
ment"), inconsistent ("made the same mistake three times"), or
irrelevant ("took the elevator to the third floor"). In a subsequent
memory test, individuals recalled more inconsistent behaviour
descriptions (mean recall proportions amounted to 54%) than trait-
consistent (43%) or irrelevant behaviours (34%). In another experiment, Hastie and Kumar varied the proportion of inconsistent
behaviours in the list. The recall rate of inconsistent items increased
from 59% to 77% as the number of inconsistent items out of 16
decreased from 6 to 1. The more unusual or exceptional an item, the
more likely it could be recalled later.

Does this contradict the aforementioned advantage of consistent
information? Not really. More recent research on person memory has
clarified the different ways in which both expectancy consistent and
inconsistent information is recalled. When we try to write down
everything that happened on a day, we can reproduce events that
were so salient and important that they can be recalled individually.
The remaining output, however, is not due to especially strong
memory traces of salient events. Rather, the largest part of information is *reconstructed*, using systematic world knowledge about what
happens normally on a day. Based on such organized knowledge, we
can reconstruct that we must have got up in the morning, that we took
a shower, had breakfast, went to the subway, entered the office, drank
a coffee, etc. Such a script of a normal work day will at least be used to
form hypotheses of what could have happened, which can then be
tested against fragments of experience that are still in memory.

As Stangor and McMillan (1992) have recently demonstrated in a
meta-analysis of many relevant studies on this topic, inconsistent
observations are likely to grab much attention and to be encoded very
deeply. As far as recall relies on the strength of individual items'
memory traces, these outstanding events will have an advantage.
However, very often, recall is of the reconstructive, context-sensitive
type such that systematic knowledge is used to reconstruct what must
have happened. By definition, this systematic reconstruction gives a
huge advantage to information that is consistent with schemas and
scripts. Thus, with respect to the basic Theme 1 introduced in Chapter
2, extended bottom-up processing is responsible for the basic recall
advantage of inconsistent information, whereas top-down processing
explains the reconstruction advantage of consistent information.

Cogent evidence for this interpretation comes from several experiments in which distractor tasks were used to manipulate the amount
of available cognitive resources. In line with Theme 3 on the impact of

processing capacity and processing motivation on the amount of processing (see Chapter 2), it was expected that memory for inconsistent information would decrease with decreasing stimulus processing when cognitive resources are restricted. Indeed, when participants were required to rehearse an 8-digit number during encoding (Macrae, Hewstone, & Griffiths, 1993), or when they were given only 1.8 s for encoding (Dijksterhuis & Van Knippenberg, 1995), the extra encoding effort for inconsistent information was precluded and expectancy-consistent information was remembered better than inconsistent information. When cognitive resources were not constrained, the advantage of inconsistent encoding could unfold.

In fact, the very advantage of consistent information is that new observations *need not be encoded*. For instance, if tennis player A beats B, and B beats C, we need not lose much time encoding that A beats C, which can be derived by transitivity. The price for this economy is typical reconstructive errors. We may "remember" A beating C although this never actually occurred. Likewise, if a person is a member of an ethnic group and that group is known to be rather sociable and cheerful, we may "derive memories" of cheerful behaviour in that person that were not really observed. In other words, memory for consistent information is not only characterized by many recall hits (correct reconstructions), but also by many false alarms (intrusion errors).

According to this more refined account of the self-regulation of memory, we do not run the danger of being paralyzed in a frozen memory of mutually consistent cognitions. Although, or exactly because, our basic knowledge structures are so tightly organized, being confronted with unexpected, surprising information elicits more attention and more cognitive effort than experiencing expected observations that are largely redundant with already existing knowledge. Thus, the very economy of a consistently organized memory, which greatly reduces the mental work needed to encode and understand consistent data, entails the potential for expending more effort in the processing of inconsistent input that does not appear to fit the remaining structure. Although people are often successful in selectively exposing themselves to desired, attitude-congruent information, once they have stumbled across an unexpected event, they can hardly ignore it and have to elaborate on it more than on expected events. How can we make sense of the Greenpeace member, with all his environmentalist and pacifist habits, who is observed torturing animals? We have to go a long mental way to reconcile this with remaining knowledge, and this elaboration will create many new associations leading to strong memory traces of the unexpected event. To be sure, a flexible, mature memory will eventually find a way to reconcile the deviant observation with the remaining knowledge, for instance, by inferring that the Greenpeace member is insane or by reinterpreting the alleged torturing episode as black humour, or as a bad joke.

Controlling the consequences of activated information

Throughout this chapter, we have taken for granted that subsequent judgments shift towards the meaning of previously activated information. For instance, in the already-mentioned experiment of Gilovich (1981), activating the historical analogy of the Vietnam war led participants to conclude that military intervention to help another country should be avoided. Thus, current judgments or decisions were biased towards the activated historical lesson. Similarly, the priming of positive categories led to more positive judgments, or the activation of the category black led to a facilitation effect when recognizing trait words related to black people. So by default, it is assumed that the priming or activation of knowledge in memory causes an *assimilation* effect: Subsequent cognitive processes should shift in the direction of the activated information.

However, this need not be the case. There is systematic evidence for the reverse outcome, a *contrast* effect. Subsequent judgments may shift away from the activated schema or category. Thus, when the politician makes up his mind whether military intervention is appropriate in a particular case, the Vietnam model may not be applicable for some reason, or the Vietnam analogy may not be used for some reason, or the politician may feel that he is about to be influenced by the Vietnam model and correct his decision in the opposite direction. Various models have addressed the mechanisms that result in contrast effects. Below we will first briefly discuss three different theoretical approaches (see also Chapter 5), and then discuss correction effects in the stereotype domain.

Direct correction

Not surprisingly, individuals are sometimes aware that their initial interpretation and judgment of a situation (person, object, etc.) has been influenced by the preceding situation. For example, we know that after having held our hand in very cold water, a moderate temperature will then "feel" very hot. When asked to judge temperature, individuals may take this context effect into account and correct their judgment accordingly. Sometimes they may even overcorrect, resulting in judgments distorted in the opposite direction—a contrast effect (for related evidence in this respect see Wegener & Petty, 1997; for related theorizing see also Strack, 1992).

Recomputation

Instead of simply subtracting or adding something to their judgment according to a subjective theory of influence, individuals may engage in a different strategy. They may re-compute the judgment, thereby attempting not to use the information that may bias their judgment. In this respect, Martin and colleagues (Martin, 1986; Martin, Seta, & Crelia, 1990) have argued that individuals may engage in a "reset" mechanism. According to this assumption, individuals try to avoid information when they believe that this information contaminates the judgment. They may thus subtract the information through a "reset" mechanism. For example, when individuals are aware that some activated positive information may bias their judgment, reset means they recompute a judgment without considering positive information. By doing so, however, too much positive information may be discounted and the resulting judgment may be *less* positive.

Differential use of activated information

Another approach addressing the emergence of assimilation and contrast effects, the inclusion/exclusion model (Bless & Schwarz, 1998; Schwarz & Bless, 1992a), holds that activated information can be used differently and, depending on the use of the activated information, assimilation or contrast effects will be more likely. When individuals *include* the activated information for constructing a mental representation of the judgmental target, the judgment will assimilate towards the activated information. For example, when the concept "friendly" is activated, this concept can be used for the mental representation of a subsequently perceived behaviour, and the behaviour will be perceived as more friendly than when the concept had not been primed.

However, for various reasons individuals may *exclude* activated information from the representation of the target, for example, because they are aware of a potentially unwanted influence. In this case the activated concepts may be used to construct a standard of comparison, against which the judgmental target is evaluated. For example, "friendly" can be used as a comparison standard against which the target behaviour is evaluated, and consequently the target behaviour is perceived as less friendly (contrast) than when the concept had not been primed.

Within the inclusion/exclusion model, it makes sense that unobtrusive, unconscious priming has been repeatedly shown to elicit more congruent judgment effects than priming effects of which judges have become aware (Lombardi et al., 1987; Strack et al., 1993). When judges have clear memories of the priming episode (that is, they are aware that certain trait words such as reckless, conceited, aloof, as in Higgins et al., 1977, were activated), they are likely to exclude these prime stimuli as clearly separate events that should not be assimilated to, or contaminated with, the judgment task at hand. When judges notice the priming treatment, its experience may be excluded. Of course, one appropriate means of avoiding awareness of priming influences is to present primes very briefly (30 to 100 ms) so that conscious recognition is impossible. Indeed, such subliminal priming has been shown to effectively influence a wide variety of behaviour (Bargh & Pietromonaco, 1982; Dijksterhuis & Van Knippenberg, 1998; Murphy & Zajonc, 1993).

The inclusion/exclusion model (Bless & Schwarz, 1998; Schwarz & Bless, 1992a) may also explain another intriguing moderator effect that was recently demonstrated by Stapel, Koomen, and Van der Pligt (1996). Judgment outcomes are likely to reflect assimilation effects when the prime is an abstract trait category, but contrast effects when the priming links the trait to a concrete person, with a name and photo. The priming task involved the unscrambling of word groups to form several sentences revolving around a trait topic (dependent). In the trait priming condition, the resulting sentences did not contain any subject but only the predicates related to the common trait. In the exemplar priming condition, however, the groups of sentences referred to a concrete subject name (e.g., Linda). Afterwards, participants engaged in a judgment task in which an ambiguously described person had to be judged on various dimensions. On the primed dimension, dependence, judgments exhibited assimilation when the mere trait had been primed, but a contrast effect when a concrete person exemplar had been primed. Apparently, a primed trait is more likely to be included in the category of the stimulus person to be judged, whereas an exemplar is a clearly different target who is likely to be excluded and used as a comparison standard.

Similar findings have been obtained for the priming of manifest actions. Following Bargh et al. (1996), who had already shown that priming the stereotype of the elderly can induce reduced walking speed in people, Dijksterhuis et al. (1998) demonstrated that priming people with the stereotype of a professor (versus a top model) can influence performance on a knowledge test modelled after the Trivial Pursuit game. However, importantly, the direction of this influence again depended on whether the category or an examplar was primed. When participants were asked, on the preceding task, to think about a professor (rather than a top model) in general (category), intellectual performance increased (assimilation). When, however, they were asked to think of Professor Albert Einstein (vs. top model Claudia Schiffer) in particular (exemplar), their performance decreased.

Automatic control of stereotyping

One of the most important applications of priming studies in current social psychology concerns the thesis that automatically activated knowledge provides an essential component of social stereotypes. Thus, regardless of whether we strive for the ideal to be nonsexist and honestly try to control and eliminate any sexist tendencies, we are all equipped with knowledge structures that provide the basis for sexist discrimination. That is, we know the contents of sexist knowledge even when our attitude does not support prejudiced behaviour. However, as soon as our well-motivated self-monitoring to avoid prejudiced thought and behaviour is set off and behaviour is no longer under the control of conscious attitudes, we may nevertheless fall pray to sexist tendencies. We are here concerned with Theme 4, the interplay of automatic and controlled processes.

The interplay of both automatic and controlled processes to stereotype priming was neatly illustrated by Blair and Banaji (1996). These researchers used gender-related words as primes, and the experimental task was to decide whether the following target was a male or a female first name. Decision latencies were clearly lower when the target names matched the gender meaning of the preceding prime word than when there was a mismatch. This effect occurred quite automatically, at SOAs of 350 ms and even 250 ms. Then participants were induced with a deliberate goal intention to counteract the automatic gender associations, that is, to be prepared for a male name when seeing a female prime word, and vice versa. This attempt to detach later responses from priming influences and to achieve voluntary control was only successful for a long SOA of

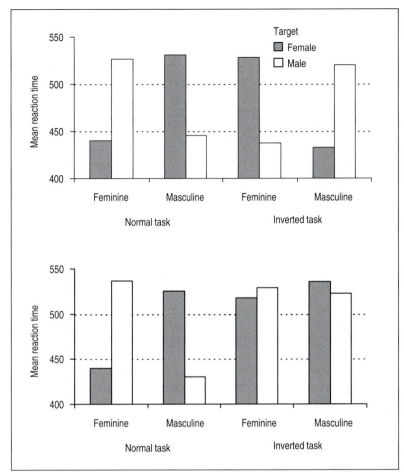

Figure 3.4.
Priming and identifying gender. Mean reaction time to identify gender of a female or male target name when the preceding prime was feminine or masculine. In the normal (inverted) task condition, participants expect target of same (opposite) gender as prime. The priming effect can be inverted voluntarily for a long SOA = 2000 ms but not for a short SOA = 350 ms (after Blair & Banaji, 1996).

2000 ms. However, the voluntary control failed for a short SOA of 350 ms (see Figure 3.4). Apparently, the relative ability to control one's stereotypical associations voluntarily is restricted. If cognitive resources are scarce—that is, under time pressure or cognitive load, when distracted or emotionally aroused—the individual may not be able to counteract the unwanted impulses.

Will these automatically activated associations have a notable effect on social judgments? A recent investigation by Lepore and Brown (1997) suggests an empirical answer. Participants were either high or low in prejudice against blacks. In a preceding, allegedly unrelated experiment, they had to detect letter strings appearing for a very brief period on different areas of the computer screen. Using one

Figure 3.5.

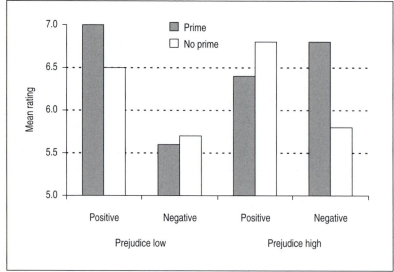

Mean ratings of a
target person on
positive and negative
trait scales as a
function of priming of
the category Black and
judges' degree of
prejudice against Black
people, after Lepore &
Brown (1997).

of two response keys, they had to indicate whether the string appeared on the left or on the right of the screen. The presentation time was 100 ms, immediately followed by a mixed-letter mask. The locus of presentation was at an angle of 2–6 degrees of visual angle away from a fixation point on the screen. This warrants parafoveal perception: The image on the retina falls outside the fovea, the point of maximally clear vision. Under such viewing conditions, conscious perception is normally impossible. In one condition, 13 prime words were thus presented that were all related to the category of black people: blacks, Afro-Carribean, West Indians, coloured, afro, dreadlocks, Rastafarian, reggae, ethnic, Brixton, Notting Hill, rap, and culture. In a control condition, no real words were presented but the mask flashed up twice.

Immediately after the priming task, a person was described by eight behaviours, of which two referred to each of four stereotypically black traits: athletic, fun-loving, aggressive, and unreliable. The impression formed of this "synthetic person" was then rated on 21 trait dimensions that were descriptive of the same two positive dimensions (athletic, fun-loving) and negative dimensions (aggressive, unreliable). Figure 3.5 shows the mean ratings on positive and negative trait scales by high- and low-prejudice participants, separately for the prime and no-prime condition. Indeed, the subliminal, unconscious priming of associations to the category black did influence the judgments of a target person described by a constant set of eight behaviours, compared with the no-prime condition. However, the pattern of this effect was reversed for the two prejudiced groups. When the stereotypical prime words preceded the person judgment, prejudiced judges gave higher ratings on negative than on positive scales, whereas nonprejudiced judges gave higher ratings on positive than negative scales.

Lepore and Brown's (1997) findings have two notable implications. First, automatically primed sexist knowledge does have a sizeable effect on social judgment. However, second, although stereotyping can be activated subliminally, well below the level of controllable reactions, this does not mean that everybody is manipulated by the same collective knowledge (however, see Devine, 1989). While the knowledge about blacks is activated in both prejudiced and nonprejudiced people, it is linked to negative reactions in the former but to relatively positive responses in the latter. Apparently, prejudiced attitudes can be overlearned to such a degree that priming effects are channelled into different judgmental pathways.

Using implicit social cognition for diagnostic purposes

The creative application of the priming paradigm has fostered many new insights into the organization of knowledge in general, and stereotypes in particular. This renewed interest in unconscious processes has pointed out many ways in which stereotypes arise quite automatically as an inextricable component of culturally shared knowledge. People may implicitly use a stereotype even when they are not explicitly committed or they may not even notice that the stereotype has an influence on their behaviour.

One recent stream of research is devoted to the development of diagnostic procedures to assess such implicit, unconscious sources of stereotyping. Most prominent within this new approach is Greenwald and colleagues' (Greenwald, McGee, & Schwartz, 1998; see also Greenwald & Banaji, 1995) implicit association test (IAT), which has become tremendously popular and instigated countless studies on implicit stereotype diagnostics within only few years. The test is freely available on the Internet and can easily be modified to apply to many different purposes. In its original and simplest application to the assessment of the cognitive underpinnings of racial stereotypes, the test starts with a first block of trials in which typically black or typically white first names are presented on the computer screen, and the participant has to press different response keys for black and white names under speed instructions. In the second trial block, participants have to sort positive versus negative trait words using the same two response keys. Later on, then, another trial block includes both race-related names as well as valence-related concepts. This double-sorting task is done under two different instructions. In the stereotype-compatible condition, the task is to sort black names together with negative terms onto the same response key and white names with positive terms. In the stereotype-incompatible condition, the task is to sort black and positive together onto one key and white and negative together on the other key. The measure of interest is the difference in time required for these two double-sorting blocks. The test has turned out to be extremely sensitive. Many participants, even those who would emphatically pretend to be nonracist, take much longer to associate blacks with more positive meanings than to associate whites with positive meanings.

It is obvious that sometimes individuals' implicit associations allow the same, but sometimes different, implications than explicit judgments do. In the latter case, an important question will be under which conditions implicit associations and under which conditions explicit judgments are better at predicting subsequent judgments and behaviours. Florack, Scarabis, and Bless (2001) have suggested that implicit association is a particularly good predictor if individuals engage in little processing when forming their judgments. The researchers assessed implicit associations and explicit judgments of German participants toward Turks in general. Participants were then provided with a description of a specific Turkish target person and asked to evaluate this target. The implicit associations were a better predictor for these evaluations than the explicit judgments about Turks in general for participants low in need for cognition (Cacioppo & Petty, 1982), that is, for participants who can be assumed not to think extensively about the specific target person. However, for individuals high in need for cognition, the explicit judgments about Turks in general allowed a better prediction than the implicit associations.

The IAT and the insights gained from priming experiments reflect but one aspect of a two-sided message. Individuals are not necessarily imprisoned in associative networks of automatically activated knowledge. They may counteract this influence. Moreover, stereotypes are not only maintained because of automatically activated structures. Apart from this implicit component, stereotypes are also protected by explicit reasoning processes and by the freedom gained from sophisticated knowledge structures to interpret each and any piece of evidence in several ways. The more flexible and multi-faceted an individual's knowledge, the less necessary it is that stereotypes have to change in the light of contradicting evidence. Evidence contradicting the implications of prior knowledge can often be dismissed as exceptions, thus rendering a change of the knowledge structure unnecessary (e.g., Kunda & Oleson, 1995).

This latter aspect suggests that a sophisticated knowledge structure is not only a closed box with uncontrollable associations. It is also a flexible instrument for reconciling unexpected data with pre-existing knowledge, or for rationalizing and reinterpreting threatening information that might disconfirm one's comfortable stereotypes and harm one's self concept. Further illustrations and experimental demonstrations of the creative flexibility with which people manage to find confirmation for their stereotypes and expectancies, and to evade disconfirmation, will be provided in Chapter 6, which is devoted to the process of social hypothesis testing.

Chapter summary

(1) In order to understand how social information is organized in memory, different types of knowledge structure should be distinguished: categories, schemas, stereotypes, scripts, or associative networks.

(2) Because the entire content of long-term memory is not entirely accessible at any time, the actual influence of memory on behaviour is contingent on selective retrieval. As memory retrieval depends crucially on appropriate retrieval cues, experimental research is concerned with the question of how to activate memorized information effectively. The so-called priming paradigm affords the major research tool for this endeavour.

(3) Different subtypes of priming have been developed within this paradigm, such as semantic priming, evaluative priming, mood priming, procedural priming, or direct-action priming.

(4) Retrieval of knowledge from memory is not only a function of externally provided primes but is also determined by self-generated retrieval cues. Information that was encoded with reference to the self has a similar retrieval advantage to other information that has been processed deeply.

(5) Inconsistent or unexpected information is particularly likely to elicit deep processing, to make sense of the inconsistencies. Accordingly, inconsistent information has a retrieval advantage. Recall of consistent information can also be facilitated, if it can be derived from superordinate memory structures.

(6) The ultimate impact of retrieved knowledge on behaviour depends on the possibility to suppress, control and correct the behavioural impulses suggested by memory outputs.

Discussion questions

(1) Access an Internet page demonstrating the implicit association test; for example, http://buster.cs.yale.edu/implicit/. Work on one of the example tests. Try to find out whether you can "beat" the IAT.

(2) How could subliminal priming be utilized for advertising?

(3) Try to find examples for different types of priming within the applied domain of advertising. How can consumer behaviour be influenced through priming-like effects?

(4) Does information have a better chance of being kept in memory if it is consistent or inconsistent with prior knowledge? Is there a single correct answer to this question?

(5) How can self-referent encoding be profitably used for academic learning and textbook reading?

(6) Find examples of different kinds of knowledge structures in the area of sports.

Recommendations for further reading

Bargh, J. A. (1994). The four horsemen of automaticity. In R. S. Wyer & T. K. Srull (Eds.), *Handbook of social cognition* (pp. 1–40). Hillsdale, NJ: Lawrence Erlbaum Associates Inc.

Uleman, J. S. & Bargh, J. A. (Eds.) (1989). *Unintended thought*. New York: Guilford Press.

Judgmental heuristics in social cognition 4

In the previous chapter, we discussed how information is stored and retrieved from memory. In this respect, it was inevitable that we should already have addressed judgmental processes. The following two chapters will take a closer and more extensive look at how individuals form judgments. Chapter 4 focuses on how individuals base their judgments on *general* judgmental heuristics, that is, on general rules of thumb that can be applied to a very wide spectrum of judgments. The subsequent Chapter 5 will then address how individuals base their judgments on the content of information that is relevant for a *specific* judgment.

Introduction

"To err is human," as the well-known saying goes, and error seems almost emblematic of human judgment (cf. Nisbett & Ross, 1980). However, the discrepancy between the judgments of individuals and reality is not simply a shortcoming that we need to recognize, deplore, and correct when necessary. It is also a source of insight that can contribute to our understanding of the dynamic of judgmental processes. The injunction "to learn from mistakes" applies also to scientists and researchers.

A classic example of this phenomenon is optical illusions, whose analysis forms the central focus of many perception theories. In the process, ever since Helmholtz (1903, p. 96), "the study of so-called tricks on the senses (*Sinnestäuschungen*) . . . has been a

Figure 4.1.

A visual illusion. The arrows in the Müller-Lyer Illusion create the impression that one segment is shorter than the other. In the domain of social perception, judgments may also be distorted by systematic influences.

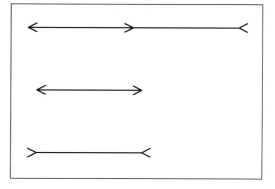

crucially important part of the physiology of the senses. It is precisely those instances in which external impressions create in us perceptions that do not correspond to reality that are especially revealing when it comes to discovering the processes and means by which normal perception occurs."

The study of the erroneous perception of reality also plays an important role in social psychology research; more precisely, in the field of social cognition (see Strack, 1988). For many years now, researchers have been studying systematic distortions in the perception of other people and their characteristics (cf. Ash, 1946) as well as in the understanding of social situations (cf. Ichheiser, 1949), with the goal of learning something about general cognitive processes. The field of cognitive deceptions also includes judgmental heuristics, which are the topic of the present chapter. Specifically, we will describe these heuristics, present research findings that illustrate their psychological functioning, and discuss their role in social psychology. Finally, we will present some alternative views to account for some of the phenomena.

Before entering into the discussion of these aspects it is important to realize that by focusing on situations in which individuals seem to err, researchers do not necessarily imply that human judgment is best characterized by its errors. On the contrary, in most situations judgmental heuristics provide accurate and efficient judgments. However, it is often the errors that allow the best access to an understanding of cognitive processes.

What are judgmental heuristics?

Imagine that you would like to invite a good friend to a gourmet dinner. Since you have just moved to a new city, you do not know many restaurants. How can you decide which restaurant is most suitable for the dinner you have in mind? Theoretically, one possibility would be to start sampling all restaurants in the city several months prior to the invitation, rate the food according to criteria important to you, draw up a ranking of the restaurants, and choose the one that comes out on top. While this method would presumably lead to a fairly reliable decision, it would also take up a lot of time, energy, and money.

A simpler method for solving the task would be to open a restaurant guide and use its ratings as the basis for your own judgment. No doubt that would be a reasonable approach, since restaurant guides, in most instances, offer accurate assessments of a restaurant's quality. However, in some cases the ratings are influenced by factors other than the actual quality of the cuisine. Perhaps the critic was in a bad mood when he visited a particular establishment. Perhaps the publishers of the guide only tested a selected number of restaurants. Perhaps a personal relationship between the critic and the management of a restaurant led to a more positive evaluation than would otherwise have been the case. By relying on the guide you may, under certain conditions, misjudge the quality of a restaurant.

We can use this example to illustrate the essential elements and characteristics of heuristic judgment: An individual seeks to locate an object of judgment (in this case the restaurants in his home town) on a judgmental scale (quality of the cuisine). Various judgment strategies are available to achieve that end. Some strategies have a high likelihood of leading to a "correct" judgment but take up much time and energy (testing all restaurants). Fortunately, in many cases information exists that is readily available (in this case the evaluations in the restaurant guide) and relevant to the judgmental scale. This information is called heuristic stimuli or cues. If the individual knows how the cue is related to the judgmental scale ("If the restaurant guide has a positive rating the food is usually good"), the cue can be used as the basis for judgment. Judgmental strategies that combine cues and judgmental scales are called *judgmental heuristics*. Judgmental heuristics are thus simple "rules of thumb" that are applied to readily available information and that allow a person, with little processing effort, to arrive at a judgment that is in most instances sufficiently accurate. However, since the connection between the cue and the actual location of the judgment object on the judgmental scale is frequently not perfect, systematic judgment distortions (biases) occur under certain conditions. In other words, an individual will reach a judgment that is based on the heuristic but does not reflect the actual location of the judgment object on the judgmental scale.

This explanation reveals why the study of judgmental distortions or judgmental mistakes is an important tool for studying judgmental heuristics. Since cues are, in most cases, fairly precise indicators of the actual location of the judgmental object, heuristic judgments for the most part agree with judgments that are rendered on the basis of more elaborate processing. That is why the use of judgmental heuristics is often only revealed when a "wrong judgment" is made. The primary purpose of the study of judgmental errors is therefore not to demonstrate the faulty nature of human thinking. Rather, the goal is to gain insight into the mechanisms of "normal" thought.

Why do judgmental heuristics exist? If we wish to accomplish our goals, we must understand the regularities in our environment and be able to explain events and, to some extent, predict them—for example, the consequences of our actions. This task resembles that of a scientist, even though in many cases the scientist searches for knowledge without a concrete purpose in mind. But while the scientist has complex methods, elaborate tools, and a lot of time at his disposal in his effort to arrive at "good theories," the individual, in his role as "intuitive scientist," is much less well equipped. Rarely is it possible to observe the cognitive object systematically (e.g., by varying the framework conditions). Only the characteristics immediately accessible to the sensory organs can be processed, and there are limitations to the reception and storage of information. Moreover, the intuitive scientist generally has limited time available (see Theme 2 of Chapter 2 on limited processing capacities). Decisions usually have to be made quickly and require an abbreviated judgmental process. This is precisely what judgmental heuristics accomplish.

What kinds of judgmental heuristics exist? Each individual has at his or her disposal a variety of simplifying judgment rules, some of which are shaped to fit the personal environment and can be applied to very specific cues. Beyond that, however, there are a number of heuristics that are highly *general* in nature. They are characterized by the fact that they can be applied to cues that are available in many different situations. These heuristics are primarily used to assess frequency and probability, categorize persons, make value judgments, and estimate numerical quantities.

Amos Tversky, Daniel Kahneman, Richard Nisbett, and Lee Ross placed the "idea of judgmental heuristics" at the centre of their theoretical reflections in the 1970s, providing the impetus to the heuristics and bias research programme that has profoundly influenced the psychology of judgment down to the present day.

The discussion that follows will begin by introducing three cognitive heuristics that form the starting point for the research programme on judgmental heuristics. First we will describe the availability heuristic, which is used primarily in judging frequency or probability. Second we will address the representativeness heuristic, which is used in assigning single elements (e.g., persons) to larger categories (e.g., groups), but is also put to use in estimating frequency and probability. The third judgmental heuristic we will look at is described as "anchoring and adjustment" in the literature, and plays a role in many different judgments. This will be followed by examples illustrating that individuals also use affective and non-affective feelings as heuristic cues. Finally, we will sketch alternative explanations and recapitulate the importance of heuristics in the judgment process.

Availability heuristic

In assessing the frequency or probability of an event (or the co-occurrence of several events), individuals often employ a strategy that is based on the difficulty (or ease) with which bits of information can be retrieved or generated from memory. An employer wishing to gauge the rate of unemployment in his community may go to the trouble of obtaining the relevant information from official sources. But if he is not motivated or able to do that, he can try to think of his unemployed friends or acquaintances. The more easily he is able to do so, the higher will be his estimate of the rate of unemployment. Tversky and Kahneman (e.g., 1973) called this judgment strategy the "availability heuristic." Formulated as a rule, we can describe it as follows: "If I can recall an event with ease, it probably occurs frequently," or "If I can easily imagine an event, it is likely that it will occur with greater frequency." What lies behind this strategy?

Ease of retrieval as the basis of judgment

The availability heuristic is an inversion of a fundamental insight in memory psychology about the connection between the frequency of presentation of an association pair and memory. The greater the frequency with which two stimuli occur together (e.g., an English word alongside a German word in foreign language learning), the greater the ease with which one stimuli can be retrieved from memory when the other stimuli is presented. This general principle of memory now becomes, in inverted form, an explanation for judgments of frequency and probability. The greater the ease with which an event can be retrieved from memory, that is, the more readily the event is accessible, the higher the assessment of its frequency or probability.

And in fact the ease (or difficulty) with which information can be recalled is closely connected to the frequency with which it occurs. Events that a person can recall without any difficulty are usually events that occur often and with a high degree of probability. However, our powers of memory are influenced not only by the frequency of the information to be remembered, but also by factors that have no or only an indirect connection to frequency.

Vivid accounts of events, the presence of events in the media, events that happened to us recently—all these are remembered better than events recounted less vividly, events neglected by the media, and events that happened some time ago. Moreover, certain characteristics of our memory can cause certain information to be remembered better during some tasks, even though there is no difference in the frequency with which it is experienced. For example, we know that information is remembered better if the context of remembering resembles the context of learning. We will presently look at two experiments that illustrate the possible dissociation between availability and frequency. After that we will show that perceived ease of retrieval is indeed used as a basis for judgment.

Dissociation between ease of retrieval and frequency

A classic experiment on the use of the availability heuristic (Tversky & Kahneman, 1973) involves the not infrequent task of judging the size of subsets: How many of your acquaintances are female? What percentage of your books is poetry? What percentage of restaurants in your home town offers Italian cuisine? The participants in the experiment by Tversky and Kahneman were given a similar task. They were presented with a list of proper names, and two of the features of the persons mentioned varied: their gender and their fame. One list had 19 names of very famous men and 20 names of less famous women, the other list had 19 names of very famous women and 20 names of less famous men. After reading over the list, participants were asked to estimate whether the list contained more men than women. If one assumes that well-known names are more readily stored than unknown names, the availability heuristic would lead one to expect an overestimation of the number of men in the first case, and an overestimation of the number of women in the second case. In fact more than 50% of the participants remembered the very famous names better than the less famous ones. Moreover, about 80% of participants overestimated the proportion of the gender associated with the very famous names. In this case the use of the availability heuristic leads to erroneous judgments, since the availability was determined by a factor other than group size, namely that of fame.

Another factor, which does influence the ease with which examples can be generated but which is not necessarily connected to frequency of occurrence, is the specific organizational features of our memory. Similar to a book in a library or a word in a dictionary, the concepts stored in human memory are also "catalogued" (among other things) according to the first letter. Just as names that start with a certain letter are easier to find in a phone book than names where the same letter appears as the third letter, concepts can be more readily retrieved from memory with the help of the beginning letters of the words that describe them. If individuals use ease of retrieval as a basis for judgment, the variation of the "number criterion" (How many words begin with the letter "r" as opposed to how many have "r" as the third letter?) would invariably lead to distorted frequency judgments. Tversky and Kahneman (1973) tested this hypothesis with a simple experiment. They selected five consonants that were shown, through extensive word counts, to appear more frequently in the third position than the first in the English language. Participants in the experiment were asked to indicate for each letter whether it was more likely to appear in first or third place, and to indicate the relationship of probabilities. The result: 70% of participants expected a given letter to be in the first position. The estimated probability relationship was 2:1 in favour of the first position.

Perceived ease of retrieval

Tversky and Kahneman (1973) interpreted these findings as evidence for the use of the availability heuristic: As the beginning letter represented a better retrieval cue than the same letter in the third position, the relevant words were recalled more easily and their actual frequency was overestimated. Because people remember the names of famous persons more easily, their share of the group was overestimated. However, what remains unclear in these and other studies is the precise way in which heightened availability influences judgment. On the one hand, individuals can use the feeling of easy retrieval as a heuristic cue. On the other hand, it could simply be the case that heightened availability caused the individual to generate or remember more exemplars, and that the judgment was made on the basis of this "distorted" sample. Here it is not the *ease* (or difficulty) of retrieval that determines the judgments, but the *contents* of the available information. In that case the influence of heightened availability is trivial, in the sense that all judgments can be rendered only on the basis of what comes to mind for the person making the judgment. The following experiment (Schwarz, Bless, Strack, Klumpp, Rittenauer-Schatka, & Simons, 1991a) makes it possible to distinguish the two possible modes of influence. In a preliminary condition, participants were given the task of writing down either 6 or 12 examples of their own self-confident (or non-self-confident) behaviour. Retrieving and listing 6 behaviours was easy in the pre-test, whereas retrieving and listing 12 behaviours was difficult in the pre-test. Afterwards they were asked to rate the degree of their self-confidence. In this situation, the ease and the content explanation make different predictions with respect to participants' judgments. Given the content explanation, participants should feel more confident after writing down 12 rather than 6 self-confident behaviours (and the converse after writing down non-self-confident behaviours) because more information was activated. However, different implications are derived from the ease explanation. Because retrieving 6 self-confident behaviours is easier than retrieving 12 behaviours, individuals may conclude more self-confidence when retrieving only 6 self-confident behaviours (and the converse for non-self-confident behaviours). The results indicate the use of ease of retrieval as a basis for judgment: Individuals who had to generate many examples of their own self-confident behaviour (= difficult) judged themselves as less self-confident than individuals who were asked to report only a few examples (= easy). Even though the first group remembered things that they were very "confident" about with respect to content, the difficulty they experienced in remembering the examples led them to the conclusion that they couldn't be all that "self-confident." By contrast, participants in the group that was asked to generate the examples of "non-self-confident" behaviour judged themselves as more self-confident if they were asked to come up with 12 examples as opposed to 6; for a similar paradigm in the domain of consumer information processing see Box 4.1.

Based on these findings, Schwarz and colleagues (1991a) argued that ease of retrieval should only affect subsequent judgments when individuals relate ease of retrieval to the amount of information stored in memory. Replicating the design described above, participants listed either 6 or 12 self-confident or non-self-confident behaviours. In addition, while writing down the behaviours, participants listened to meditation music. Half of the participants were told that the music would make the retrieval task easier; the remaining participants were told that the music would make the task more difficult. As a consequence, in some conditions participants could attribute the ease (difficulty) to the music when the task felt easy

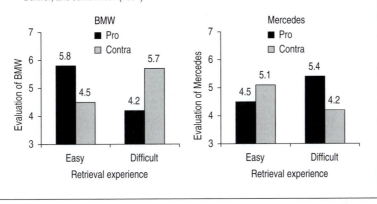
(difficult) and the music ostensibly made the task easy (difficult)—thus reducing the informational value of the experienced ease. In other conditions participants could attribute the ease (difficulty) of retrieval to the retrieval itself—when the task felt easy (difficult) and the music ostensibly made the task difficult (easy). When the informational value was not questioned by the information about the music, individuals based their judgments on the ease of retrieval and judged themselves as more self-confident after retrieving 6 rather than 12 self-confident behaviours (and the converse for non-self-confident behaviours). However, when participants could attribute the ease of retrieval to the music—thus reducing the informational value of ease of retrieval—individuals based their judgments on the content of the retrieved information and judged themselves as less self-confident after retrieving 6 rather than 12 self-confident behaviours (and reversely for non-self-confident behaviours).

A third, critical test of the availability heuristic consists of manipulating the feeling of ease of retrieval directly while keeping the effort associated with the cognitive activity constant. This is precisely what Stepper and Strack did (1993, Exp. 2) by instructing participants to remember six examples of self-confident behaviour. Half of the participants were told to knit their brows, a movement that goes hand in hand with feelings of tension and effort. By contrast, the other half was asked to smile. The result: Participants who knitted their brows and thus experienced a feeling of effort judged themselves to be less self-confident than did participants who smiled. This study, along with a number of other experiments, provided impressive confirmation that individuals indeed use perceived ease of retrieval as the basis for judgments (e.g., Grayson & Schwarz, 1999; MacLeod & Campbell, 1992; Rothman & Schwarz, 1998; Wänke, Bless, & Biller, 1996; Wänke, Schwarz, & Bless, 1995; for an overview see Schwarz, 1998).

The availability heuristic in social judgments

The studies discussed above reveal that the availability heuristic is used both for frequency judgments and for judgments about one's own personality. In addition, a whole series of additional judgmental phenomena are connected with the availability heuristic.

One example is risk assessments. One factor that leads to a natural dissociation between availability and actual frequency is the frequency with which events are reported. For example, Lichtenstein, Slovic, Fischhoff, Layman, and Combs (1978) found that causes of death frequently reported in the press were greatly overestimated in terms of their frequency. While heart disease causes 85% more deaths than accidents, only 20% of those surveyed thought that heart disease was the greater risk. The conspicuousness of events also influenced their availability. For example, in the study by Lichtenstein et al., the overestimated causes of death were especially dramatic and sensational (murder, flood, automobile accident), while the rather inconspicuous causes of death (heart disease, cancer, diabetes) were underestimated.

Events that we know from personal experience are also more readily available than events we only know about through third parties, and at the same time we consider these events to be more plausible (Greening, Dollinger, & Pitz, 1996). The following studies demonstrate the direct influence of perceived ease of retrieval on the assessment of risk: One group of subjects in the experiment by Rothman and Schwarz (1998) rated the risk of a heart disease higher when they were asked to list three instead of eight factors that increased their own risk. Participants in a study by Grayson and Schwarz (1999) considered the risk of becoming a victim of a sexual crime to be lower when they were asked to list four instead of eight behaviours that increased the risk.

Attitudinal judgments about everyday topics are also made on the basis of the availability heuristic under certain conditions. Wänke et al. (1996) reported more positive attitudes towards public transportation on the part of subjects if they had previously been asked to generate three instead of seven arguments in favour of public transportation. Wänke, Bohner, and Jurkowitsch (1997) reported similar results with respect to the evaluation of consumer products (see Box 4.1).

Another example refers to the ease with which we are able to imagine a different course of events. Let us look at the following example of counterfactual thinking: "If I had gotten up 5 minutes earlier this morning I would not have missed the train, I would not have been late for the exam and would have been able to read the one additional problem that I needed to pass the exam." What is crucial is that the ease with which we can undo an event in our mind influences our affective reaction to the event. While the person in our example would presumably feel a great deal of anger over being 5 minutes late, a person that overslept an hour instead of 5 minutes would be less angry. For a detailed account of recent findings on counterfactual thinking see Roese and Olson (1995).

Overestimation of probability: Many people are more afraid of becoming the victim of a terrorist attack (a hijacking of an airplane) than of a car accident. How does the availability heuristic contribute to this distorted judgment? Credit: Popperfoto.

Apart from these examples of judgments and affective reactions on the basis of the perceived ease of cognitive operations, the "availability principle" in its general form, that is, the finding that increased accessibility of certain contents and cognitive structures influences judgments, has stimulated a host of research in social psychology. This pertains, for example, to work on the categorization of persons (Higgins et al., 1977; Srull & Wyer, 1980), causal attribution (Taylor & Fiske, 1978), the constancy of opinions after they have been discredited (Davies, 1997a; Ross, Lepper, Strack, & Steinmetz, 1977), or the testing of hypothesis (Davies, 1997b). The interested reader should consult surveys of this topic (e.g., Higgins, 1996).

Representativeness heuristic

Representativeness as the basis of judgment

Imagine you are having lunch with a fellow student and want to make a bet about the field in which a student at a neighbouring table at the cafeteria is majoring. He is wearing a suit and is reading the business section of the paper. How could you determine the "most likely" major? You could procure information about how many students are enrolled in each major and then bet on the major with the highest enrolment. However, this is a rather time-consuming method, for surely you would neither be motivated to get the necessary data from the registrar nor able to reproduce the figures from memory.

But your memory provides you with another basis for judgment: Your knowledge of certain characteristics of various groups of people. You may have an idea about the "typical" student in education, physics, or art history. Thus you could assign the student at the next table to the group of which he is an especially good representative—in this case perhaps a business major. If you had reached your judgment in this way you would have made use of the representativeness heuristic (Kahneman & Tversky, 1972). The term "representativeness" refers to how typical an element (e.g., the student in question) is for a specific category (e.g., business student), a sample (e.g., 1000 people), a basic entity (e.g., citizens), an effect (e.g., sore throat), or a cause (e.g., viral infection). In more general terms this means asking how well a concrete case represents an abstract model. The representativeness heuristic uses representativeness as the basis for categorization and probability judgments: The more typical the concrete case is for the model, the greater the assessed probability that the case belongs to this model, and the greater the likelihood that the case will be assigned to this category.

What lies behind this judgmental strategy? In many, though not all, cases our schematic knowledge represents real connections. Students of various majors may in fact be characterized by different behaviour, and the stereotype of the "business major" contains the knowledge about these characteristics. Certain causes do in fact produce "typical" symptoms, and samples of sufficient size do indeed resemble the larger group. If our knowledge of the models is sufficiently accurate, judgments on the basis of the representativeness of exemplars often lead to correct judgments. As with other heuristics, the use of the representativeness heuristic can lead to erroneous judgments because other factors that determine the probability of occurrences are neglected or fundamental principles of the theory of probability are ignored. The following examples will illustrate this.

A single element as representative of a category: Ignoring base rates

Let us take another look at our opening example. Following the representativeness heuristic, you would probably have identified the student as a future economist. But how meaningful would such a classification be if your university had no business department and consequently the base rate, the frequency of members of the category "business students" in the student body, was below 3%? In this case the probability that this was a business student would be much lower than if the base rate were 90% (e.g., if you were eating in the cafeteria of the business department). It seems that in making category attributions, individuals chiefly consider representativeness and often neglect the base rates (Griffin & Buehler, 1999; Kahneman & Tversky, 1973; Koehler, 1996; Schwarz, Strack, Hilton, & Naderer, 1991b).

A classic experiment carried out by Kahneman and Tversky (1973) illustrates this phenomenon. Participants were presented with brief personality descriptions that matched the stereotypes of either a lawyer or an engineer. Here is an example for the second group: "Jack is 45 years old. He is married with four children. He is generally conservative, careful, and ambitious. He has no interest in politics or social issues and devotes most of his spare time to one of his many hobbies, such as woodworking, sailing, or mathematical brain-teasers."

In addition, the base rate of members of both groups was varied by telling participants that the descriptions were the result of psychological interviews conducted, in the one condition, with 70 lawyers

---

BOX 4.2.

The representativeness heuristic: An example

Frank is a good friend of this book's authors. He is 45 years old, likes poems, reads about old buildings, and spends most of his vacations in Italy.

Is Frank more likely to be an art historian or a psychologist?

If you have chosen the first option, you may have fallen prey to the representativeness heuristic by neglecting the high baseline probability that friends often share the same professional background.

and 30 engineers. Participants were asked to judge the probability that the person described was in fact an engineer (or a lawyer). Result: the different initial probabilities had virtually no influence on the judgments of the participants. Only the external description of the target person was decisive for the attribution.

A conjunction is representative of one person: Disregarding the principle of extensionality

One fundamental assumption of the theory of probability, the principle of extensionality, maintains that if a result A includes the result B, the probability for B cannot be higher than for A. Here are two examples: (1) the probability that someone is studying biology (A) cannot be greater than the probability that the person is studying the natural sciences (B); and (2) the probability that a person is a bank teller and an active feminist (B) cannot be greater than the probability that a person is a bank teller (A). In each instance, A is a more general description that contains the specific case B. Now, it is easy to construct tasks in which the use of the representativeness heuristic leads to a violation of the principle of extensionality. For example, the participants in the Tversky and Kahneman experiment (1983) were given the following description: "Linda is 31, very intelligent, and speaks her mind. She studied philosophy. As a student she was actively engaged with questions of social justice and discrimination. In addition, she participated in demonstrations against nuclear energy."

Having read the description, participants were asked to arrange eight statements about Linda according to their probability, of which the following two statements were critical for the evaluation of the experiment: (A) Linda is a bank teller; (B) Linda is a bank teller and active in the feminist movement. The more specific conjunction B cannot be more likely than A, since A includes the case "bank teller and active in the feminist movement" as well as the case "bank teller and not active in the feminist movement." But it is easy to see that conjunction B shows a greater representativeness for Linda than statement A. That Linda is active in the feminist movement fits the description of her, whereas it is hard to imagine that she works in a bank. Use of the representativeness heuristic should therefore lead participants to judge B as more likely than A. The results obtained by Tversky and Kahneman (1983) indicate the use of the representativeness heuristic: 85 to 90% of participants considered the conjunction B more likely than the statement A. This phenomenon, described as conjunction error or conjunction effect, has been shown in a number of studies (e.g., Bar-Hillel & Neter, 1993; Betsch & Fiedler, 1999; Dulany & Hilton, 1991; Epstein, Donovan, & Denes-Raj, 1999; Fiedler, 1988; Gavanski & Roskos-Ewoldsen, 1991; Shafir, Smith, & Osherson, 1990).

A sample is representative for the whole: Misperception of coincidence

Let us assume there is a family with six children. You are asked to judge the probability of the following sequence of births of boys (B) and girls (G):

BBBBBB   GGGBBB   BGGBBG

Which of these sequences do you consider to be most likely? If you chose the third sequence, your intuition is in line with that of many people. Still, your judgment is wrong. All three sequences have the same probability, if one assumes that as many boys as girls are born and that the gender of one child does not allow any predictions about the gender of the next child.

A second example will illustrate this. Let as assume a lottery where you can pick only one of two series of winning numbers. One week the following series are put out, with the same jackpot for both:

15, 3, 8, 47, 23, 14   1, 2, 3, 4, 5, 6

On which series would you bet? Once again, objectively both series have the same probability. Still, people tend to think that the probability for the first series is greater.

To what can we attribute this judgment tendency? Kahneman and Tversky (1972) maintain that this erroneous judgment indicates the use of the representativeness heuristic. While all results are equally probable, they are differently representative for a random sample. For the intuitive perception of a random sample excludes regularities of every kind. Put differently: Regularities (be it the birth of six boys or the drawing of six sequential numbers) are untypical for random processes. However, random events whose characteristic distributions are representative for random samples are considered to be more probable. In general, people expect more alternations and scattering in sequences than would be expected in a random process. Let us take another look at the sequence of boys and girls in the birth sequences. Given the preconditions mentioned, the probability for the alternation of gender after every birth is .5. However, some studies (for an overview see Falk & Konold, 1997) have shown that under these conditions people consider sequences with an alternation probability of circa .6 to have maximum randomness.

A study carried out by Gilovich, Vallone, and Tversky (1985) revealed that "misperceptions" of random sequences is not limited to the psychology lab. Gilovich et al. examined the phenomenon of the belief in the "hot hand", common among basketball fans. It describes the belief that for brief periods players will score with an especially high probability. Basketball fans, coaches, and players consistently report nonrandom scoring streaks. However, extensive analyses of actual games were unable to corroborate the existence of such scoring sequences. A comparable phenomenon is the belief in lucky or unlucky streaks among gamblers (Wagenaar & Keren, 1988).

Anchoring and adjustment

If we wish to make a judgment in a given situation, it often happens that we find an initial, rough starting point for our judgment. A student in the first semester who wants to estimate how long it will take her to finish her studies can first use the normal duration as a point of orientation, ask herself whether she will require more or fewer semesters, and then, depending on her answer, add or subtract semesters until the final figure strikes her as plausible. A tourist who wants to gauge the height of a structure can draw on the height of a known building and then increase or reduce that height as it seems appropriate. A person who receives an initial offer from a negotiation partner may first ask himself whether this offer is acceptable. If it is not, for example, because it is too low, he can raise the offer in his mind until it seems acceptable. What all these examples share is that the individuals are using a judgment strategy that Tversky and Kahneman (1974) called "anchoring and adjustment": Individuals gauge numerical size by starting from an initial value (an anchor) and adjusting it during the subsequent course of judgment to arrive at their final judgment. However, Tversky and Kahneman assumed that the adjustment of the judgment is typically insufficient and leads to judgments that are distorted in the direction of the starting value. This judgment phenomenon, the assimilation of a judgment to a starting value, is called anchoring effect or anchor assimilation.

A classic example by Tversky and Kahneman (1974) exemplifies this anchoring effect. Participants were asked to estimate the percentage of African states that are members of the UN. In order to establish different anchors for the judgment, the task was preceded by a procedure in which a kind of wheel of fortune, with numbers from 1 to 100, was turned. Participants first had to indicate whether, for example, the number 10 generated randomly in this way was larger or smaller than the actual percentage of African member states, much like the student in the earlier example asked herself whether she would take longer or shorter than the normal period of study. After this, participants were asked to estimate the actual percentage of African member states. Result: If the number 10 was randomly given, the percentage of African states was estimated at 25%. But if, for example, the number 65 was randomly given, the estimated percentage of member states rose to 45%. Dealing with a randomly selected number thus caused the judgment to be assimilated to this number.

Research on the anchoring effect was carried out in many cases using the following procedure: The anchor information was offered in the form of a preceding comparative question ("Is the true value of the object of judgment larger or smaller than X?"), followed by the absolute judgment ("What is the true value?"). However, anchoring effects are not limited to this sequence. The anchor can originate from other sources, for example, from the partial completion of a task (e.g., when a person deduces the final result from an interim result in a math problem) or from the description of a task ("Enter your answer here, for example, '150 metres'."). In addition to simple questions of knowledge, as in the example above (e.g., Strack & Mussweiler, 1997; Wilson, Houston, Etling, & Brekke, 1996), or probability judgments (e.g., Block & Harper, 1991), researchers have also studied other judgmental objects. The anchoring effect is also characterized by a remarkable robustness. In many cases, whether the judging person is familiar with the judgmental object or a layperson is of only secondary importance (e.g., Northcraft & Neale, 1987; Whyte & Sebenius, 1997). Even incentives to render especially accurate judgments, or explicit instructions not to let oneself be influenced by the anchor, do not reduce the anchoring effect reliably (e.g., Wilson et al., 1996).

What causes the anchoring effect?

The original characterization of anchoring and adjustment was more a description of the anchoring effect than an explanation. For what reason is adjustment usually insufficient? Why is the judgment assimilated to the anchor? Tversky and Kahneman (1974) provided no answers. As a result, since the publication of their study, researchers have developed a number of theories in an effort to explain the anchoring effect. Since a comprehensive review of the various approaches is not possible within the framework of this chapter, we will introduce one current approach and refer the interested reader to other discussions of this topic (Jacowitz & Kahneman, 1995; Mussweiler & Strack, 1999a; Wilson et al., 1996).

The selective accessibility model (SAM)

The selective accessibility model (see Mussweiler & Strack, 1999a; Strack & Mussweiler, 1997) explains the anchoring effect with the help of the effect of two fundamental cognitive processes: selective hypothesis testing and semantic priming.

Selective hypothesis testing, the first thesis of the SAM, occurs during the processing of the anchor information: Individuals test the possibility that the anchoring value in fact corresponds to the actual location of the judgmental object on the judgmental scale. For example, confronted with the question of whether the average price of a car in Germany is more or less than Euro 20,000, individuals will test whether the price is in fact Euro 20,000. In so doing they will try to find knowledge that corroborates this possibility. In our example it could be information such as the following: "Expensive luxury cars are a common sight," "A compact car can already cost more than Euro 15,000," and so on. This method of testing hypothesis—researchers speak of a positive testing strategy—is often used by individuals (Liberman & Trope, 1999); we will address hypothesis testing more extensively in Chapter 6. And in many cases it is also a particularly effective way of arriving at a correct judgment (Klayman & Ha, 1987). Independent of whether this selective hypothesis testing results in a positive answer ("Yes, the average price is Euro 20,000") or a negative answer ("No, the average price is lower"), anchor-consistent semantic knowledge (knowledge that supports the "correctness" of the anchor) remains cognitively accessible after the anchor information has been processed. Mussweiler and Strack (1998) tested this with the following experiment: Participants first had to decide whether the average price of a German car is more or less than Euro 10,000 (low anchor) or Euro 20,000 (high anchor). After working on this question, they were given the following task: A series of words was presented and they were asked to decide as quickly as possible whether the word presented was meaningful or not. In these kinds of lexical decision tasks, individuals are faster at recognizing words that fall into a category that is particularly accessible to them. The meaningful words included some that are associated with more affordable cars (Honda, Volkswagen) or with expensive cars (Mercedes, BMW). Participants were faster at recognizing "expensive cars" if they had worked on the high anchor. By contrast, "affordable cars" were recognized more quickly as meaningful words if participants had been given a low anchor.

How does selectively heightened accessibility lead to the anchoring effect? According to the second thesis of the SAM, the mediating process resembles semantic priming: To answer the question properly ("What is the average price?"), individuals draw on the knowledge that is especially accessible at the time the judgment is made. And according to the first thesis of the SAM, after the anchor information has been processed, the knowledge that is especially accessible is that which works in favour of rendering the judgmental object similar to the anchor. We know from work on semantic priming (for an overview see Higgins, 1996) that the only information that influences judgment is information applicable to the judgmental object. Here is an example: If a person were to receive anchor information about the height of the Brandenburg Gate ("Higher or lower than 150 metres?"), while the final question asked about the width of the gate, the subsequently more accessible information, that is, information indicating a certain height ("Double-decker buses can drive through it," and so on), would have limited applicability with respect to width. Consequently, if the anchoring information refers to a judgmental dimension that is not applicable to the judgment called for, there should be no anchoring effect. Strack and Mussweiler (1997) confirmed this hypothesis in an experiment in which the judgmental dimension was either different from (as in the example above) or identical to the comparative question and the absolute judgment.

In addition to the findings we have examined through various examples, scholars have been able to confirm other specific predictions of the SAM. Regardless of whether this model can be used to explain all phenomena related to the anchoring effect, it is presumably an adequate explanation for many of them.

Adjustment and anchoring in the formation of social judgments

Anchoring effects occur not only in knowledge questions or the estimation of simple probabilities, but also in judgments about our social environment and ourselves. One example is situations involving sales and negotiations. Researchers were able to demonstrate in a series of experiments that the size of the initial offer had a strong influence on the result of negotiations (see, e.g., Neale & Northcraft, 1991; Ritov, 1996). Whyte and Sebenius (1997) tested experimentally whether this was an anchoring effect. Two studies revealed the influence of noninformative anchors on the judgment of important subjective values in negotiations. Among business students as well as experienced managers, the initial price offer, the minimum price, and the desired price were strongly influenced by the anchor value. In a study by Mussweiler, Strack, and Pfeiffer (2000), individuals purchasing cars estimated the value of a used car at Euro 1711 on average if they were given a high anchor, and Euro 1356 on average if they were given a low anchor.

In view of the possible consequences, anchoring effects are especially relevant in the formation of legal judgments. Studies on simulated verdicts by jurors (Chapman & Bornstein, 1996) and judges (Englich & Mussweiler, 2001) revealed that the assessment of guilt and the severity of punishment could be influenced by anchors. Englich and Mussweiler (2001, Study 3) supplied experienced judges with the usual information for judging a case of rape and asked them to determine the punishment they would impose. Previously, however, the judges had been asked to judge whether the penalty of either 12 or 34 months in jail allegedly proposed by a law student was too high or too low. Result: Judges who had been asked to evaluate the high anchor imposed a sentence of 35 months on average; judges with the lower anchor, by contrast, imposed 28 months on average.

In jail for 28 or 35 months? The anchoring heuristic influences judgments of legal experts. Credit: Art Directors and TRIP.

The occurrence of anchoring effects in self-judgments was exemplified by an experiment by Cervone and Peake (1986). Subjects who had been asked to judge whether they would be able to solve more than 18 brainteasers or fewer expected to solve more of them than subjects who had been asked the same question about 4 brainteasers. From the perspective of the subjects, the anchoring effect had been chosen at random and thus had no informative value. Similar findings were reported by Switzer and Sniezek (1991).

The anchoring effect has also been invoked to explain other judgmental phenomena, for example the fundamental attribution error (Leyens, Yzerbyt, & Corneille, 1996; Quattrone, 1982)—that is, the overestimation of the influence of personal factors on the behaviour of others and the simultaneous underestimation of the influence of situational factors (Jones & Harris, 1967). Individuals, the thinking goes, usually begin by explaining the behaviour of others with reference to their attitudes or personality, and then adjust this evaluation (insufficiently) by taking other causes into consideration. Another judgmental phenomenon that has been explained through the anchoring effect is the hindsight bias (Fischhoff, 1975; Hawkins & Hastie, 1990): Given the correct solution to a problem, individuals in retrospect overestimate the likelihood that they correctly solved the problem or would have been able to do so. It is possible that the correct solution works as an anchor and influences the memory of the answer previously given (Pohl, 1992).

Other heuristics in the judgmental process

In the previous sections we have introduced three basic judgmental strategies by means of which individuals are able to form sufficiently accurate judgments with little cognitive effort, although under certain circumstances these strategies can lead to systematic distortions. The idea of heuristic information processing has subsequently been expanded to other heuristic cues, with lasting influence on theory formation in broad areas of judgmental psychology. One important category of stimuli whose significance as cues has been studied over the last 10 years is affective reactions by individuals to a judgmental object. The following discussion will present important research findings in this area. In addition, researchers have identified additional characteristics of objects as the basis of heuristic judgment formation. We will conclude the discussion by sketching findings in this area, using persuasion research as an example.

Feelings as the basis for heuristic judgment formation

Imagine you have just seen a movie and somebody asks you whether it was good or bad. How could you answer this question? If you had enough time and motivation to render a particularly precise judgment, you could begin by judging the movie according to the criteria you consider relevant for evaluating a film. How was the cinematography? Were the actors convincing? Was the story entertaining or boring? After answering these individual questions you could combine the various pieces of information into an overall judgment. However, you could also choose a simpler path by merely paying attention to the feeling you have when you think about the movie. If that feeling is positive, the movie was presumably good. If that feeling is negative, the movie was probably not good. In many ways, this strategy resembles a judgmental heuristic: Readily accessible information (a feeling connected with remembering the film), which in most cases is related to the actual judgmental dimension (the quality of the film), is used as the basis for judgment. A simple judgmental rule is used in the process: "If the feeling is good, the judgmental object is also good." By proceeding in this way, individuals follow a more general judgmental principle that Higgins (1998) has called the "aboutness principle": When individuals have a reaction, they conceive of it as being informative about something, usually about the object that triggered the reaction. However, this procedure can also lead to false judgment, for example, when the feeling was caused by a different event, such as the weather at the time the judgment was made, and this cause was not recognized. Because of these characteristics, affective feelings as well as other subjective experiences—such as experiences that accompany cognitive operations (e.g., the feeling of ease with the availability heuristic)—are seen increasingly as heuristic information (Chen & Chaiken, 1999; Strack & Gonzales, 1993). The discussion that follows will illustrate that individuals employ subjective feeling as the basis for a variety of judgments and decisions (for additional overviews see Clore, 1992; Schwarz & Clore, 1996; Strack & Gonzales, 1993).

Affective feelings

Affective feelings, such as positive or negative moods, serve individuals on the one hand as a source of information about the qualities of judgmental objects, and on the other hand as the basis for various decisions. Research on such judgmental processes is discussed under the heading "feeling as information" (Clore, 1992; Schwarz & Clore, 1996), and the underlying judgmental principle has been described by Schwarz and Clore (e.g., Clore, Schwarz, & Conway, 1994; Schwarz & Clore, 1988) as the "How-do-I-feel-about-it?" heuristic: Instead of undertaking elaborate analyses of judgmental objects, individuals ask themselves "How do I feel about it?" and use this feeling as the basis of judgment.

By applying the "How-do-I-feel-about-it?" heuristic, individuals can short cut their judgmental processes. When evaluating a particular target, for example another person we are talking to at a party, we no longer need to integrate various different pieces of information. We can simply "consult" our affective state and base our judgment on this information. As a result, the same judgmental target is usually evaluated more positively when individuals are in a positive than in a negative affective state. We will return to the underlying processes of this heuristic in Chapter 7, when we discuss the impact of affect on cognitive processes more extensively.

Nonaffective feelings as the basis of judgment

Cognitive activities are frequently accompanied by subjective feelings: Above, we have discussed the ease of retrieval as one such subjective feeling. Besides ease of retrieval, other subjective feelings may accompany individuals' cognitive activities, for example the feeling of effort (e.g., when working on brainteasers), the feeling of familiarity (in seeing a face), or the feeling of uncertainty (in making a prediction) (for overviews see Bless & Forgas, 2000; Schwarz & Clore, 1996). One thing that distinguishes such "nonaffective" feelings from affective feelings is the fact that they contain little valence; they are not primarily positive or negative. The discussion of the representativeness heuristic has already shown that nonaffective feelings can also be used as the basis for heuristic decision making. In that particular heuristic, it is the feeling of ease of cognitive operations that is used as the basis for frequency and probability judgments. The following discussion will describe the significance of the feeling of familiarity as a basis for heuristic judgment.

Jacoby and colleagues (e.g., Jacoby & Woloshyn, 1989; Kelley & Jacoby, 1998) demonstrated in a series of experiments that the feeling of familiarity for a person's name was used as the basis for judgments about the person's fame. The relevant heuristic could be formulated as follows: "If a person's name seems familiar to me it probably belongs to a famous person." In one experiment (Jacoby, Kelley, Brown, & Jasechko, 1989), presented as a study of accent, participants were asked to read out loud a list of names of exclusively nonfamous individuals. In the second part of the experiment, participants judged the fame of both new and previously presented names. In accordance with the assumption that familiarity is used as the basis of judgments of fame, names were judged to be famous more frequently if participants had read them before. However, individuals used familiarity as the basis of judgment only if they were not aware of the reason for their familiarity: The described results occurred only if 1 day had passed between the reading of the names and the judgment of their fame, but not if the judgment was solicited immediately after the reading of the list.

What conveys the feeling of familiarity? What feels familiar to us are objects we encounter regularly and events we experience frequently. It is possible that repeated experience renders such objects or events more easily perceivable (Jacoby & Dallas, 1981). Do individuals use the feeling of ease as a cue for the familiarity of an object? One experiment by Strack and Neumann (2000) provides evidence in

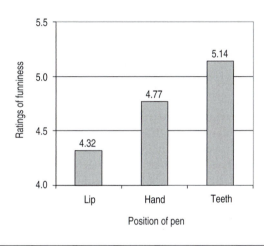
support of this hypothesis. Participants were presented with pictures of famous and nonfamous persons and asked to judge their fame. In addition, in half of the participants the feeling of tension was induced by having them knit their brows while processing this task (cf. Stepper & Strack, 1993), and in fact these participants judged the pictures of famous and nonfamous persons as less famous than did participants who raised their eyebrows during the task (see also Box 4.5 for another example of how individuals use their "motoric feelings" in the form of facial feedback as a basis for judgments).

The experiments described above offer only a few examples for a host of additional findings and theoretical approaches on the significance of nonaffective feelings for judgment formation. The interested reader can find extensive discussions of the topic in Bless and Forgas

(2000), Clore and Parrott (1991), Schwarz and Clore (1996), and Strack and Gonzales (1993).

Specific stimulus characteristics as the basis for heuristic judgments

Above we have discussed various forms of heuristics that individuals apply to simplify their processing. The described heuristics were all very general in their nature and can be applied independently of a particular content. In addition to these general heuristics, individuals can simplify their processing by relying on other heuristics that are usually more related to content. These heuristics imply the use of prior general knowledge that can be applied to new specific situations (in several parts of this book we have already pointed out individuals' reliance on general knowledge structures as one way to simplify cognitive processes).

In particular, in the domain of person perception and attitude change such heuristics have received considerable attention. For example, when evaluating another person, individuals can base their judgments primarily on available individuating information about a specific target person. They may, however, simplify their processing by basing their judgment on the implications of a target person's category membership. In this case, judgments reflect the perceiver's general knowledge about the category to which the target is assigned, i.e., the implications of the stereotype.

Similar considerations can be applied when individuals are confronted with a persuasive message and are forming an attitude judgment. On the one hand, they may carefully consider the content of the message, paying close attention to the implications of the presented arguments. Again, they may simplify this task and rely on heuristic cues, such as the communicator's expertise, likableness, attractiveness, or the sheer length of a message.

In both domains, various models have been proposed to conceptualize the different processes of arriving at a judgment. Addressing attitude change, two models of the processing of persuasive communication—the elaboration likelihood model (ELM; Petty & Cacioppo, 1981, 1986; Petty & Wegener, 1999) and the heuristic systematic model (HSM; Bohner, Moskowitz, & Chaiken, 1995; Chaiken, 1987; Chen & Chaiken, 1999)—involve the use of persuasion heuristics as one of two processing modes (see Eagly & Chaiken,

1993). Under conditions of low motivation or capacity, the change of attitudes depends primarily on the expression of certain superficial, easily processed characteristics. The strength of presented arguments, however, recedes as an effective factor. Persuasion heuristics, such as "Experts can be trusted" or "Many arguments speak for the message," are less general than the heuristics we have examined previously. They are applicable especially to the context of the communication, since they refer chiefly to characteristics of a communicator (e.g., likeability or expert knowledge) or a message (length, number of arguments).

Similar models have been developed in the domain of person perception. Again, these models distinguish between two different processing strategies (Brewer, 1988; Fiske & Neuberg, 1990). Again, processing motivation and processing capacity play a key role in determining whether judgments are based on a heuristic strategy, i.e., on the implications of the stereotype, or whether judgments are based on a more elaborative strategy, i.e., on a consideration of all the individuating information that is target specific. The key assumptions hold that judgments based on category membership information are more likely if processing capacity and/or motivation is low, whereas judgments based on individuating information are more likely if both components are sufficiently high (see Fiske & Neuberg, 1990; Kruglanski, 1989a; for reviews see Bodenhausen et al., 1999; Hamilton & Sherman, 1996).

Despite the importance of these models, we will not further elaborate on these aspects because person perception and attitude change are discussed extensively in other volumes of this series.

Alternative explanations and further developments

This discussion of the research programme on judgmental heuristics would be incomplete if we failed to point out that researchers have proposed and experimentally tested alternative explanations for some of the judgmental phenomena we have described. The section that follows will sketch some explanatory approaches.

Task understanding

At the very beginning of this chapter it had already become clear that in many cases the use of judgmental heuristics was and is determined by the fact that the judgments of test subjects deviate from the "actual" manifestation of the judgmental object. However, in the processing of a judgmental task, the result depends not only on our judgmental strategy but also on how we understand the task (see Bless, Strack, & Schwarz, 1993; Hilton, 1995; Schwarz, 1996; Strack, 1994). Since the elements contained in a task are not always unambiguous, they first need to be interpreted. Studies have in fact shown that some of the judgmental phenomena described here are in part due to the fact that the test subjects understood the task differently from the way in which the experimenter intended. For example, let us look at the neglect of base rates in regard to person information. As in the experiment described above (remember "Jack," who resembled either a typical lawyer or a typical engineer), the person information in many studies was described as the product of psychological interviews. Moreover, each test subject was confronted with several person descriptions in the experiment, with the base rates always remaining the same. Both characteristics could have led participants to believe that the person information was more important and more relevant than the base rates for the judgment they had been asked to make. Schwarz et al. (1991b) examined this possibility by, on the one hand, presenting the problem either as a predominantly "statistical" one or as a predominantly "psychological" one, and on the other hand by varying the base rates and keeping the person descriptions constant in one condition, and keeping the base rates constant and varying the person descriptions in another condition. Result: If the task was presented in a "statistical" context, the influence of the base rate was significantly higher than in the "psychological" context. In addition, the influence of the person information was strongly reduced if it was kept constant. This finding is supported by a number of other experiments (for overviews see Koehler, 1996; Schwarz, 1994, 1996).

The conjunction effect, as well, can be partially attributed to a certain task understanding on the part of the test subjects. Tversky and Kahneman (1983) already considered the possibility that test subjects understood the statement "Linda is a bank teller" not in the comprehensive sense, that is, one that includes all other additions, but as "Linda is a bank teller and not active in the women's movement." But if this interpretation is correct, the conjunction effect is no longer a judgmental error. Dulany and Hilton (1991) tested the meaning of the interpretation of the statement in four experiments. Individuals were, among other things, confronted with the "Linda problem" and their understanding of the statement "Linda is a bank teller" was ascertained. The study (Exp. 1) produced two important results: Under conditions that were comparable to the experiments of Tversky and Kahneman (1983), only 55% of the participants interpreted the statement "correctly," that is, in the comprehensive sense. Among these individuals, the rate of conjunction error was indeed strongly reduced: While Tversky and Kahneman reported error rates in excess of 80%, in this experiment they were between 20 and 26%.

Other cognitive processes

The following alternative explanations have emerged out of a fundamental critique of the heuristics and biases approach. This critique maintains that the proposed judgmental heuristics are merely descriptions of the judgmental phenomena they are supposed to explain. Our discussion of the explanatory power of the anchoring heuristic clearly reveals the background of this critique. The logical consequence of this critique was the development of new explanatory models for the respective judgmental phenomena. The model of selective accessibility described in the section on adjustment and anchoring (Mussweiler & Strack, 1999a) is a good example of this. Other theories refer, for example, to the conjunction effect or to the misperception of random sequences (on this see Falk & Konold, 1997). Some authors have thus assumed that the conjunction effect is attributable not to the use of the representativeness heuristic, but to the use of simple though false arithmetic rules (Gavanski & Roskos-Ewoldsen, 1991; Yates & Carlson, 1986). Gavanski and Roskos-Ewoldsen constructed a series of conjunction problems in which the conjunction had no representativeness whatsoever for the person to be judged. One example: "On one planet live Gronks. The probability that a Gronk has blue hair is ___%. What is the probability that the first Gronk you meet on the plant has blue hair and three eyes?" Result: Even with a task like the one just described, the rate of conjunction error was about 40%. Moreover, the majority of test subjects reported that they determined the probability of the conjunction by simply forming the medium value of the two individual probabilities.

Presentation format

One fundamental critique of the heuristics and biases approach is directed against the fact that many problems are expressed in the form of probabilities (see, e.g., Cosmides & Tooby, 1996; Gigerenzer, 1991; Gigerenzer & Hoffrage, 1995). This critique contains two aspects: First, the principles and algorithms of probability theory were developed to describe relative frequencies, and applying them to individual results, as is the case in many experiments, lacks a normative basis. For that reason it is also inappropriate to speak of "errors." However, the related question, whether in fact we are dealing with errors, is of little interest from a psychological point of view. By contrast, the question of how individuals form judgments on the basis of probability statements is relevant, regardless of the normative appropriateness of how individual questions are framed. This is not the case because dealing with probabilities is something individuals frequently have to do.

The second aspect of the critique is more significant psychologically. It contains the thesis that our cognitive system, in the course of evolution, adjusted itself to the processing of frequencies but not to the processing of probabilities. The concept of probability rests on abstract concepts and their linguistic representations and is thus relatively recent in the developmental history of humanity. In fact, a number of studies were able to show that judgment errors, such as the neglect of base rates (Cosmides & Tooby, 1996; Gigerenzer & Hoffrage, 1995) or the conjunction effect (Fiedler, 1988), disappear in the judgment of probabilities if these are presented in the form of relative frequencies or if judgments are solicited in this format. For example, Fiedler (1988) presented one group of test subjects with the Linda problem and other tasks in the form used by Tversky and Kahneman (1983), and another group with the same problem and tasks in a slightly altered form. The first group was asked to rank individual statements about Linda ("Linda is a bank teller," etc.) according to their *probability*. The other group was asked to indicate to *how many* of 100 women each statement of the Linda problem applied. Result: While on average 73% of participants violated the conjunction rule if the question asked about probability, the number was only 23% under the frequency format of the question (Exp. 1).

In the above-mentioned studies, the use of the frequency format led to a reduced occurrence of judgment distortions attributed to the use of the representativeness heuristic. Manis, Shedler, Jonides, and Nelson (1993) also demonstrated similar effects for distortions attributed to the availability heuristic. In one experiment, judgments about the frequency of specific names ("Frequency of the name Jack"), but not judgments about the size of subgroups ("Frequency of male names"), were determined by the actual presentation frequency.

However, it must be noted that the use of the frequency format is presumably less reliable in causing a reduction of judgmental errors than was initially assumed (on this see Griffin & Buehler, 1999).

Moreover, the finding that judgmental errors occur less frequently in the frequency format does not explain their occurrence in the probability format. Nor should we deduce from the sample findings on task understanding that the judgmental heuristics described by Tversky and Kahneman are meaningless for the judgmental phenomena we have looked at. Rather, the reason we have considered some of the critiques of heuristics is to show that their use is one factor among many, a factor that presumably plays a fairly minor role in some phenomena (e.g., in anchoring effects), and a profound role in others (e.g., the use of the availability heuristic).

Concluding remarks

We conclude this chapter by noting an important change that is taking place in our understanding of the role of judgmental heuristics in the judgment process. For a long time the research programme on judgmental heuristics was characterized by the fact that the person was seen as a "cognitive miser" who employed simplifying judgmental heuristics in a relatively rigid manner, virtually automatically, and independent of the situation or actual goals.

Research findings of the last few years, however, have given rise to a more subtle picture. They have shown that the presumed rigidity and stability of judgmental errors apply only to some judgmental heuristics or individual judgmental distortions. In many cases the judging individual can be described more with the image of a "manager" or "motivated tactician" (Fiske & Taylor, 1991), who pursues various goals with temporally and cognitively limited resources and who must and is able to coordinate these resources. In this picture, judgmental heuristics are a subgroup of the "tools" that the "resource manager" has at his disposal to accomplish his task.

What task does this resource management entail? First, it is necessary to make sure that more resources are allocated to important judgments than to unimportant judgments. Second, under conditions of strongly constrained resources, "more parsimonious" judgmental strategies must be employed than under conditions of less constrained resources. Third, a judgmental strategy must be changed when it apparently does not lead to the desired goal, for example when the information to which the judgmental strategy can be applied is not representative or because the strategy proves unsuccessful during its application. The following research findings illustrate that these three tasks can be fulfilled for some heuristics or judgmental areas, but that a number of preconditions must be met.

Possibilities and conditions of the flexible use of judgmental heuristics

The study by Rothman and Schwarz (1998) (see the discussion on the availability heuristic) offers one example for the significance of the importance or relevance of the judgmental task for the use of judgmental heuristics. Rothman and Schwarz asked a group of participants to list three or eight factors that increased (or decreased) their risk of heart disease. The personal relevance of the judgment was varied by comparing individuals with a family history of heart disease (high relevance) to individuals with no such family history (low relevance). Result: Under the condition of low relevance, individuals used the ease with which they were able to generate risk factors in assessing their personal risk. Under the condition of high relevance, by contrast, judgments were determined by the number of listed risk factors. In other words, the availability heuristic was used only when the judgment was less important.

A study by Siemer and Reisenzein (1998) showed that the use of judgmental heuristics depends on the available temporal or cognitive resources. Siemer and Reisenzein varied processing capacity on four levels and found that participants made greater use of their mood as the basis for judgments about life satisfaction the more they were distracted by another task or the greater the time pressure they were under. Many other studies have demonstrated that some judgmental heuristics are used in judgment formation primarily when the judgment is unimportant or the individual has little processing capacity at his or her disposal (for overviews see Eagly & Chaiken, 1993; Kunda, 1990).

Another reason for exerting a regulating effect on the judgment process occurs when the representativeness of heuristic information is in question (cf. Strack, 1992). We have already encountered a typical example of this in the section on the experienced ease of retrieval. For example, when the representativeness of the subjective ease of recall was reduced by informing some of the test subjects that the background music to the test made it easier (or more difficult) to remember self-confident behaviour, judgments were determined less by the ease of recall and more by the amount of recalled information (Schwarz et al., 1991a). Similarly, the impact of perceived familiarity was reduced when participants attributed their feeling of knowing the name in question to a prior presentation in the experiment (Jacoby et al., 1989).

A study by Stapel, Reicher, and Spears (1995, Exp. 5), offered one example for the flexible use of a judgmental heuristic (in this case the availability heuristic) as a function of its appropriateness for the task. The researchers presented participants with lists of 19 female and 20 male names (or vice versa), whereby the less frequent names were more famous than the more frequent ones. Participants were simply asked to listen carefully. Subsequently they were asked to judge whether the list contained more female names or more male names. As was expected from the use of the availability heuristic, the majority of participants judged the category made up of famous names to be bigger, even though in every case it was smaller than the one with less famous names. Unlike the participants in the study by Tversky and Kahneman (1973), however, participants in this study had the opportunity to work on the task three additional times—in this case, of course, with knowledge of the actual task, i.e., estimating the share of female and male names. Result: The "availability bias" was reduced to the point that in the fourth run-through only 7 of 22 participants came up with false judgments. Evidently the participants had abandoned their original judgmental strategy and had chosen a more successful one.

The flexible use of judgmental heuristics that we have sketched in the preceding sections makes demands on the judge (cf. Kunda, 1990; Petty & Wegener, 1993; Strack, 1992; Strack & Hannover, 1996) that are frequently not met. For example, the individual must have knowledge of and control over those processes that influence his or her judgment in order to be able to assess their appropriateness and, if need be, to take regulative action. The anchoring heuristic is a good example of the case in which this condition is not met. As was described above, even incentives for precise judgments or warnings do not diminish the anchoring effect, let alone eliminate it. The explanation is probably that the anchoring effect is attributable not to the knowing application of a judgmental heuristic, but to basic cognitive mechanisms that are not immediately accessible to the individual. If that is the case, another possibility of judgment regulation gains in importance (cf. Strack, 1992; Strack & Hannover, 1996): Individuals are able to develop subjective theories about the conditions under which their judgment is distorted by certain information, in which direction and to what degree. If an individual has such theories, he or she can make corrections to a rendered judgment; corrections that balance out this distorting influence.

Outlook

The heuristics and biases approach founded by Tversky and Kahneman (1973, 1974) has unquestionably led to important insights in various fields of psychological research. First, this research programme has contributed to a fundamental change in the image of the human being in psychology. While in the 1960s distortions and errors in judgment formation were attributed primarily to the effect of specific motives, from the perspective of the heuristics and biases approach they result from the use of simplifying and useful judgmental strategies. Second, research carried out as part of the heuristics and biases approach moved a number of previously unknown or neglected judgmental phenomena into the centre of attention and stimulated related research (for overviews see Hell, Fiedler, & Gigerenzer, 1993; Jungermann, Pfister, & Fischer, 1998). Third, the idea of heuristic information processing was also shown to be fruitful in research fields other than those originally studied by Tversky and Kahneman. On the one hand, researchers uncovered new heuristic cues and related heuristics, e.g., moods or nonaffective feelings (see Strack & Gonzales, 1993); on the other hand, entire classes of theories were influenced by this idea, for example in attitude and stereotype research (see Chaiken & Trope, 1999; Eagly & Chaiken, 1993).

However, this substantial influence was accompanied and intensified by varied debates about the strengths and weaknesses of the heuristics and biases approach (cf. Gigerenzer, 1996; Kahneman & Tversky, 1996). In addition to other arguments, critics have rightly lamented a lack of theoretical integration of the individual judgmental heuristics and their related judgmental phenomena (see, e.g., Dougherty, Gettys, & Ogden, 1999; Gigerenzer, 1996). Which heuristic is used under which conditions? How is the effort that is invested in a judgmental task regulated? How are the processing methods that go hand in hand with specific heuristics or judgmental phenomena embedded in the entire process of information processing? The further development of more general judgmental theories is one obvious consequence of this criticism and is currently being studied from various theoretical perspectives. An account of the various approaches lies beyond the scope of the present chapter. The brief comments that follow are intended to point the interested reader in the direction where deeper research can be pursued.

With the support theory, Tversky and colleagues (Rottenstreich & Tversky, 1997; Tversky & Koehler, 1994) have developed a comprehensive theory of subjective probability. The support theory assumes that individuals do not assign events as such to certain probabilities, but rather descriptions of events. With the help of this basic assumption and some others it is possible to explain, among other things, the influence of different descriptions of a logically identical event. The recently developed MINERVA-DM theory (Dougherty et al., 1999) explains a number of judgmental phenomena that occur in the assessment of probabilities and frequencies with the help of basic memory processes. Other important theories of probability and frequency judgments, developed in connection with the heuristics and biases approach, are the theory of probabilistic mental models (PMM) put forth by Gigerenzer, Hoffrage, and Kleinbölting (1991) and the Brunswickian induction-algorithm for social cognition (BIAS) formulated by Fiedler (1996). Which of these approaches in their present or expanded form will prove to be the better model of simplifying judgmental strategies is a question that must be answered by the results of future research.

Chapter summary

(1) The process of generating a judgment can be simplified by using "rules of thumb," which are called "heuristics." They allow people to reach a judgment under suboptimal conditions.

(2) Three heuristics have been identified by Amos Tversky and Daniel Kahneman, as devices to afford "judgments under uncertainty." The *availability* heuristic posits that the ease with which information can be brought to mind determines judgments of frequency and probability. The *representativeness* heuristic uses perceived similarity to judge category membership. Finally, the *anchoring and adjustment* heuristic describes how quantitative judgments are orientated toward the starting point of a numeric operation.

(3) Although the underlying cognitive mechanisms have long been unclear, recent evidence has contributed important insights into the mediating processes.

(4) Beyond Tversky and Kahneman's original three heuristics, other means of simplifying judgments have been described. For once, feelings or "subjective experiences" have been identified to serve as judgmental rules of thumb. Also, people were found to use cues to judge the strength of persuasive communications without pondering over the arguments.

(5) Although some of Tversky and Kahneman's experimental procedures have been criticized for conversational demands (see Chapter 5), more recent research has basically confirmed, substantiated, and extended their judgmental heuristics.

Discussion questions

(1) Do errors in social judgment always reflect human irrationality?
(2) What are the benefits and costs of judgmental heuristics?
(3) How may the ease of retrieval exert effects on judgments that are different from those exerted by the amount of the retrieved information?
(4) Some people believe that a powder made from a rhino's horn will be effective as an aphrodisiac. How does this belief reflect the representativeness heuristic?
(5) How may anchoring play a role in negotiation, where each party has to come up with a starting offer?
(6) Recently, the conditions under which individuals resort to judgmental heuristics have been studied. Under which circumstances are heuristics most and least likely to be employed?

Recommendations for further reading

Nisbett, R. E., & Ross, L. (1980). *Human inference: Strategies and shortcomings of social judgment.* Englewood Cliffs, NJ: Prentice-Hall.
Tversky, A., & Kahneman, D. (1974). Judgment under uncertainty: Heuristics and biases. *Science, 185,* 1124–1131.

The use of information in judgments 5

In Chapter 4 we discussed how individuals form judgments on the basis of general heuristics. In this chapter we focus on a different aspect of human judgment and decision making by discussing how individuals use activated information. In doing so, we will first briefly address the possibility that individuals use whatever information comes to mind. We will then turn to different aspects that influence whether and how individuals use activated information.

One trademark of the science of social cognition is undoubtedly that it construes the person as an active processor of information. This perspective has its roots in Bartlett's (1932) work on memory. Specifically, Bartlett showed that the process of recalling past events includes constructions and inferences that "go beyond the information given" (Bruner, 1957a). In one of his experiments, participants who were asked to report the content of a fairy tale they had read previously did not rely solely on the encoded information. Instead, their reports were "enriched" by general knowledge that was suitable for filling the gaps. Thus, the task of remembering was not solved simply through the activation of memory contents, but through an active reconstruction of the past that involved "schemata" and inferences.

These mental activities are akin to what many researchers of social cognition (most recently Kunda, 1999) have highlighted as the role of "making sense" of the behaviour of others. That goal is best achieved by detailing and understanding "why" a given behaviour has occurred. For example, if the cause of Person A's pushing Person B is found in A's intention to hurt B or in A's slipping on a wet floor, each cause leads to a fundamentally different understanding of the observed event. Not surprisingly, theories of causal attribution have been developed in social psychology (e.g., Jones & Davis, 1965; H. H. Kelley, 1967) and have played an important role in detailing the process of how people explain. Individuals use these attributional principles not only to explain the conduct of others, but also to understand their own behaviour (Bem, 1967; Jones & Nisbett, 1972). Most importantly, researchers have found that people apply the logic of attribution to make sense of their own private feelings and experiences (Jacoby et al., 1989; Schachter & Singer, 1962; Schwarz & Clore, 1983), which allows them to use these feelings and experiences as a source of knowledge for their judgments.

The science of social cognition has adopted this perspective and has made the regulation of judgments an integral part of its theorizing. In this spirit, the dynamics by which individuals construct a judgment provide an important means of understanding how a judgment is generated and how it is communicated in a social context.

Using what's on your mind!

Imagine you are asked to indicate on a 7-point scale how happy you are with your life as a whole. Chances are that you do not have a ready-made answer. Rather, you will need to think about various aspects of your life to form a judgment (Schwarz & Strack, 1999). However, there is no reason to assume that people engage in a *complete* review of all their positive and negative experiences. Instead, they will use the information that can easily be brought to mind. What comes to mind, however, is not randomly determined. In part, it depends on what individuals were thinking about previously (see

Rodin's "The Thinker".
Credit: Art Directors and TRIP.

the recency principle discussed in Chapters 2 and 3). That being the case, it should be possible to influence judgments of happiness by inducing people to think about certain events. That is exactly what Strack, Schwarz, and Gschneidinger (1985) did when they asked experimental participants to think about three positive or three negative events of their present life. When the same individuals had to report their happiness in a different context later on, more positive ratings were obtained if they had been induced to think about positive events and more negative ratings if they had been induced to think about negative events. In other words, judgments were based on what was on people's minds. The result is an "assimilation effect," that is, participants' judgments were in line with the implications of the activated information.

Basing a judgment on the contents of one's mind is a way to reduce the complexity of judgment formation. In Chapter 4 we have learned that judges use simplified procedures to arrive at "satisficing" (H. A. Simon, 1957) solutions under suboptimal circumstances. The study of "heuristics" has greatly contributed to our understanding of social judgments (Nisbett & Ross, 1980), which often have to be generated under such conditions. In addition to these described heuristics, it could be argued that the most general means of simplifying a judgment seems to be the unqualified use of whatever comes to mind.

This becomes apparent if you consider the task of forming an impression of another person based on her behaviour. In this endeavour, you first identify the nature of the behaviour. For example, you may interpret an act as "aggressive." Then, the simplest way of describing the actor is to use the activated behavioural descriptions. That is, the aggressiveness of the behaviour serves as a basis for inferring that the person is aggressive (see Trope, Cohen, & Maoz, 1988). Of course, this simplification (named the "fundamental attribution error," Ross, 1977) neglects the situational circumstances under which the behaviour occurs and may be completely unjustified if the aggressive behaviour was, for example, caused by an attempt to assist another person who was being attacked. This neglect of mediating circumstances is particularly likely if the perceiver is not motivated to form an accurate impression or if the impression has to be created under adverse conditions, such as time pressure (e.g., Martin et al., 1990). By contrast, when people are given sufficient time to form their impression, they are more likely to consider situational determinants (e.g., Gilbert et al., 1988). Similarly, a person who has the goal of generating a judgment quickly should be more likely to base it solely on the accessible information, while a person who has the goal of being accurate is inclined to include mediating circumstances (Kruglanski, 1989b).

When relying on what comes to mind, individuals need to integrate that information into a judgment, thus giving weight to various judgment-relevant information (N. H. Anderson, 1981). The aim of this chapter, however, is not to describe how people form and simplify their judgments by relying on whatever comes to mind. Instead, we want to explore the conditions under which the most accessible contents and experiences are *not* used as the sole basis for a judgment, and to identify the qualifying strategies that individuals employ (a) to increase the accuracy of a judgment, and (b) to assure that the judgment is correctly understood if it is communicated to a third person (note that we have already discussed this aspect briefly in Chapter 3). As we shall see, these endeavours require the type of active and goal-directed information processing that goes beyond what is on a judge's mind. In pursuit of these goals, judges draw inferences on the basis of knowledge about the world, of knowledge about others, and of knowledge about themselves.

Cognitive aspects of information use

Awareness of being influenced

One of the most surprising findings in the domain of social cognition is that the force of an influence may be negatively correlated with its success. This phenomenon was convincingly demonstrated in the domain of priming, where the activated information was more likely to become the basis of judgment if the priming was subtle (e.g., Bargh & Pietromonaco, 1982; Martin et al., 1990). The counterintuitive nature of these results disappears if one takes into account that a forceful and blatant priming not only activates semantic information that is relevant for the judgment, but may also direct the judge's attention to the activation episode, which may be completely irrelevant to the judgment at hand. For example, a judge may become aware that her interpretation of a behaviour as "aggressive" has been caused by a previous but unrelated act of aggression. That is, the judge becomes aware that her impression is "contaminated" (Wilson & Brekke, 1994) by an event that had nothing to do with the target of the judgment (Strack, 1992). In this case, the person may try to purge the unwanted influence from the judgment.

In natural situations, recollecting the priming episode depends on the determinants of episodic memory (Tulving, 1983). For example, Jacoby and his collaborators (Jacoby et al., 1989) found that individuals used the feeling of familiarity to judge a person's fame (see also Chapter 4). That is, if test subjects were presented with a name that "felt familiar," they judged that person to be famous. In these studies, however, participants' feelings of familiarity were under the experimenter's control, because the names had been used in a preceding memory task. Knowing that the feeling of familiarity was caused by circumstances that are not representative of the required judgment should provide the judge with the possibility of disregarding the feeling as a basis of judgment. Whether this regulation was, in fact, an option depended on how much time had passed. The episode of learning the name list was more likely to be remembered if it occurred immediately before the judgment and less likely if it occurred a day before, although the elicited feeling did not decay over time. As a result, feelings of familiarity were more likely to influence judgments of fame if the temporal distance made it difficult to retrieve the priming episode and to "decontaminate" the judgment. However, if the episode occurred in close temporal proximity such that it came to mind along with the feeling, participants had the chance to evaluate the "representativeness" of this source. That is, if the judge attributed the experienced familiarity to the name's appearance on the learning list, the feeling was understood to be unrelated to fame. However, if the prior exposure was attributed to a newspaper headline that contained the relevant name, the feeling of familiarity (along with the implications of the episodic knowledge) could remain the basis of judgment.

Experimentally, it is possible to direct people's attention to the episode of the influence. Instead of decreasing the probability that the priming episode will be in people's focus of attention by presenting the information subliminally (Bargh & Pietromonaco, 1982), Strack et al. (1993) conducted a study in which participants were led to focus on the priming episode—note that we have addressed this issue briefly in Chapter 3. In particular, participants were required to perform what they thought was a series of perceptual and cognitive tasks. In one task they heard a series of tones that were paired with words: They had to classify the tones as low or high and to write down the words. For half of the participants, the words had a positive valence (e.g., friendship); for the other half, they had a negative valence (e.g., dishonest). After the tone–word task, participants had to form an impression of a person whose behaviour (e.g., stole exam questions for a desperate friend) was ambiguous and open to interpretation in terms of the positive and negative primed concepts.

To manipulate participants' attention toward the priming episode, the experiment included a control condition in which participants had to perform the tone–word task before generating the impression. In the experimental condition, other participants were asked to answer some questions about the tone–word task (e.g., how successful they had been in discriminating the tones) before forming their impressions. This interpolated task served to remind participants of the priming episode that had caused the positive or negative words to be highly accessible. Replicating earlier priming studies (e.g., Higgins et al., 1977), we found that impressions of the target person were assimilated to the activated concepts when participants were not reminded of the priming episode. However, when participants were reminded, the activated concepts were not used as a basis for the impressions. Rather, a contrast effect was obtained: Participants gave more positive ratings if the prime words were negative, and vice versa. These findings suggest that while a concept may be highly accessible, if judges are aware that it has been activated by an event that is not representative for the judgment, it may not be used for interpreting the target information (see also Lombardi et al., 1987).

The finding that directing people's attention toward possible determinants of a judgment may induce them to avoid being influenced was also obtained in the domain of stereotypes. Although they did not intend to test this notion, Darley and Gross (1983) conducted a study in which participants had to predict the academic achievement of a group of children from a minority group. In one condition, participants saw a videotape of the children playing in impoverished housing conditions that were characteristic of their ethnic group. In another condition, these children were shown filling out a scholastic aptitude test. Darley and Gross found that the observers of those videos expressed more positive expectations if they saw the children in their typical environment than if this context was removed. Although there are no findings to corroborate this interpretation, this result is consistent with the notion that participants did not want their judgments to be influenced by ethnic stereotypes. That possibility, however, became salient when judges' attention was directed at stereotypic context. As a consequence, observers may have corrected their judgments under this condition.

Content or experience?

As you may have noted, the mechanism outlined above is essentially the same as in the study by Jacoby and his collaborators, in which the use of experienced familiarity depended on participants' awareness of the eliciting circumstances. However, there are also differences in both phenomenology and the processes of influence. First of all, subjective experiences are associated with a specific phenomenal quality that is often described as a feeling of which people are aware. Second, such feelings serve as the basis for inferences (see our discussion in Chapter 4). In contrast, the activation of information does not necessarily result in a state of awareness and its influence is not mediated by the fact that it provides a basis for inferences. Instead, people focus on the target of the required judgment (see C. M. Kelley & Jacoby, 1990) and associate the activated contents with the characteristics of the target. For example, a participant primed with the word "adventurous" and asked why she had assigned this characteristic to a target will justify her judgment with behavioural manifestations of the target person (see Higgins, 1997), unless, of course, attention is directed toward the priming episode. By contrast, a person who is asked why she thought a particular name belonged to a famous person may respond that the name felt familiar to her. In other words, judges have more introspective access to the basis of their judgment if it is based on a feeling than if it is influenced by previously activated information.

In many situations, both content and experience may be used as a basis for a judgment. Often their implications can be similar, but sometimes they may be quite different. In Chapter 4 we addressed this aspect when we discussed the study by Schwarz et al. (1991a) in which participants had to recall either 6 or 12 episodes in which they had (or had not) behaved assertively. In this situation, different implications were derived from ease versus content. The findings suggested that individuals relied on the ease of retrieval, which probably was the first aspect that came to their mind. Note, however, that the experience of mental effort did not influence the judgment if participants were led to attribute it to some external determinant, such as a specific kind of music. Thus, it seems again as if individuals do not rely on highly accessible information when they assume that incorporating this information into a judgment is not appropriate and would result in a biased judgment (see also Schwarz & Bless, 1992a).

Typicality and representativeness

Obviously, one of the first questions individuals need to address is whether activated information is at all relevant for the judgment or whether it came to mind due to some unwanted influence. Above, we have seen that in this case individuals attempt to avoid the influence, often resulting in contrast effects. Sometimes, although being relevant, information may be perceived as atypical, in which case the reliance on this activated information seems not appropriate. Suppose, for example, you were asked to evaluate the financial situations of African Americans in general. Suppose further that in this context two prominent African-American athletes, Michael Jordan and Tiger Woods, come to mind. On the one hand, these celebrities belong to the social category of African Americans. On the other hand, you may consider these celebrities as atypical of African-Americans in general (see Bodenhausen, Schwarz, Bless, & Wänke, 1995). Consequently a judgment based on this information would potentially be biased and individuals may try to avoid this influence.

Obviously, the perceived typicality of the activated information plays a crucial role as to whether or not individuals rely on it. Evidence for this assumption is, for example, provided by research in the stereotype change domain. An activated exemplar (e.g., a specific target) is more likely to change judgments about the group when the exemplar is perceived as typical rather than an atypical exception (Bless et al., 2001; Hewstone, 1994; Kunda & Oleson, 1995; Weber & Crocker, 1983). Directly addressing the role of typicality, Bless and Wänke (2000) demonstrated that, when perceived as typical, activated information resulted in assimilation effects (i.e., activated positive information resulted in more positive judgments), whereas contrast effects resulted (i.e., activated positive information resulted in more negative judgments) when the same information was perceived as atypical.

Indirectly related to these findings, Herr and colleagues (Herr, 1986; Herr, Sherman, & Fazio, 1983) found in their studies that a target (an animal or a prominent person) was judged as more hostile when it was presented in the context of another moderately hostile exemplar (assimilation), but was judged as less hostile when it was presented in the context of an extremely hostile exemplar (contrast). They argued that assimilation and contrast depend on the extremity of the context information. Assuming that extreme exemplars are perceived as atypical, whereas moderate exemplars are perceived as typical (see also Philippot, Schwarz, Carrera, Dr Vries, & Van Yperen, 1991), these findings converge with the conclusion that perceived typicality plays a crucial role in whether and how individuals rely on activated information (see also Lambert & Wyer, 1990;

Maurer, Park, & Rothbart, 1995; Rothbart & Lewis, 1988; Schwarz & Bless, 1992a).

Applicability

Even when activated information is considered typical and even when its use is potentially appropriate, the activated information does not necessarily enter directly into the judgment. Sometimes, potentially relevant information is simply not applicable to the judgment in question. Imagine, for example, you were asked to rate the trustworthiness of a specific politician Smith, and due to some other previously performed task the scandal-ridden politician Miller comes to your mind. Obviously, this information could be relevant. However, the scandalous politician Miller cannot easily be "included" into the politician Smith. In this case, Miller can serve as a standard against which Smith can be compared. As a consequence, Smith seems more trustworthy than without the activation of Miller. Imagine now a different judgmental task. You were asked to rate the trustworthiness of politicians in general. In this case, scandal-ridden Miller can be included into the category in question, and consequently, you would consider politicians in general as less trustworthy when the scandal-ridden politician is activated. Evidence reported by Schwarz and Bless (1992b) demonstrates this seeming paradox: A specific untrustworthy exemplar may decrease rating of other exemplars but increase the trustworthiness of the category politicians in general. The logic that activated information needs to be applicable to the judgmental target is also inherent to the finding that judgments about a target person are likely to reflect assimilation effects when the prime is an abstract trait category, whereas contrast effects are likely to emerge when the prime is a concrete specific person (Stapel et al., 1996). Apparently, a primed trait is more likely to be used or included into the mental representation of the stimulus person, whereas this is often not possible for the primed specific exemplar.

Interestingly, the contrast effects, usually elicited by other exemplars ("compared to the Nobel prize winner Prof. Fabulous, the achievements of Professor Jones next door seem rather minor"), can be eliminated under some conditions. When common aspects of the context and the judgmental target are emphasized ("Hey, both Prof. Fabulous and Prof. Jones work in the same department") contrast effects are reduced or even eliminated (see Wänke, Bless, & Igou, 2001).

The communication of judgments

To assess the psychological dynamics of human judgments, people are typically requested to express their opinion or attitude in a direct manner. For example, they are asked to indicate how happy they are with their life or how dangerous they think the neoNazis are for democracy. It is important to note that responses are frequently not given on a scale with objective numerical or categorical response options (e.g., "How long is the River Seine? 700–750 km, 750–800 km, or 800–850 km?"), but on a subjective rating scale (e.g., "How long is the River Seine? Not very long/somewhat long/extremely long").

For the objective format, the response depends on the information that is mentally accessible, which is not only influenced by the target of the judgments but also by preceding mental operations (Mussweiler & Strack, 1999b; Strack & Mussweiler, 1997; see also Chapter 4). Otherwise, the judge simply wants to communicate what he or she thinks is the truth. In the second case, however, judges must take additional considerations into account. In particular, they need to consider the recipient's situation. Imagine that the recipient of the judgment is a person living in a city by the Mississippi River. To describe the River Seine (actually 780 km long) as "extremely long" would be misleading to such a person, who may be expected to use his or her experience (the Mississippi River is 3780 km long) as a point of reference. In contrast, for a person who has never seen a river but only small creeks, "extremely long" would be an appropriate characterization of the Seine.

This is an example of how different response formats require respondents not only to report a judgment that is correct, but also to make sure that a recipient understands it in the intended way. In the domain of social judgments, both formal rating scales and informal assessments of attitudes require the communicator to adopt the recipient's perspective. For example, if the person who is asking you to rate the quality of your favourite family-style restaurant is known to be an exceptional gourmet, you would probably come up with more moderate ratings than if the recipient typically goes to fast-food restaurants.

These examples describe what the linguist Paul Grice (1975) has named the "cooperation principle," which expresses the insight that any communication is an interaction whose success depends on the participants' cooperation. More precisely, this principle includes several rules ("maxims") that people are expected to obey. For our purposes, Grice's maxim of relation is of particular importance. It requires participants to make their contribution to an exchange relevant to the aims of an ongoing conversation. If it is the aim of communicators to convey an accurate impression of a target (be it a river, a restaurant, or a third person), they must take the perspective of the recipient into account and craft their message accordingly (see also Higgins, 1981; the "communication game"). Conversely, recipients may assume that a communication comes with a "guarantee of relevance" (Sperber & Wilson, 1986; for discussion see also Schwarz, 1994, 1996).

To tailor a message in such a manner that it will be understood in the intended way, it is necessary to take the recipient's state of knowledge into account. For example, if you are asked where the Eiffel Tower is, your response will be "in Paris" if the question is asked in Rome, but perhaps "two blocks from here" if the same question is asked in Paris. In this example, the context serves as a basis for inferring what recipients already know and what information they want to add to their knowledge. The quest for new information that is tied to existing knowledge structures is captured in Grice's maxim of quantity. In everyday conversations, we need to keep track of what is already conveyed and what is new. This type of monitoring an ongoing exchange has been called the "given-new-contract" (Clark & Haviland, 1977; see Box 5.3), which needs to be observed to make a conversation successful (Krauss & Weinheimer, 1966).

Adding new information to what is already known is a principle that is not only the basis of natural conversations; it may also guide the processing of information in standardized settings. When responding to a survey (e.g., Schwarz & Strack, 1991), participating in psychological experiments (Bless et al., 1993), or filling out a questionnaire or a form, people expect that what they are asked to convey should go beyond what they have previously contributed.

It is important to take this principle into account, because its implications may override influences of mere accessibility. For

BOX 5.3.

An example for the "given–new contract"

Consider the following two conversational exchanges:

(a)   How is your wife? . . . . . . And how is your family?
(b)   How is your boss? . . . . . . And how is your family?

In which case is the answer to the inquiry about the family's well-being more likely to include the wife's happiness? How does the "given–new contract" (Clark & Haviland, 1977) determine whether accessible information is used?

example, in a study by Strack, Martin, and Schwarz (1988a), American college students were given a questionnaire in which they were asked how happy they were with their dating and how happy they were with their life in general. Principles of cognitive accessibility suggest that applicable information will become the basis for subsequent judgments, in this case specific information about happiness with dating for judgments of global happiness (but not vice versa). In fact, correlations between reports of specific (dating) happiness and happiness with life in general were much higher (.55) if the questions were asked in this order than if the order was reversed (.16).

Like in a natural conversation, if one person asks you about the well-being of your wife and another person about the well-being of your family, chances are that you will base the second judgment on the implications of the first. However, if both questions are asked by the same person, you will be more likely to obey the Gricean norms and add new information to what you have already conveyed. That is, you would be less likely to use your wife's well-being but include other information about your family to generate the judgment. In a standardized situation, it is often not clear whether two questions belong to the same conversational context. In fact, designers of questionnaires often break up perceptions of relatedness by mixing up the questions or by interspersing unrelated filler items. Conversely, one might establish a conversational context by indicating that two questions belong together. Under such conditions, the conversational principles should be applied and the global judgment should go beyond the specific judgment. As a result, the correlation between the answers should be reduced.

This is exactly what happened in the described study (Strack et al., 1988a) when respondents were explicitly told that they would be asked two questions about their life, (a) how happy they were with their dating, and (b) how happy they were with life in general. Although the specific question was asked first, the correlation was dramatically reduced from .55 to .26 (see also Schwarz, Strack, & Mai, 1991c).

The same reasoning applies to questions that are very similar in content. Let us assume that one person asks you how happy you are with your life and another person, in a different context, asks about your satisfaction. Chances are that your responses will not be all that different. However, if the two questions are asked by the same person in close succession, you will differentiate between your report of happiness and that of satisfaction. Again, this prediction was tested and confirmed in a questionnaire study (Strack, Schwarz, & Wänke, 1991) in which participants were asked to indicate both how happy and how content they were with their life. More importantly, the questions were presented in different contexts such that in one condition the happiness question was placed at the end of one questionnaire while the satisfaction question was presented as the first question in a new and ostensibly unrelated questionnaire. In another condition, both questions were presented at the end of the same questionnaire and were introduced by the joint lead-in "Now we have two questions about your life." As expected, respondents' reports of happiness and satisfaction did not differ substantially (Ms = 8.0 and 8.2 on a 11-point scale) and were highly correlated ($r = .96$) if the questions were not perceived as belonging together. However, if respondents assumed that the questions were part of the same conversational context, respondents differentiated between happiness and satisfaction. In particular, they reported higher happiness ($M = 8.1$) than satisfaction ($M = 7.4$) and the correlation between the two measures dropped to $r = .75$.

These findings show that the goals of conversation operate not only in situations that consist of direct exchanges between two or more people. They are also effective if a recipient is merely "implied" (Allport's definition of social psychology) in the interaction. This is, of course, the case not only in assessment procedures, like surveys, but also in psychological experiments in which participants may tailor their responses to the presumed needs of the questioner (Bless et al., 1993; Schwarz, 1996). Unlike in natural situations, where communicators may resolve ambiguities by asking for clarifications, standardized conditions greatly restrict behavioural options. As a consequence, participants must rely on minor and seemingly irrelevant aspects of the research procedures to infer what information they should provide. The results of attempts to obey conversational norms may be confounded with influences of other variables and lead to an over-estimation of the focal effect. An example is a famous study by Kahneman and Tversky (1973), in which participants were given a short description of a target person who bore a slight resemblance to the prototype of an engineer assigned to that category, although the baseline probability was very low. The result was interpreted as having been caused by the representativeness heuristic (see Chapter 4), which suggests that similarity is the primary basis for categorizations. Subsequent research (Schwarz et al., 1991b), however, has demonstrated that the neglect of the baseline information also depended on minor aspects of the experimental situation that led participants to infer that the description of the target person was deliberately selected for it to be used as a judgmental basis. If they were told that the information about the target person was "randomly" compiled by a computer, participants were much more likely to take the baseline probability into account. Although the judgments were strongly influenced by such conversational aspects, the results still supported the representativeness heuristic.

The inclusion/exclusion model

Above we have discussed various cognitive and communicative aspects that influence whether and how individuals use the information that comes to their mind. We have discussed variables that influence how particular activated information is used. The inclusion/exclusion model (Schwarz & Bless, 1992a; see also Bless & Schwarz, 1998) attempts to integrate the variables that influence information use. The model holds that evaluative judgments (e.g., judgments about the trustworthiness of politicians) that are based on features of the target require two mental representations, namely a representation of the target and a representation of a standard (Kahneman & Miller, 1986) against which the target is evaluated. Both representations are formed on the spot, drawing on information that is chronically or temporarily accessible. Information that is used in forming a representation of the target results in assimilation effects; that is, the inclusion of positive (negative) information about the target results in a more positive (negative) judgment. For example, positive information about the target politician will result in more positive judgments. Conversely, information that is used in forming a representation of the comparison standard results in a contrast effect; that is, more positive (negative) information results in a more positive (negative) standard, against which the target is evaluated less (more) favourably. Hence, the *same* piece of accessible information can have opposite effects, depending on how it is used.

The inclusion/exclusion model holds that three filters channel information use. First, individuals will exclude accessible information when they believe that this information was brought to mind by some irrelevant influence (see above discussion about awareness of being influenced; Lombardi et al., 1987; Martin, 1986; Strack et al., 1993). Second, information is excluded when it is not considered representative of the target. This decision is driven by the numerous variables known to influence the categorization of information, including the information's extremity and typicality (e.g., Bless et al., 2001; Bless & Wänke, 2000), as well as the presentation format and related context variables (for reviews see Martin, Strack, & Stapel, 2001; Schwarz & Bless, 1992a; see above discussion about typicality and representativeness). A third filter pertains to the norms of conversational conduct that govern information use in conversations. Information is likely to be excluded when its repeated use would violate conversational norms of nonredundancy (see above discussion about the communication of judgments; e.g., Schwarz et al., 1991c; for a review see Schwarz, 1996). Information that passes all three filters is included in the representation formed of the target and results in assimilation effects. Information that fails any one of these tests is excluded from the representation formed of the target, but may be used in forming a representation of the standard, resulting in contrast effects.

Motivational aspects of information use

In the above sections we have discussed how individuals may attempt to avoid the influence of activated information if the use of this information is considered not appropriate for a variety of reasons. Obviously, individuals strive for adequate judgments of the social situation, that is, an unbiased construction of social reality, and they want to communicate adequate judgments to others. As we have outlined in the beginning of this chapter, not directly using what comes to mind may require additional processing. Given the variability of individuals' amount of processing, individuals' processing motivation and their processing capacity may play a crucial role in the use of information. Processing motivation can be influenced by a variety of aspects, such as the perceived importance of the judgment, accountability to others, individuals' motivation not to be influenced by stereotypes, or by individuals' disposition to think carefully ("need for cognition," see Cacioppo & Petty, 1982). We will address these aspects in turn.

Content versus experience—a question of processing motivation

Above we have discussed that in many cases, individuals seem to rely on the ease with which information comes to mind rather than on the content per se. However, the preference for feelings is not a universal law of human judgment. In fact, conditions exist under which people prefer to use the activated information. This was demonstrated in a series of studies by Rothman and Schwarz (1998), who found that content was more likely to serve as the basis of judgment when people were motivated to be accurate. Specifically, these authors asked participants to recall either three (easy condition) or eight (difficult condition) instances of their own behaviour that would, depending on the condition, increase or decrease their risk of heart disease. When they were subsequently asked to indicate their susceptibility to this condition, respondents who had been asked to recall risk-increasing behaviours reported themselves to be more susceptible if the task was easy (three instances) than if it was difficult (eight instances). The opposite was true if they had to recall risk-reducing behaviours. However, these results, which replicated the earlier findings on self-assertiveness (Schwarz et al., 1991a), were obtained only if the participants did *not* have a family history of heart disease. In fact, respondents who had such a history were more influenced if they had to retrieve eight rather than three instances. This result does not replicate the previous findings. Instead, it suggests that people's choice of using the activated information instead of the elicited feeling reflects a desire for greater accuracy, which in turn is due to a greater involvement in the issue. In general, these results suggest that the need for accuracy determines whether people follow their feelings or engage in a more elaborate processing of relevant information (see also Wänke & Bless, 2000, for a discussion of the possibility that increased processing motivation may increase the influence of ease of retrieval).

Accountability and reasons

It is often the case that a judgment needs to be justified. Imagine you are an employee and have purchased a car for your company. Of course, your boss wants to know why you bought this particular car rather than a different one. Most likely, you would not justify your decision by invoking a particular feeling that you had when you purchased the car. Instead, you would come up with arguments that support your choice. More generally, whenever we have to justify an action to a third person, we typically offer reasons and not subjective experiences. If this is the case, people who expect that they will have to justify their decisions before they generate a judgment will be more likely to use content instead of feelings as their basis. Labelled "accountability," this insight has been translated into an experimental manipulation that has been used by Phil Tetlock (1992) to induce participants to attempt to increase their judgmental accuracy. Interestingly, increasing accountability does not necessarily increase accuracy. Sometimes, thinking more about potential reasons may in fact decrease accuracy (Tetlock, Skitka, & Boettger, 1989). A nice example for coming up with reasons for a judgment (rather than basing the judgment on a feeling) is provided by Wilson and colleagues (Wilson et al., 1993). Their participants were asked to select one free poster from a set of six different posters. Half of the participants were asked to think of reasons for their selection, whereas the remaining half was not asked to provide reasons. When participants were asked how satisfied they were with their choice 6 weeks later, it turned out that participants who had based the selection on their feelings were more satisfied (e.g., still had the poster on their wall) than participants who had thought about reasons for their selections (see also Wilson, Dunn, & Kraft, 1989). This suggests that a "rational choice" (as opposed to an "intuitive choice") may neglect the affective component that also contributes to people's satisfaction.

Individuals' motivation to avoid the impact of stereotypes

In the domain of social judgments, accuracy is particularly important when it comes to stereotypes. That is, a person who wants to be accurate in assessing the characteristics of another person may try to avoid being influenced by preconceptions that apply to the group to which the target belongs. Certainly, knowledge about the target person's group may serve as a heuristic and help simplify the judgment (see Bodenhausen & Lichtenstein, 1987) if the goal is speed or the reduction of mental effort. However, if accuracy is of primary importance, individuals should avoid generalization and give preference to individuating information. In Chapter 3 we discussed individuals possibly being motivated to counteract the influence of an activated stereotype. In Chapter 4, we saw that when individuals have a high processing motivation, their judgments are less likely to reflect the implications of the stereotype but rather the individuating information (cf. Fiske & Neuberg, 1990). Additional evidence for this assumption is provided by a series of studies (Strack & Mussweiler, 2001) in which participants had to rate an applicant for a job on a variety of dimensions. It turned out that if they were not instructed otherwise, judges used the applicant's gender as a basis for inferences and assigned more technical skills to the male applicant and more empathic abilities to the female applicant. However, if additional information about the applicant was available and if participants were instructed not to be influenced by the target's gender, judgments were more likely to be based on this individuating information.

Individuals' need for cognition

Not surprisingly, individuals may differ with respect to how much they engage in elaborative cognitive processes. Some individuals have a need to think extensively before making a judgment (high in need for cognition) whereas other individuals may attempt to avoid extensive, effortful processing (low in need for cognition; see Cacioppo & Petty, 1982). Relating the need for cognition construct to the present discussion, it seems a straightforward assumption that individuals low in need for cognition should be more likely to base their judgments on what comes to mind, whereas individuals high in need for cognition engage in additional processing. Evidence in this respect is reported by Martin and colleagues (Martin et al., 1990), who found assimilation towards activated context information when participants were low in need for cognition but contrast effects when participants were high in need for cognition.

The role of knowledge

Depending on how individuals attempt to correct for an unwanted influence, they may require information about its direction and strength. Where does this information come from? Introspectively,

BOX 5.4.

How strong is your need for cognition?

"Yes" responses indicate a high need:

- I would prefer complex to simple problems.
- I prefer my life filled with puzzles that I must solve.
- I really enjoy a task that involves coming up with new solutions to problems.
- I would prefer a task that is intellectual, difficult, and important to one that is somewhat important but does not require much thought.
- I find it especially satisfying to complete an important task that required a lot of thinking and mental effort.

"Yes" responses indicate a low need:

- Thinking is not my idea of fun.
- I don't like to have the responsibility of handling a situation that requires a lot of thinking.
- I only think as hard as I have to.
- I find little satisfaction in deliberating hard and for long hours.
- I try to anticipate and avoid situations where there is a likely chance I will have to think in depth about something.

Items from the Need for Cognition scale (Cacioppo & Petty, 1982).

people have little awareness of the impact of specific determinants of their psychological processes (Nisbett & Wilson, 1977). They must therefore use their knowledge or beliefs about the influence a particular variable may have on them. In other words, people may use their intuitive psychological knowledge to regulate the generation of their judgments. Of course, the more accurate this type of self-knowledge, the more accurate the resulting judgment. The operation of these mechanisms has been investigated in the domain of memory, where Bartlett (1932) has demonstrated the importance of inferences. However, unlike Bartlett's studies, the basis is not knowledge about the world but knowledge about the judges' own psychological functioning.

In a first set of studies (Strack & Bless, 1994), we created a situation in which people would use their metamnestic knowledge (knowledge about how their memory works) to infer whether a particular stimulus had been presented. In particular, we assumed that recollective inferences are more likely if people have no—or no clear—memory trace of what has happened. This is the case if there was no experience in the first place. Take the following example. You are asked whether your professor wore a white blouse during last week's lecture while, in fact, she wore a yellow blouse. Of course, you have no recollection of a white blouse. At the same time, however, you are not sure if you *would have* remembered such a nondescript piece of clothing. In contrast, imagine that you are asked whether your professor wore a blouse with red and blue stripes. In this case the absence of such a recollection is more diagnostic because you know that you would have remembered such a distinct piece of clothing. This inference is based on your knowledge that something that stands out is more likely to leave a memory trace. And if no such trace can be found, its absence tells you that the stimulus (here, the colourful blouse) was not there to begin with.

This logic was translated into an experimental setting where participants were shown slides of 30 tools and of five objects that were not tools. It was assumed that the absence of a clear memory trace would raise the question whether the object would have been remembered had it been presented. If participants are asked whether they saw a particular tool that was not presented (a so-called "distractor" item), they would be less likely to say "no" because they were not really sure if they would have remembered the object had it been presented. By contrast, if a nontool is used as a distractor, the absence of a recollection would allow participants to conclude that it was not presented. The reason: Nontools were in the minority and therefore stood out against the majority of tools. Because we know that salient objects are more likely to be remembered, the absence of a recollection is diagnostic for the possibility that the object was, in fact, not presented.

This knowledge about our own memory not only helps us reconstruct a past event; it may also serve as a safety guard against unwanted social influences. From work by Elizabeth Loftus (1975) we know that the use of the definite article elicits an affirmative response. In one study participants were shown a video that contained, among other things, a yield sign. Half of the participants were then asked if they had seen a stop sign. The other half was asked if they had seen *the* stop sign. This leading question proved highly successful because a greatly increased proportion of the participants provided affirmative responses. To test whether this suggestive influence could be counteracted by people's knowledge about their own memory, we varied the wording of the question such that half of the participants were asked if they had "seen *the* [name of the object]" while the others were asked if they had "seen *a* [name of the object]."

In fact, the results of the study confirm the expectation that the salient nontools were more frequently rejected as targets than the nonsalient tools. They also replicated the finding by Loftus and her colleagues that questions using the definite article lead to more affirmative answers. However, this was only the case if the (non-salient) tools were used as distractors. By contrast, salient nontools were consistently rejected as distractors, regardless of whether the question employed the definite or the indefinite article. These findings suggest that knowledge about ourselves not only helps us to use our experience for further inferences (in this case the absence of a recollective experience to decide whether or not an object has been presented); it also serves as an antidote to outside influences and suggestions. Conversely, social influence has its greatest effects if people cannot rely on knowledge about themselves (for a more detailed discussion of this point, see Bless & Strack, 1998).

While these experiments merely suggest that people use knowledge about psychological functioning to infer what they would have remembered, subsequent studies (for a review, see Strack & Förster, 1998) addressed this issue in a more direct fashion. In one experiment, participants had to encode words on different levels of encoding depth. Specifically, half of the participants had to count syllables, which is likely to induce a phonological representation, while the others had to find spelling errors, which induces a deeper, semantic representation. As memory research suggests (e.g., Craik & Lockhart, 1972), words that are semantically encoded have an advantage when it comes to recall. In fact, this was the case if people had to recognize a word that had been previously learned. However, if they had to reject a word that had not been presented previously, the response depended on what participants believed. That is, if they believed that memory is improved more by finding spelling errors, they were more likely to reject distractors belonging to this category. Conversely, if they believed that counting syllables is the better procedure, they were more likely to reject distractors from the category for which they had done the counting. This result is in line with the previous finding in that participants used their knowledge about what they would have remembered to decide whether the absence of a recollection is due to the fact that a stimulus was not there in the first place.

Because this evidence is only correlational and does not allow definite conclusions about the causal impact of people's beliefs, we conducted yet another study in which we created conditions that suggested to participants that their memory would be affected in opposing ways. Specifically, we had them memorize words while listening to music. More important, the results led people to believe that the music had either improved or worsened their memory performance. As expected, the induced beliefs had an impact on the solution of the subsequent recognition task: Words from the category where memory would be improved through music were more likely to be rejected as distractors.

In summary, these results show how idiosyncratic knowledge about oneself may help to interpret the quality of a subjective experience to be used as a diagnostic indicator of what has happened in the world. In this respect it is important to see that it is the knowledge about one's own functioning rather than a general mechanism that applies to other people. This suggests that philosophy's recommendation to "know thyself" is valid not only as an exercise of egocentric self-actualization, but as a viable means of exploring the world. Of course, the more accurate the knowledge about ourselves, the more valid the inference we draw about what is happening in the world.

In the domain of attitudes, Petty and Wegener (e.g., 1993) have demonstrated how people use their beliefs about the influence of preceding judgments to correct subsequent assessments. These authors were able to show that corrections occurred in a "flexible" manner and depended on how judges believed they had been influenced. In one experiment (Petty & Wegener, 1993), participants were asked to estimate the number of sunny days in Hawaii prior to being asked to assess work satisfaction in Hawaii or the pleasantness of the weather in the American Midwest. The crucial manipulation consisted of directing judges' attention toward a possible contaminator and requesting them to prevent the subsequent judgment from being affected by the previous judgment task. The results showed that participants who were asked to "decontaminate" their judgment did so in opposing ways, depending on the nature of the second judgment. That is, if the task was to appraise work satisfaction in Hawaii, the correction led to a contrast effect: the higher the estimated number of sunny days, the lower the rating of work satisfaction. By contrast, if the focus was on the pleasantness of Midwest weather, correction occurred in the form of assimilation effect: the higher the estimates for the sunny days in Hawaii, the higher the pleasantness ratings for Midwest weather.

As the authors were able to show, the different ways of adjusting judgments depended on participants' beliefs about the direction of the particular distortions. With respect to judgments of Hawaii work satisfaction, judges believed that the contaminating influence of estimating the number of sunny days was assimilative, meaning that work satisfaction would be overestimated. To compensate for this influence, judgments were adjusted in a downward direction. With respect to judgments of the pleasantness of Midwest weather, participants believed that the prior estimate would produce a contrast effect, meaning that the pleasantness of the weather would be underestimated. Correction therefore entailed an assimilation toward the value of the preceding judgment.

These findings further support the notion that people may correct for a contaminating influence by adjusting the judgment. However, to engage in this procedure, one must not only be aware of the distorting influence but also know (or believe one knows) how this influence operates. In combination with the reported findings on memory judgments, these results underscore the importance of knowledge about one's own psychological processes as a basis of social and nonsocial judgments. While the domains of the judgment may differ, the basic principles remain the same.

Chapter summary

(1) To understand people's judgments in a social context, it is not sufficient to explain what is on their mind. Rather, it is necessary to determine whether information is used and how it is used, given that it is activated.

(2) Under suboptimal circumstances (i.e., little time or motivation) people are most likely to use accessible information as a basis of a judgment. This will result in an assimilation effect. Contrast effects are the result of excluding information or using it as a

standard of comparison, and often requires additional mental effort or capacity.

(3) The use of subjective experience versus informational content depends on the representativeness of the experience and the goal of the judgment. In particular, if an experience appears to be elicited not by the target of the judgment but by some extraneous source, it is less likely to be used. Also, if people's primary goal is to be accurate, they are more likely to use information about the target than subjective feelings.

(4) Natural and standardized conversations are governed by rules of cooperation. The Gricean maxims have been successfully applied to predict the use of information in contexts of communication.

(5) People's knowledge of their own psychological functioning has been shown to be an important mediator in the use of subjective experience. In particular, it has been demonstrated that to decide that an event did not happen, the absence of a recollective experience is not sufficient. Rather, people must believe that they would have had such an experience if the event had occurred. We found subjective theories about one's idiosyncratic memory processes to play a central role.

Discussion questions

(1) Judgments depend on what is on the judge's mind. However, what is on the mind will not always become the basis of a judgment. What determines the use of accessible information?

(2) *How* is information used in different ways and what are the determinants?

(3) Why is it necessary to include the rules of communication to understand people's judgments in a social context?

(4) What are the psychological implications of the claim that in social contexts, contributions to a conversation come with a "guarantee of relevance"?

(5) What determines whether people base their judgments on their feelings (subjective experiences) or on the content of the information that is on their mind?

(6) How does knowledge about one's own psychological functioning moderate experience-based judgments, e.g., about past occurrences?

Recommendations for further reading

Schwarz, N. (1996). *Cognition and communication: Judgmental biases, research methods, and the logic of conversation.* Mahwah, NJ: Lawrence Erlbaum Associates Inc.

Strack, F. (1994). Response processes in social judgment. In R. S. Wyer & T. K. Srull (Eds.), *Handbook of social cognition* (pp. 287–322). Hillsdale, NJ: Lawrence Erlbaum Associates Inc.

Testing hypotheses in social interaction: How cognitive processes are constrained by environmental data

6

Referring back to Chapter 1, in which we have emphasized that the construction of social reality comprises the input from the environment, prior knowledge, and the cognitive processes operating on them, we may recognize that all preceding chapters have been mainly concerned with cognitive processes and with the knowledge structures that support them. Although it was implicitly presupposed that input data are required to trigger these cognitive processes, the stimulus data themselves have not been under focus. This is the purpose of the present chapter. We now turn to intriguing research findings that demonstrate how external data constrain the internal processes. Or, to use another phrase, we shall consider the intriguing interplay of environmental and cognitive factors that characterizes human interaction in particular situations and institutions.

Social hypothesis testing: Updating knowledge in the light of environmental data

Throughout the preceding five chapters, we got to know diverse experimental tasks that have been constructed to study social-cognitive phenomena. For instance, recall or recognition tasks were used to study person memory, courtroom sentencing scenarios to study guilt attribution, priming procedures to study social stereo-types, and probability judgment tasks to investigate cognitive biases and fallacies. However, in reality these various tasks are not presen-ted in isolation by an experimenter but they appear in combina-tion, intertwined and embedded in all kinds of active social interaction—as people try to get acquainted with each other, as they try to achieve social influence, to buy or sell products, to evaluate performance or moral conduct, as they compare themselves and their own group to others and other groups, in dating, fighting, and deception episodes.

A feature that all these interaction episodes have in common is the goal to test a social hypothesis. Social hypothesis testing is the unifying paradigm of the present chapter. As people are interacting with each other, they are permanently involved in hypothesis tests related to all kinds of problems: How much interest does the other person show in my personality, in my private thoughts, in my feelings? How much can I attract the other? How much are the goods that I want to sell worth? How far can I go in pursuing my interests without appearing unfair? How do I compare to others in terms of morality and ability? How does my in-group compare to out-groups? Does my conversation partner tell the truth or try to deceive me? Is that person my friend or enemy?

Social life is replete with such hypothesis tests. It is fair to say that a great proportion of all social interaction can be subsumed under the hypothesis-test paradigm. This central role assigned to hypothesis testing is nothing but a logical consequence of the generalized assumption, emphasized throughout this book, that social cognition is an active, knowledge-guided process, rather than a merely passive reaction pattern to new stimuli. To the extent that people approach the world with prior knowledge and meaningful social concepts in mind, the resulting information inevitably takes the form of an active hypothesis-testing process. The most prominent phenomena in social cognition—such as person memory, attribution, stereotypes, probability judgments, cognitive fallacies—are embedded in this active interplay, or competition, between an individual's guiding hypotheses and new stimulus data that often deviate from prior expectancies.

The built-in tendency towards confirmation

Hypothesis-testing episodes have their own internal structure and rules. One of the most intriguing features is that the hypotheses that people use to explore their social ecology seem to have a built-in device for confirmation. All other things being equal, hypothesis tests are more likely to end up with an affirmative than a negative answer. If we want to find out whether somebody else is mad, it is not unlikely that we will find some supportive evidence. If we try to find out whether somebody is ingenious, we will presumably find some pertinent evidence as well. Tests for dishonesty will be likely to reveal dishonest people; tests for fairness and altruism will identify fair and helpful people. It is this affirmative, YES-responding echo of social interaction (Snyder, 1984) that makes experimental approaches to hypothesis testing so interesting, for testing appropriate hypotheses, and avoiding others, can be used to confirm social stereotypes (Slusher & Anderson, 1987), support attributions (Trope, 1986), attain social influence (Wegner, Wenzlaff, Kerker, & Beattie, 1981), justify performance evaluation (Rosenthal, 1991), and carry through political and economical strategies (Ray, 1983). The persistent tendency towards verification will be the central topic of this chapter.

Beliefs, desires, and external origins

A substantial part of social interaction is driven by two prominent classes of hypotheses that have intrigued philosophers and psychologists alike (Greve, 2001), namely, *beliefs* and *desires*. People are either concerned with hypotheses about the truth of some belief, or about the means of fulfilling some desire. Some problem situations involve a mixture of both goals; people must find a compromise between an accuracy goal (find the truth about beliefs) and a motivational goal (realize some desire). In other words, cognitive as well as motivational influences suggest themselves to explain the pervasive tendency towards verification (Kunda, 1990; Pyszczynski & Greenberg, 1987; Snyder, 1984). Obviously, many hypotheses tend to be verified because they reflect the individual's prior beliefs or personal motives.

However, supplementing this insight, another intriguing lesson of the research reviewed below is that in addition to these internal (cognitive and motivational) origins, external environmental factors may also contribute a lot. Indeed, even when prior beliefs and desires are eliminated, the very structure of social interaction, and the very distribution of stimulus data in the environment, can lead to hypothesis confirmation.

The next sections are devoted to three research paradigms, which highlight that the data input itself can explain the bias towards one hypothesis and the neglect of others. First, hypothesis testers may *select* particular data and ignore others, due to selective attention or selective availability of information in memory. For instance, a journalist with an inclination to favour a particular political party may selectively expose herself to information about the preferred party. Second, hypothesis testers may actually *produce*, in the target person, the data that are needed to support a hypothesis. The journalist, for instance, may apply an interview strategy that leads or misleads a politician to provide evidence for some hypothesis. The third possibility is that the external *environment affords* more access to some stimulus data than to others. For instance, as undesirable information about political activities is more likely to be concealed than desirable information, a positivity bias in publication will mainly benefit the party to which the journalist pays most attention. Let us now consider empirical findings related to all three types of stimulus data.

Self-selected data: The information search paradigm

One classical investigation of information search leading to confirmation bias was conducted by Snyder and Swann (1978), using a simulated interview task that was later adopted in numerous subsequent studies. Participants were instructed to find out, in a kind of get-acquainted interview, whether their interview target was extraverted or, in another condition, whether the target person was introverted. For this purpose, participants could select suitable interview questions from an extended list. These questions could then be administered to the target persons who could provide their responses, and the outcome of this planned conversation could finally be presented to nonparticipant observers.

The behavioural evidence elicited in the target and the resulting personality impressions of the target were systematically biased toward the starting hypothesis. Across a series of four experiments, more evidence for an extraverted person was created when the interviewer tested the extraversion hypothesis. In contrast, when the interviewer focused on the introversion hypothesis, the resulting evidence pointed to an introverted person (Figure 6.1). This was evident in analyses of the interviewees' responses and in passive observers' impressions, as well as in the interviewers' own inferences. Thus, as mentioned before, there was a general tendency to find confirmation for whatever hypothesis the participants happened to test.

Note that personal desires and prior beliefs could not be responsible for these findings, because the direction of hypothesis was manipulated and participants were allocated at random to the

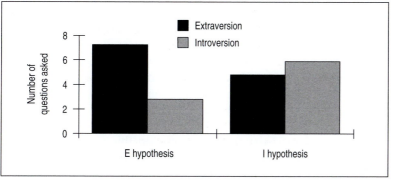

Figure 6.1.

Mean number of
extraversion and
introversion questions
asked when testing an
E hypothesis (interview
partner is an extravert)
versus an I hypothesis
(interview partner is an
introvert), as reported
by Snyder & Swann
(1978, Investigations 1
& 2).

two experimental groups instructed to focus on extraversion or introversion, respectively. Note also that interview partners could not see or hear each other directly so interviewers could not subtly communicate the hypothesis through nonverbal or paraverbal communication, as in Rosenthal's (1966) famous work on experimenter effects. Moreover, the results did not reflect selective memory for hypothesis-confirming interview responses or distorted judgment processes that were only sensitive to observations congruent with the starting hypothesis. Rather, the resulting impressions were completely determined by the strategies of information search, which solicited more evidence for extraverted behaviour in the extraversion condition and more evidence for introverted behaviour in the introversion condition.

How could this happen, given that prior beliefs and desires were controlled? Analyses of the very questions selected as suitable for the interview revealed that the confirmation process originated in the initial stage of information search. Interviewers of the extraversion group had typically selected questions that created rich opportunities for targets to exhibit extraverted behaviours. Examples of such questions are "What would you do if you wanted to liven things up at a party?", or "What kind of situation do you seek out if you want to meet new people?" In contrast, interviewers of the introversion group found it more appropriate to ask questions such as "In what situations do you wish you could be more outgoing?", or "What things do you dislike about loud parties?" Such questions would typically solicit more introverted and less extraverted responses in the interview target.

For several reasons, an explanation in terms of the hypothesis-tester's biased search alone cannot be upheld, given the current state of the art. Rather than blaming the information search process per se, we must look for additional factors in the hypothesis verification process. First, it should be underscored that interviewers had no vested interest or need to convey any personal expectancies. Nevertheless, participants may have been influenced by what they *believed* to be the experimenter's attitudes. Thus, in spite of the randomised allocation to hypothesis conditions, participants may have internalised the task hypothesis they were assigned to, assuming that "If I am to look for extraversion, extraversion must be a reasonable guess. The experimenter must know why the task is chosen this way." So does the verification effect reflect the influence of directly or subtly conveyed expectancies?

Prior expectancy or arbitrary hypothesis focus?

Semin and Strack (1980) were quick to demonstrate that no expectancies need to underlie the hypotheses that tend to be verified. Strack and Semin manipulated expectancies and hypothesis focus in an orthogonal design. In two experimental conditions, information about the interview target's profession was used to create the expectancy that the target is probably an extravert (salesman) or an introvert (librarian). Within both expectancy groups, different subgroups of participants were instructed to find out whether their interview partner was an extravert or an introvert. The latter manipulation clearly governed the process of information search, whereas the expectancy manipulation had little influence. Regardless of whether the target was a salesman or a librarian, interviewers instructed to test the extraversion hypothesis asked more questions about extraverted topics (parties, jokes, friends), whereas interviewers in the introversion-test condition asked relatively more questions about introverted topics (privacy, meditation, contemplation). Thus, even when interviewers were not biased towards prior expectancies or beliefs but simply cooperated with the experimental task instructions, they asked different questions that solicited different interview responses.

The role of suggestive influence

Another aspect of Snyder and Swann's (1978) original paradigm that might have suggested some kind of manipulation in the interviewer's information search is that the questions offered by the experimental materials contained rather blatant *presuppositions*. For instance, rather than asking, in open format, *whether* the target is occasionally the one who livens up the party, the question presupposed that the target always does and merely asked *how* they fill this role. Using this kind of presupposition as opposed to open, unbiased questions is a common linguistic device used for leading questions and suggestive manipulation, as evident from research on eyewitness testimony (Loftus, 1979).

However, the phenomenon of hypothesis confirmation is by no means confined to such a tricky conversation strategy. When similar experiments were conducted using open questions rather than presuppositions (e.g., Semin & Strack, 1980; Zuckerman, Knee, Hodgins, & Miyake, 1995), the outcome remained largely the same. Depending on the hypothesis focus, participants would search more information about typically extravert situations when testing the extraversion hypothesis, but more information about typically introvert behaviours when testing the introversion hypothesis. Together, these findings corroborate what can also be concluded on logical grounds alone: The site of a confirmation bias cannot lie in the questions. Questions alone can provide neither confirmation nor disconfirmation; which outcome occurs obviously depends on the target person's answers.

Positive testing

Accordingly, Klayman and Ha (1987) suggested a more adequate term to characterize information search by the notion of *positive testing* (see Box 6.1), denoting the prevailing tendency to look out for positive examples of the hypothesis being tested (e.g., for examples of

---

BOX 6.1.
Positive testing

Positive testing is a highly common, widely applied strategy of information search, in everyday problem solving as in scientific discovery (Mynatt, Doherty, & Tweney, 1977). When we want to figure out whether there are some problems with the used car we are about to purchase, we ask questions and make tests that focus on these potential problems (e.g., prior damage, new tyres, rust), rather than losing much time with questions about the car's assets (such as nice colour, powerful engine, much space) that are already obvious and not of current interest. The example illustrates what several scholars have proven formally, namely, that positive testing is not irrational at all, but reflects an economical and rather diagnostic strategy of information search that promises high information gains under many conditions (see Klayman & Ha, 1987; Oaksford & Chater, 1994; Trope & Bassok, 1983). People who want to purchase a used car do not want to waste much time and effort with questions about alternative hypotheses; they are mainly interested in the potential deficits of this particular car, and not in other aspects of the same car, or assets and deficits of other cars. Therefore, the information value to be expected from positive testing is particularly high.

extraverted behaviour when testing the extraversion hypothesis). Questions about extraverted situations (like parties) promise to provide maximally diagnostic information about extraversion. Positive information for the target showing extraverted behaviour provides more cogent evidence than negative information that the target does not show introverted behaviour. In other words, the negation of introversion does not strictly imply high extraversion, because the social world is not strictly dichotomous. Somebody may be neither introverted nor extraverted, nor high in both extraversion and introversion. Therefore, because the dimensional constraints on antonyms (e.g., extraversion vs. introversion) are very weak, performing direct positive tests is a rational and effective strategy most of the time—although the price for this strategy is that positive testing can foster a serious confirmation effect, as we have seen.

Motivated information search

Thus far, we have seen that hypothesis testers cannot—or cannot always—be blamed for one-sided strategies of information search. Even when no prior expectancies (beliefs) and vested interests (desires) are involved, and even when the information being searched is high in information value, biases towards the hypothesis being tested can remain. This is not to claim, conversely, that wishful thinking, lop-sided expectancies, or personal motives may never cause or reinforce the confirmation effect. There is no doubt that there is very strong evidence for the contention that under conditions of high pay-offs, ego-involvement, or strong expectancies, information search may be strongly biased towards the kind of evidence that people believe in or desire. Such examples of motivated biases are evident, for instance, when a patient refuses to learn information about his terminal disease, when we are more willing to recognize our own success and others' failure, when parents wish to conserve the belief that their son or daughter is high in academic achievement, or not involved in drug abuse, or when researchers selectively expose themselves to evidence that confirms their own theory and disconfirms alternative theories.

However, at least some of the time some of the people are not determined by such ego-threatening, motivational goals and they are able to strive for accurate hypothesis tests in an attempt to find out the truth. Assuming that strong motivational goals have been ruled out and that search strategies are rational or even optimal, the intriguing question remains as to what process may cause the illusion in favour of the focal hypothesis. Thus far, we have considered the possibility that the hypothesis tester might elicit the whole process. Other evidence suggests, at first glance, a causal role played by the target person. Let us briefly review the pertinent evidence for the role of the target in the confirmation process, before we cease to blame individual roles and try to understand that fully "innocent" communication rules can bring about the whole phenomenon, in the absence of any cognitive or motivational bias in individual interaction partners.

Self-produced data: The self-fulfilling prophecy paradigm

The entire phenomenon that was introduced in the last section—from the lop-sided selection of interview questions soliciting differential target responses to the resulting confirming impressions, even in nonparticipating observers—is reminiscent of the famous notion of a self-fulfilling prophecy (Jussim, 1991; Madon, Jussim & Eccles, 1997; Rosenthal & Jacobson, 1968). Interviewers in the present experimental situation seem to behave like teachers who expect lower-class children to be less talented than middle-class children and who therefore treat students from different social classes differently, until lower-class children actually show lower performance than middle-class children, producing the data required for hypothesis confirmation. Thus, the target persons eventually confirm and justify the hypothesis that guided the entire process. In this scenario, the hypothesis tester (teacher) is the causal origin of the self-fulfilling prophecy; the outcome originates in his or her one-sided tendency to treat targets in accordance with their hypothesis and thus to artificially produce the confirming evidence needed to confirm the hypothesis. It is within such a scenario of a self-fulfilling prophecy that many experiments like those of Snyder and Swann (1978) have been explained in terms of a biased search for hypothesis-confirming evidence.

Acquiescence tendency

By what rule is the target "obliged" to follow the hypothesis tester's question contents? Using the same simulated interview situation as in Snyder's early work, Zuckerman et al. (1995) demonstrated how the interviewer's strategy of asking positive questions is complemented by the interviewee's tendency to give positive answers. In one condition, the hypothesis to be tested focused on the positive poles of four trait dimensions: Trusting – suspicious, calm – worried, extraverted – introverted, optimistic – pessimistic. In a second condition,

Figure 6.2.

Positive testing and
acquiescence
response tendency as
mediating factors in the
illusory confirmation of
social hypotheses;
after Zuckerman et al.
(1995).

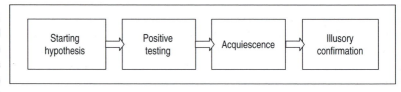

the task focus was on the negative poles. In a third condition, both hypotheses were presented and participants had to find out which one of the two hypotheses was correct. As in previous work, most participants who tested one-sided hypotheses applied a positive-test strategy, asking more questions about the hypothesis under focus than about the opposite hypothesis. Thus, when testing positive attributes, they tended to ask more questions about positive attributes and fewer questions about negative attributes than when focusing on the negative poles. However, at the same time, a so-called *acquiescence* tendency was demonstrated in the interviewees. Regardless of which type of question they were asked, they tended to provide confirming answers. Such a YES-responding bias is long known to students of survey research and interview methodology (Ray, 1983). Together, these two tendencies, interviewers' positive-test focus and interviewees' acquiescence bias to provide positive responses, seem to describe the social interaction rule that results in confirmation for the hypothesis under focus (cf. Figure 6.2.).

Cooperative communication

What might such a positive communication game be good for? Even though real social interaction may serve several motives, at least part of the acquiescence bias can be attributed to Grice's (1975) principle of cooperative communication (see Chapter 5). For communication to remain interesting and socially rewarding, communication partners must be aware of, and adhere to, several maxims. The maxim of quantity obliges communicators to provide enough information to be understood, but not more information than is needed by the conversation partner. Thus, the contents of verbal messages must be neither too impoverished nor too long-winded and circumstantial. The maxim of quality entitles communication partners to provide information on which one can rely and that is consistent with the empirical facts of the extra-verbal communication context. The maxim of relevance says that communication partners should use words and phrases that are relevant to the communication goal and to the preceding utterances in the conversation.

According to these rules, it makes sense that interviewers whose task is to test the extraversion hypothesis do not lose themselves in too many other questions (maxim of quantity) or even irrelevant questions (maxim of relevance), but tap directly into the focus of interest where they can expect maximally informative responses (trusting in the maxim of quality). Interviewees, in turn, can show cooperation in that they take on the same reference words as introduced by the interviewer (maxim of relevance), treating the topics, behaviours, and situations suggested by the interviewer as valid (maxim of quality) and mostly confining themselves to the topics introduced by the interviewer (maxim of quantity).

It seems plausible that the best way to fulfil these multiple rules is by accepting the interviewers' invitation to talk about those topics that seem to be considered common ground. There seems to be common ground that (almost) everybody is extraverted some of the time. So if my conversation partner invites me to talk about parties, friends, and jokes, I am not entitled to question the premise that everybody has something to say about such topics—and I cooperate, or acquiesce. Similarly, if my conversation partner invites me to talk about reading a book when alone at the beach or listening to good music in a dark room, I will cooperate as well. Rejecting these invitations—or starting awkward meta-communication about the justification of such premises—would mean questioning Grice's (1975) communication contract and would be experienced as a communication anomaly. As Snyder (1984) has emphasized repeatedly, social interaction is essentially cooperative, and by this virtue confirmative. Part of the overwhelming tendency to confirm and maintain hypotheses can thus be understood as a by-product of genuinely cooperative behaviour, driven by prosocial motives, rather than tricky strategies or manipulative intentions.

One intriguing implication from this cooperative communication approach says that, to a considerable extent, the answer of a communication cycle is already in the question (Semin & De Poot, 1997; Semin, Rubini, & Fiedler, 1995). That is, the questions asked by one person can shape or even predetermine the answers given by another person, and this can of course be exploited by skilful interviewers or journalists. As already mentioned in Chapter 3, by using a different verb in an otherwise constant question, somebody might ask "Why do you *read* the New York Times?" or "Why do you *like* the New York Times?". The first question uses an *action verb* that implies internal attribution; the subject person who decides to read is herself perceived as the cause of such intentional, deliberate behaviour (cf.

Brown & Fish, 1983). In contrast, the second question uses a *state verb* that implies external causation; to like the Times means to express that something about the stimulus, the Times, is responsible for the behaviour. In accordance with this reasoning, the two different questions elicit different causal inferences about the Times and the respondent's personality. Of course, less mundane, more existential episodes are also possible. Asking somebody mad questions over an extensive period of time may solicit actually mad behaviour.

Grice's communication contract is so strong and common that observers need not even wait for the responses to draw inferences from questions. This was demonstrated in an intriguing study conducted by Swann, Giuliano, and Wegner (1982). In the familiar extraversion–introversion paradigm, some participants were again asked to select questions appropriate to test one or the other hypothesis. Participants in different experimental conditions were presented with (a) the set of questions selected along with the target person's responses, (b) only the target's responses, or (c) only the questions, without the responses. Interestingly, apart from some minor differences, the same basic confirmation effect was apparent in all conditions. Regardless of whether judges saw the questions plus the answers providing affirmative evidence, or only the affirmative answers, or only the questions, they judged targets to be more extraverted in the extraversion condition but more introverted in the introversion-hypothesis condition (Figure 6.3).

Apparently, then, hypothesis verification can be understood in part as a by-product of cooperative communication. As the aforementioned research by Zuckerman et al. (1995) has shown, interviewers and interviewees behave like cooperative players of the game "Let's talk about extraversion." Interviewers cooperate by raising many extraverted topics, and interviewees cooperate by providing many positive examples related to extraverted behaviour. The outcome is rich evidence for extraversion, which seemingly justifies the impression that the target (interviewee) is actually an extravert.

Once more, it is interesting to note that such a process is not inherently biased or irrational. Just as we noted before, that the interviewer's positive testing may be reasonable and diagnostic, the interviewee's yes-responding tendency may not be meant to selectively favour one hypothesis. Rather, the principle of cooperative communication predicts a global, nonselective tendency to answer YES, regardless of whether the question refers to extraversion, introversion, or some other topic. Again, we see that a fully "innocent,"

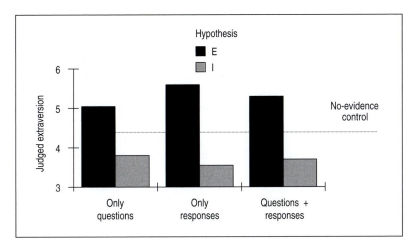

Figure 6.3.
Influence of hypothesis being tested (E = extraversion, I = introversion) on judged extraversion under three different conditions: when only interview questions, only responses, or questions + responses are given; after Swann et al. (1982).

unbiased, undirectional process, driven by the well-motivated principle of cooperation, can lead to illusory hypothesis verification.

Distribution of environmental data: Hypothesis testing and learning

However, something is still missing in the emerging theoretical account. Upon closer inspection, positive testing and acquiescence alone cannot fully explain why the hypothesis should be *confirmed*. Asking many extraversion questions that elicit many YES responses may afford *rich* support for the focal hypothesis, but no *distinctive* support. This is evident from Figure 6.4.

Number of observations or learning trials

Assuming twice as many extraversion as introversion questions and twice as many yes as no responses, the cooperative process may result in 8 yes responses to 12 extraversion questions and 4 yes responses to 6 introversion questions. Thus, the relative proportion of confirmation for extraversion and introversion is the same: $8/12 = 4/6 = 67\%$; only the absolute amount of support is higher in the former case. This means that in order to explain that interviewers and observers arrive at more extravert impressions of the target, one has to assume that a ratio of $8/12$ observations is worth more, psychologically, than a ratio of $4/6$. Although this may appear strange at first glance, it is easily understood upon some reflection. Just like any learning process, learning that a hypothesis tends to be confirmed increases with the number of learning trials. Even though the ratio of

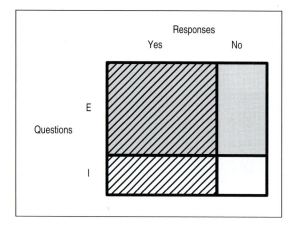

Responses
Yes   No

E

Questions

I

Figure 6.4.

Graphical illustration of the fact that although a high prevalence of extraversion questions (grey area) comes along with a high proportion of YES responses (dashed area), the relative proportion of YES responses is the same for both extraversion (E) and introversion (I) questions.

confirmation is the same, there are 12 trials to learn the 67% confirmation rate for extraversion but only 6 trials to learn the same rate for introversion—thus affording more complete learning for the focal hypothesis.

Such a simple learning approach helps us to understand why cooperative communication can result in illusory hypothesis verification. However, the learning approach is more general, because different numbers of observations or learning trials for different hypotheses can be due to other reasons besides cooperative communication. An investigation by Fiedler, Walther, and Nickel (1999) substantiates this point. In a diagnostic task context, participants were to find out whether the problems of a heterosexual couple, Peter and Heike, are due to different aggression styles in male and female people. Concretely, they had to test the (double) hypothesis that the male partner (Peter) tends to show *overt* aggression whereas the female partner (Heike) shows more *covert* aggression. They could search information in a database represented on the computer, asking over 32 trials whether particular behaviours (selected from a pull-down menu) had been observed or not in Peter or Heike. On each trial, they could choose to ask a question about Peter or Heike, and they could select a question referring to either overt aggression or covert aggression. The feedback rate was held constant at the same rate of 75% affirmation. That is, regardless of whether Peter or Heike, or overt or covert aggression, were being considered, the computer confirmed the behaviour in question with a 75% probability. Thus, the computer was programmed to display the very acquiescence effect observed by Zuckerman and colleagues.

After the learning stage was over, participants were asked to estimate the relative frequencies with which overt and covert aggression had been observed in Peter and Heike. They also rated their impressions of Peter and Heike on trait dimensions related to overt and covert aggression. As in previous experiments, information search was again characterized by a marked tendency towards positive testing; that is, participants asked more questions about overt aggression in Peter and about covert aggression in Heike than about the reverse combinations. Although the "communication" was with

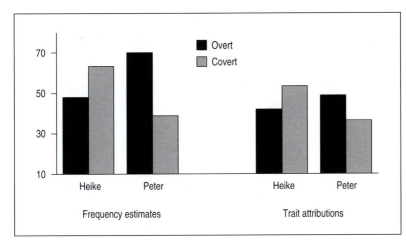

Figure 6.5.
Illusory verification of the hypothesis that aggression tends to be covert in female persons (Heike) and overt in male persons (Peter), as demonstrated by Fiedler, Walther, and Nickel (1999).

the computer's database rather than a human discussion partner, and although the confirmation rate for all question topics was held constant at 75%, the unequal numbers of observations led to illusory verification. Frequency estimates as well as trait ratings reflected more overt than covert aggression attributed to Peter but more covert than overt aggression attributed to Heike (see Figure 6.5). This effect was exclusively due to the fact that a larger absolute number of observations were drawn about the Peter-overt and Heike-covert combinations than about the Peter-covert and Heike-overt combinations.

Additional experiments corroborated this conclusion. Thus, when participants were to test the opposite hypotheses, that Peter's aggression is covert and Heike's aggression is overt—contrary to gender stereotypes—they still found confirmation for the focal hypotheses. Moreover, when active information search was eliminated so that participants could only passively observe how another (fictitious) participant gathered information on Peter and Heike, it was possible to vary the number of observations independent of the direction of the hypothesis. Thus, even when the hypothesis said to find out whether Peter's aggression is overt and Heike's is covert, it was possible to simulate *negative testing*, that is, most observations could refer to Peter's covert and Heike's overt aggression (holding affirmation rate constant). What would determine the subsequent judgments in this condition?

Interestingly, the results showed that the crucial factor is the number of observations. Even when task instructions focused on Peter-overt and Heike-covert, observing larger samples on Peter-covert and Heike-overt led to an opposite illusion. Peter was judged higher in covert than overt aggression and Heike received higher ratings in overt than covert aggression. These findings demonstrate that the number of learning trials can provide a very simple, parsimonious explanation for hypothesis verification—though clearly not the only one. Although the confirmation rate remains constantly high for all kinds of question, the stimulus environment affords more trials to learn this confirmation rate for some hypotheses than for others. These findings eventually illustrate what it means when we say that social hypothesis testing is constrained by the distribution of stimulus data in the environment, quite independently of motives and stereotypical beliefs.

Illusory correlations against minorities

At the same time, the simple rule that environmental learning increases with the number of trials can explain a very prominent type of illusory correlation. Hamilton and Gifford (1976) conceived the following experimental analogue of minority group derogation that fascinated researchers to such a degree that hundreds of follow-up studies used the same basic paradigm. Hamilton and Gifford reasoned that minorities are by definition less numerous than majorities, and it can also be assumed that undesirable (i.e., norm-deviant) behaviours are less frequent than desirable (i.e., normative) behaviours. Mapping this reasonable assumption about the social ecology onto a group-judgment experiment, they constructed a stimulus series covering 39 behaviour descriptions shown by members of two social groups, denoted A and B (to avoid associations with actual existing groups). The distribution of these 39 stimulus behaviours over the 2 × 2 combinations of groups (A vs. B) and evaluation (+ vs. −) is given in Figure 6.6. Although Group A, the majority, appeared more frequently than Group B (the minority), and positive behaviours were more frequent than negative behaviours, the *proportion* of positive behaviours was exactly the same for both groups (18 out of 26 for Group A = 9 out of 13 for Group B). In other words, the correlation between groups and evaluation was carefully controlled at zero value.

Nevertheless, a systematically more favourable impression was created of the majority than the minority, in spite of the constant rate of desirable behaviour

Figure 6.6. Illusory correlations according to Hamilton & Gifford (1976). Although the same high ratio of desirable to undesirable behaviours holds for both groups, the majority group A is associated with relatively more positive behaviours than the minority group B.

	Majority group A	Minority group B
Desirable behaviours	18	9
Undesirable behaviours	8	4

in both groups. The illusory correlation was evident in several dependent measures. Frequency estimates of the number of positive and negative behaviours shown by Group A and B members were biased against B. Group ratings on trait scales reflected more favourable impressions of A than B. And in a cued-recall test, erroneous reproductions of the group associations of the stimulus behaviours were also to the advantage of the majority. These findings—which have been replicated in numerous experiments—are extremely provocative because they suggest a permanent source of bias against minorities. In a world in which minorities are smaller than majorities and norm-deviant behaviours are less frequent than normative behaviours, a systematic illusion will discriminate against minorities—even when there is no stereotype or sentiment against them.

Originally, Hamilton and Gifford (1976) explained this illusory correlation phenomenon in terms of the assumption that negative behaviours of the minority, the most infrequent stimulus class, are most distinctive and salient in the stimulus list. However, the learning approach offers an even simpler explanation. Even when all stimuli are equally distinctive or salient, the very fact that there are twice as many observations about Group A than B (cf. Figure 6.6) predicts that the high positivity rate should be learned more readily and more completely in A than in B.

Completing the hypothesis-testing paradigm: Verification effects at various stages of cognitive processing

Thus far, diverse experiments have been reported to demonstrate the important role of environmental data in the process of social hypothesis testing. We have been concerned with three mechanisms through which stimulus data may contribute to a pervasive bias towards hypothesis verification: self-selected data, self-produced data, and the distribution of stimuli afforded by the external environment itself. All three mechanisms exert an influence on the initial process of information search, that is, on the input data of the entire cognitive process. We now turn to the question of how social hypotheses fare during the subsequent cognitive processes, from perception and encoding to memory retrieval, judgment, and communication. As we shall see, these subsequent process stages are more likely to reinforce than to correct for the verification bias. Just as a leading hypothesis can bias the initial information search, it can also bias perception, memory, judgment, and communication.

To illustrate this point, consider for example the commonly held national stereotype—conveyed in the media and in the popular literature—that Germans are high in organizational skills. A number of social-cognitive phenomena, as introduced in the preceding chapters, may all help to conserve the (questionable) belief that Germans are well-organized people. As already shown, during the initial stage of *information search*, people may attend more to, or may be more likely to be exposed to, information about the combination *Germans & well-organized* than to alternative combinations. At the next stage of social *perception*, the same behaviour that is interpreted as reflecting organization in Germans may be interpreted as reflecting some other attribute in non-Germans. Thus, if many Spanish people possess cell phones, this may be perceived as Spanish playfulness rather than reflecting an organizational mentality. Or the same qualitatively unambiguous behaviour, such as being punctual, may be noticed more sensitively, or experienced more intensely, in Germans than in Spanish people. At the next stage, *memory encoding*, episodes of Germans showing seemingly well-organized behaviour may be more likely to be integrated in long-term memory, because a corresponding knowledge structure (i.e., the stereotype of Germans) is available to facilitate the encoding process. Similar memory structures will not be available for encoding, making sense, and remembering the same episode in Spanish people. Indeed, different schemata for the Spanish will serve to encode punctuality-related behaviour as evidence for much leisure time. Later on, *retrieval processes* may again give an advantage to "meaningful information" about Germans being well organized (see Chapter 3), compared with other information for which no such meaningful categories exist. To the extent that retrieval is not a passive process but guided by active prompts and expectations, information that confirms hypothetical knowledge is more likely to be recalled than contrahypothetical information. Finally, as information is *communicated* from one person to others—in face-to-face settings, in newspapers, electronic media, or in the literature—evidence that speaks to the focal hypothesis is again more likely to gain a special status. The focus of a current hypothesis or expectancy is not only more likely to be mentioned at all, but also more likely to be expressed with confidence and at a high level of linguistic power and generality (Maass, 1999; Semin & Fiedler, 1988; Vallacher & Wegner, 1987).

Indeed, a huge body of research evidence exists to support the contribution of all these processing stages to the conservation and (illusory) confirmation of social hypotheses. And, indeed, the manner in which we have just depicted confirmation biases in perception, encoding, retrieval, and communication appears plausible and in line with common intuition. As in the previous sections concerned with information search, the first explanation for these phenomena that comes to mind is in terms of beliefs and desires, that is, cognitive and motivational biases within the individual. Once more, however, we shall see that we need not always blame sloppy and wishful thinking. To explain hypothesis confirmation, we need not always assume biased psychological processes. Moreover, we shall see that the confirmation tendency is not as unconstrained and catastrophic as it might appear from the above sketch. Rather than perpetuating infinitely, the processes are confined by specific boundary conditions, which are interesting in their own right.

Perception and encoding

In most studies described thus far, we have mainly considered the process of social hypothesis testing in (experimental) situations in which prior expectancies (i.e., beliefs and desires) have been minimized. A priori there is little reason to suspect that a formerly unknown interview partner is either extraverted or introverted, and an unspecified, fictitious "Group A" is no more positive than "Group B." However, in reality, most judgments and decisions do not take place in a vacuum. Very often, hypothesis testing is not simply a matter of learning and accurate assessment but is driven by the individual's beliefs and desires, goals, and vested interests. Such preconceptions may blind social hypothesis testers to unwanted information and exaggerate the perceived support for "beloved" hypotheses. Of course, such instances of motivated or "hot" cognition can contribute strongly to the pervasive verification bias.

The very same behaviour can be perceived differently depending on the perceiver's motives and expectations. For example, when a female outperforms males in a male performance domain, such as technical problem solving or car driving, the unexpected female performance may be overlooked or reattributed to good luck or chance. Likewise, given the stereotypical expectation that overt aggression is a male phenomenon, instances of female overt aggression may be diminished and may not be perceived as overt or intense. How this

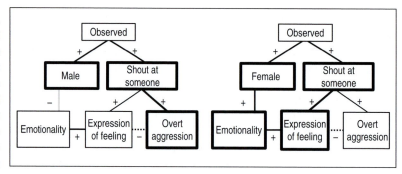

Figure 6.7.
An associative model of how the same behaviour (shouting at someone) may be perceived and encoded differently, depending on the gender of the subject. If the person is female rather than male, the emotionality concept will be activated, thus increasing the likelihood that the behaviour will be interpreted as an expression of feeling, rather than an overt aggression.

phenomenon of expectancy-dependent perception works is illustrated in Figure 6.7, borrowed from Kunda and Thagard (1997). An ambiguous motor reaction (shouting at someone) can be perceived as an act of overt aggression when the stimulus person is male but as an act of emotional expression when the person is female. This is because older information in an associative network can either support or inhibit an aggressive interpretation. As the node for the attribute *female* is more strongly associated with *emotionality* than is the node for the attribute *male*, the associative path from the stimulus behaviour to the target trait (*overt aggression*) is inhibited in the former case.

One reason for the plasticity of expectancy-driven perception is that many social attributes do not exist objectively but have to be construed subjectively. Whether a person is honest, fair, or attractive cannot be determined for sure but depends on the way in which these attributes are construed in terms of relevant features. Different persons may use different features to construe, say, the meaning of fairness, putting an emphasis either on leniency or on open competition. An experiment by Kunda and Oleson (1995) nicely illustrates the manner in which the same information can be given different meaning in a genuinely constructive process. In pilot testing, these authors first made sure that lawyers are typically expected to be extraverted, rather than introverted. Then participants in a main experiment were presented with a vignette describing a particular lawyer in terms of introverted behaviours. One experimental group, who were told that the lawyer was employed in a large company, arrived at the explanation that this exceptional lawyer was introverted because he worked in a large company. Another group, who were told that the lawyer was employed in a small company, concluded that his introversion was due to his working in a small company. Thus, opposite features (small vs. large company) could be used for the purpose of maintaining the assumption that "normal" lawyers are extravert whereas only lawyers in particular companies happen to be introverted.

Sometimes hypotheses are motivationally very important for the individual's goals or self-esteem, such as the hypothesis "I am a likeable person" or "I am unlikely to become the victim of a serious crime, accident or disease" or "my soccer team is better and more attractive than rival teams." Especially in these motivated cases, social perception can be severely biased towards the ego-involving beliefs. Just as food looms larger for a hungry person, the subjective perception of one's own behaviour or one's in-group is biased towards a positive self-image (Kunda, 1990).

There is ample evidence to support this notion, from everyday anecdotes as well as controlled experiments. One often-studied phenomenon with obvious implications for risk-taking and health-related behaviour is unrealistic optimism (Weinstein, 1980). The risk associated with particular behaviours (e.g., breaking a leg, being robbed, getting divorced) is perceived to be systematically lower for oneself than for other people. For instance, most people agree that car driving entails a sizeable accident risk but they assume that this risk only holds for other people—not for themselves. Similarly, the probability of contracting AIDS through unsafe sexual intercourse is generally admitted, but much less for oneself than for other people.

Misperceiving or reinterpreting stimulus events is but one means of reconciling conflicting information with motivationally important hypotheses. Another strategy is to deny the relevance or pertinence of discrepant observations, as in the so-called subtyping paradigm (Hewstone, 1994; Kunda & Oleson, 1995, 1997; Weber & Crocker, 1983). For instance, imagine a female person who wants to maintain the belief that women are unlikely to become the victim of rape and sexual offence. When such a woman is confronted with the case of another woman from her neighbourhood who was raped on her way home the previous night, she may exclude this women as belonging to a subtype of women who are not typical or representative of women in general (see section on typicality in Chapter 5). For instance, she might assume that the victim belongs to a subcategory of women of particularly provocative appearance, or stupid women who lack the ability to recognize danger and risk situations, or women with criminal companionship. To the extent that the victim is classified as not belonging to her own group but belonging to the subtype, the threat is absorbed, and the pleasant invulnerability hypothesis can be upheld.

Indeed, subtyping cannot only maintain but even strengthen the motivated hypothesis, as Bless et al. (2001) have shown (see also

Kunda & Oleson, 1997). After subtyping is used to explain contradictions to prior knowledge, the subtype can then be used as a comparison standard to judge one's own group (see discussion on inclusion/exclusion processes in Chapter 5). Relative to the subtype, one's own group can then appear even safer and better than before. Thus, the woman can say to herself: In contrast to this subtype of women who dress themselves that way and who are in contact with those obscure people, I am clearly different and therefore particularly unlikely to become a rape victim as well (cf. Bohner, Weisbrod, Raymond, Barzvi, & Schwarz, 1993).

Selective retrieval

Social hypothesis testing is not only a matter of selective information intake via processes of information search, perception, and encoding. The outcome of hypothesis testing also depends on recall and retrieval of information from memory. There are (at least) three ways in which selective memory can contribute to the pervasive tendency to verify certain focal hypotheses and to neglect equally likely alternatives: motivated recall, constructive memory intrusions, and deductive retrieval structures. These phenomena are discussed in the present section, along with an opposite mechanism that works against a pervasive verification bias.

Motivated recall

Whenever hypotheses are charged with emotions and strong motives, memory can become extremely selective, favouring expected or desired outcomes. Common sense and everyday experience provide ample evidence for this notion. People recall nice things about the persons they love or admire, and they recall nasty things about the persons they hate. Members of one political party remember different actions from the last government period than members of a rival party. Fans of one soccer club will remember different events from the same match than fans of the opponent club. Or, after participating in a discussion, we selectively remember arguments that are consistent with our own attitude, while forgetting those arguments that are inconsistent.

One explanation for such a motivated bias is in terms of the chronic accessibility of emotion-laden concepts in memory. Thus, the thoughts of a teenage girl who is a great fan of the Backstreet Boys will chronically revolve around this concept. Whatever she is doing, the beloved concept "Backstreet Boys" will be accessible. When this girl is asked to write down—in a free recall test—what she has done the day before, any experience related to this pop group is very likely to be recalled with priority. She will presumably recall if she had a debate with other teenagers about pop groups, that she bought a CD, or listened to music. It is close to impossible for her to forget how she went to a Backstreet Boys concert.

As explained in Chapter 3, the notion of *accessibility* refers to the readiness to find a concept in memory very quickly and without much effort. The notion of *availability* refers to the question of whether some information has been encoded in memory at all. Affectively very important concepts are typically high in both accessibility and availability, because these concepts are likely to be retrieved and used very often and they are likely to be associated with multiple personal experiences. However, highly accessible material that governs memory recall is not restricted to extremely desirable objects, or targets of wishful thinking. One important source of high accessibility is self-reference of all kind. What I have done or experienced myself, what I have said, or what has been merely related to my self-concept, has a clear-cut memory advantage over comparable information without self-reference (see Chapter 3 for more evidence on this self-reference advantage).

The so-called *egocentric bias* in attribution provides another example of how selective memory for self-referent information can serve to confirm specific hypotheses or convictions. In one of the most prominent studies, Ross and Sicoly (1979) asked people who were involved in close relationships to judge their own and their partner's relative responsibility for various joint activities, such as planning leisure activities, doing housework, starting arguments, etc. Most participants claimed to contribute more than their partners to the majority of activities. This difference held not only for desirable behaviours but even for many undesirable behaviours (such as starting debates), suggesting that the egocentric bias is not confined to a self-serving function. As both partners were included in the study, judgments about the same activities in the same dyad could be compared. As it turned out, the sum of both partners' percentage estimates of their own contribution to most activities exceeded 100%. Thus, the results cannot be explained by the assumption that the more active partners happened to participate in this study.

Additional findings supported the assumption that the bias in favour of egocentric hypotheses was due to enhanced accessibility in memory of self-related information. Ross and Sicoly also included a memory task, in which participants were asked to recall particular

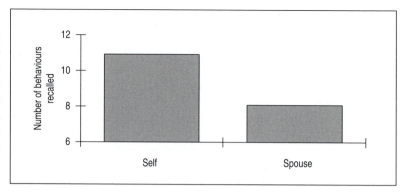

Figure 6.8.
Egocentric recall as a source of egocentric attribution in partnership, after Ross & Sicoly (1979). On average, participants recall more of their own activities than activities of their spouse.

behaviours associated with the various activities in their partnership. In this memory task, too, there was a clear-cut bias towards enhanced recall of self-related information. In other words, one's own actions were more accessible in memory than other people's actions, even those of an intimate partner (Figure 6.8). Moreover, the advantage of self-related memory recall correlated markedly (r = .50) with the tendency to believe in egocentric hypotheses.

Constructive memory

The accessibility of memory contents can be manipulated artificially. If this occurs, leading hypotheses can be confirmed through constructive memory errors. For a famous illustration, imagine you have witnessed a car accident and your testimony is now being used in a legal trial. The lawyer who asks you to estimate the speed of the car driven by the accused person may use different words for the same question:

- About how fast were the cars going when they *smashed* each other?
- About how fast were the cars going when they *bumped* each other?
- About how fast were the cars going when they *hit* each other?
- How fast were the cars going when they *contacted*?

Loftus and Palmer (1974) examined the impact of this kind of variation in the wording of a question in simulated eyewitness tasks, in which participants first saw a film of an accident and then had to report what they recalled about it. Witness responses varied significantly as a function of the question wording. The average speed estimate solicited by the word *smashed* (M = 40.8 mph) was about

30% higher than the estimate solicited by the word *contacted* ($M =$ 31.8 mph).

How can this influence of questioning on eyewitness memory be explained? One possibility is that respondents are simply following *demand characteristics*. That is, they might not quite remember what they have seen and they might therefore rely on the cues provided in the question. The word *smash* suggests a higher speed than the word *collide*. Granting that the interrogator has background knowledge about the correct speed estimate, witnesses might simply use those cues to guess what they actually cannot remember. Alternatively, the biased eyewitness reports might reflect a genuinely *constructive memory* process that not merely affects the witness' response behaviour but changes the memory representation proper. Thus, when confronted with the question "How fast were the cars going when they smashed together?" the witness may mentally reconstruct the accident scene in accordance with the semantic meaning of "smashing." This self-generated memory representation, constructed to understand and answer the lawyer's question, may then merge into the original representation and cause a permanent change in the memory of the accident. Subsequently, the witness will believe, to her best knowledge, that the enhanced speed suggested by the word *smash* was actually true of the accident.

There has been a rather long debate about the merits and validity of these two alternative explanations, (1) guessing effects based on demand characteristics and (2) genuine memory effects due to constructive processes (cf. McCloskey & Zaragoza, 1985; Tversky & Tuchin, 1989). By now, there is uncontestable evidence that even though guessing-based response tendencies are possible, genuine constructive changes of memory do exist as well (Roediger & McDermott, 1995). Cogent evidence for the latter claim comes from demonstrations of counterdictional questioning effects. Even when the respondent (correctly) denies the questioner's suggested hypotheses—thereby demonstrating that she does not use the questioner's cues as a basis for guessing—the respondent's belief in the denied question contents may nonetheless increase.

For instance, Fiedler and colleagues (Fiedler, Armbruster, Nickel, Walther, & Asbeck, 1996) first presented their participants with a videotaped group discussion on an economic topic. Participants were then asked to answer a number of questions reflecting an evaluatively positive or negative hypothesis about one target discussant. When questions referred to undesirable behaviours (Did the target *attack*, *interrupt* others?) subsequent ratings on semantically matched trait dimensions (e.g., *aggressive, impolite*) increased in comparison with another experimental group that saw the same film but answered questions related to desirable behaviours (Did the target *encourage, delight* others?). Most interestingly, this tendency to provide confirming ratings for either question contents held even in those cases in which judges had denied having seen the behaviour. Thus, even when judges denied having seen that the target had attacked or interrupted others in response to the behavioural questions, the negative questions led to increased ratings of the matched traits aggressive and impolite, respectively. Merely considering the possibility of various negative behaviours, or merely construing the target person in the semantic space of these behaviours for the sake of question answering, caused a constructive bias towards the question contents. Demand effects or guessing based on question cues could hardly account for these findings, because participants had rejected the question contents as false in the first place. Moreover, participants could not have believed that the experimenter had intentionally chosen positive or negative questions because they could themselves choose their question list at random from different lists. Thus, the influence of hypothetical questions on memory-based judgments must be due to a genuinely constructive process of memory change or update.

Deductive retrieval structures

In Chapter 3, it was already mentioned that surprising, unexpected information (e.g., a priest engaging in immoral behaviour) is often encoded particularly well and therefore has a recall advantage. Note that this extra salience of unexpected information would work against the verification of prior hypotheses or expectancies. However, there is also a place for the opposite principle, namely, that under certain conditions hypothetically expected information has a recall advantage and thereby supports the guiding hypothesis. This is the case whenever recall proceeds deductively within the associative structures of world knowledge.

For example, when somebody believes in the hypothesis "I am an industrious person who contributes a lot to housework" and when this person is asked to recall what he has done the day before, the hypothesis may guide a deductive recall process. Thus, the person may first deduce what categories of housework can be done in a normal day and thereby scan, in a one-sided fashion, his memory for positive examples of such behaviours that he has actually done. Similarly, when recalling information about a priest, a deductive process may follow knowledge about what priests normally do. Or when recalling information about a stigmatized group, the group stereotype may serve as a deductive guideline. In these cases, recall will also—much like the other processes reviewed in this chapter—serve to confirm a starting hypothesis.

When, however, recall does not proceed deductively but is driven by the salience and outstanding value of singular events, then we often find an opposite effect, as noted in Chapter 3. Surprising events that disconfirm an expectancy or hypothesis will then be recalled particularly well (cf. Stangor & McMillan, 1992).

Judgment and decision making

If selective recall favours one hypothesis over others, one would expect that subsequent judgments and decisions are biased as well. This plausible principle suggests that judgments and memory tests should normally be correlated strongly. In fact, for a long time, social psychologists have assumed that selective recall is a major predictor of judgments and decisions, just as attitude change was believed to be determined by selective recall of relevant arguments. Meanwhile, it has been acknowledged that the correspondence between memory and judgment is often very low. Judgments would often exhibit no clear correlation with measures of recall.

What might be the reason for the counterintuitive negative evidence? Hastie and Park (1986) have offered a convincing explanation. These authors drew a clear distinction between two different situations, *on-line* judgments and *memory-based* judgments. The term on-line refers to the fact that people would often form immediate judgments after they have encountered and encoded new information. For instance, based on direct on-line experience, somebody may immediately judge, and store as a fixed module in memory, the wisdom that a Mercedes is an excellent car. When this person is later asked to evaluate Mercedes, he need not scan memory for relevant raw information in order to arrive at a judgment. Rather, the person can draw on his previously stored on-line judgment. Under these conditions, judgments cannot be expected to be correlated with memory, because memory is cut short in the judgment process.

In contrast, when someone has never thought before about Mercedes and then happens to be asked for a judgment, then a memory-based process is enforced. Now the judge has to scan his memory for whatever relevant pieces of information or statements of other people come to his mind. In this case of memory-based judgments, in the absence of on-line encoded modules, the correlation between judgment and recall should be substantial. In fact, Hastie and Park's (1986) review of the pertinent research literature supports this appraisal. Judgments and decisions are correlated with biased recall if the process is memory-based, but uncorrelated if the process can draw on on-line inferences.

Aside from the correspondence of judgment and memory, the various judgment heuristics described in Chapter 4 afford a rich repertoire of devices for hypothesis confirmation. As we have seen in the discussion of these various heuristics, they often imply a bias towards a starting hypothesis (for an example, see the discussion of the anchoring heuristic in Chapter 4).

Communication and sharing of social information

Early in this chapter, we have seen that social hypothesis testing begins in the environment, in the process of information search and selective exposure to stimulus ecologies, well before the individual's internal cognitive processes come into play. Now, at the end of the chapter, we must also recognize that hypothesis testing does not end with the closure of individual cognitive processes. After judgments and decisions are complete—under the influence of the antecedent stages of information search, perception, encoding, organization, and retrieval—there is still the question of how the outcomes of cognitive processes are communicated and shared with other people, or with the public. After all, individuals do not live and act in isolation but in groups and in connected systems involving many other people, with a considerable degree of interdependence and division of labour. Recent research on the role of language in social information processing provides strong evidence that rules of communication can contribute a lot to the verification and consolidation of prior expectancies and hypotheses. Moreover, this research once more started with a phenomenon that looked like a motivated bias but that turned out later to reflect a more general process of hypothesis stabilization.

Linguistic intergroup bias

The so-called linguistic intergroup bias (LIB), as originally demonstrated by Maass, Salvi, Arcuri, and Semin (1989), concerns the abstractness of linguistic terms used to describe behaviours of ingroups and out-groups. Maass and colleagues asked members of North Italian Palio teams—a traditional horse race involving deep identification with local communities—to verbally describe various social behaviours depicted in cartoons. The target persons in the cartoon whose behaviours were to be described were either characterized as belonging to the participant's local in-group, or to an out-group. The major finding, to which the term LIB pertains, showed that language users tended to describe desirable in-group behaviour in more abstract terms than undesirable in-group behaviour. In contrast, for the out-group, they used more abstract terms to describe undesirable than desirable behaviours. To measure linguistic abstractness, Maass et al. relied on Semin and Fiedler's (1988) linguistic category model, which affords a taxonomy of predicates of increasing abstractness, from descriptive action verbs (e.g., to telephone, to shake hands), interpretive action verbs (to help, to hurt), state verbs (to hate, to admire), to adjectives (aggressive, helpful). Table 6.1 indicates how these linguistic categories are defined, and illustrates the taxonomy with examples.

The LIB, which was replicated in a number of subsequent studies, reflects a language style that gives more weight and meaning to a group-serving hypothesis. Positive in-group behaviour is typically raised to the abstract level of global and stable trait words (e.g., honest, friendly, etc.), carrying all the surplus meaning of internal dispositions. However, they localize negative in-group behaviour in terms of neutral, situation-dependent verbs (e.g., to write a letter, to

TABLE 6.1
Word classes of the Linguistic Category Model (LCM)

Linguistic category	Examples	Defining features
DAV (Descriptive action verbs)	telephone kiss kick touch	Finite behavioural episode Concrete situation reference Invariant physical features Context-dependent meaning
IAV (Interpretive action verbs)	cheat hurt help explain	Finite behavioural episode Concrete situation reference Interpretation and evaluation Independent meaning
SV (State verbs)	admire hate like envy	Affective or cognitive state No situation reference Interpretation and evaluation Abstract regarding specific actions
ADJ (Adjectives)	honest aggressive nice clever	Enduring disposition No situation reference Highly interpretive Abstract regarding specific actions

Figure 6.9.

The linguistic inter-
group bias (Maass,
Salvi, Arcuri, & Semin,
1989) reflects more
abstract language used
to describe positive in-
group behaviours and
negative out-group
behaviours than to
describe negative
in-group and positive
out-group behaviours.

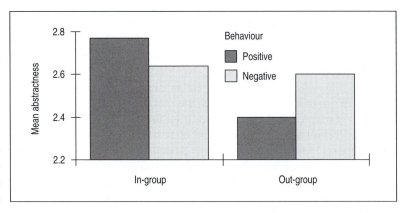

telephone, etc.), thereby avoiding evaluation and downplaying the social meaning of those negative behaviours (e.g., avoiding such interpretations as: threat or blackmail in the letter, being insulting on the telephone, being brutal or crude). Conversely, when talking about the out-group, they localize positive behaviour by using concrete, contextualized terms and raise negative behaviour to the abstract level of traits or internal dispositions (Figure 6.9). Clearly, such a language style serves to affirm an in-group-serving hypothesis in that equivalent behaviours are communicated differentially, depending on whether actors belong to the in-group or the out-group. Assuming that the LIB extends to the manner in which mass media report on events associated with in-groups versus out-groups (Maass, Corvino, & Arcuri, 1994), one can imagine that its impact on opinion formation multiplies with the power and distribution of those mass media. It seems obvious that distributing a LIB through the mass media can contribute to the maintenance and communication of stereotypical hypotheses.

Linguistic expectancy bias

Although the original LIB finding looks like an in-group-serving bias, a motivated tendency to describe groups in words with desirable implications, subsequent research has shown that the underlying motive may not be self- or in-group-orientated, but other-orientated. Results suggest that the linguistic intergroup bias (LIB) may be more adequately called a linguistic expectancy bias (LEB). That is, what drives language users to apply different words when talking about in-groups and out-groups may not be primarily the selfish tendency to present oneself in favourable terms. Rather, the motive may lie in the cooperative tendency to say abstractly what can be expected to be well known and familiar, and to express in concrete detail only what is new and unexpected. Such a language style would be well in line with Grice's (1975) principle of cooperative communication, as introduced in Chapter 5. In particular, Grice's maxim of quantity says that language users should be as precise and extensive as necessary to be understood, but should not use more words and references than are needed. Accordingly, they are entitled to abstract from unnecessary details when talking about common, stereotypical group attributes, but they should be more specific and deliver more details about unexpected behaviours that do not fit common stereotypes. Such a cooperative, partner-orientated rule of language use would "mimic" a group-serving bias. As stereotypical expectancies are confounded with evaluation—most people expect positive in-group and negative out-group behaviour—using abstract language for expected behaviour will appear to favour the in-group and to harm the out-group.

To disentangle the influence of expectedness from the positive evaluation of one's in-group, Maass, Milesi, Zabbini, and Stahlberg (1995) varied both factors in an orthogonal fashion. Using North Italians and South Italians as target groups, they studied verbalizations of positive and negative behaviours typically associated with people from the North and from the South, based on consensual ratings of people from either region. Thus, the verbal description task referred to:

(1) positive behaviours expected in North Italians but not in South Italians (industrious, emancipated);
(2) negative behaviours expected in North but not South Italians (materialistic, intolerant);
(3) positive attributes expected in South Italians but not in North Italians (hospitable, warm); and
(4) negative behaviours expected in South but not in North Italians (sexist, intrusive).

Participants from North and South Italy were asked to describe in-group and out-group behaviours, depicted in cartoons, that varied in valence and expectedness. It is clear that, say, North Italians should tend to use abstract terms to describe *expected* positive behaviours in North Italians, and they should also use abstract terms to describe negative *expected* behaviours in South Italians. However, aside from this uncontestable prediction, the crucial question is how they would describe positive *unexpected* behaviours of the (North Italian)

Figure 6.10.
Abstractness of
language use as a
function of typicality or
expectedness of
behaviour. Typically
Northern behaviour is
expressed more
abstractly when
describing North
Italians, whereas
typically Southern
behaviour is described
more abstractly when
describing South
Italians (after Maass et
al., 1995).

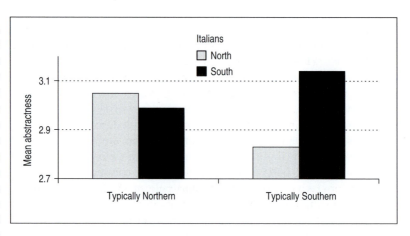

in-group, or negative *unexpected* behaviours of the (South Italian) out-group. If a group-serving bias dominates, they should still tend to describe positive in-group and negative out-group behaviours in more abstract terms than negative in-group and positive out-group behaviours, even though these behaviours are unexpected. However, when the expectedness principle overrides the group-serving motive, then unexpected behaviours should be described in abstract terms, even when the implications are unfavourable for the in-group and favourable for the out-group.

Indeed, the results reported by Maass et al. (1995) demonstrate that the crucial difference is between expected and unexpected information (see Figure 6.10). More abstract words were chosen when describing expected than unexpected behaviours, even when expected behaviours had negative implications for the in-group and positive implications for the out-group. Consistent findings have been reported by other researchers (Wigboldus, Semin, & Spears, 2000), suggesting that the LIB may to an unknown degree reflect an LEB. Thus, once more we see how an "innocent" interaction rule—to adapt to a conversation partners' information need—can result in an unintended bias which looks like a motivated, self-serving, or group-serving bias. However, it should be kept in mind that support for the LEB (i.e., raising expected information to an abstract level) does not rule out the possibility that a LIB (raising group-serving information to an abstract level) can be effective as well.

Shared information effect

Sometimes, especially in democratic systems, hypotheses have to be tested in teams or decision groups with a clear-cut division of labour.

For example, a group of jurors has to test the hypothesis that a defendant is guilty, or an election board has to decide on whether an applicant should be offered a leading position in an organization. The manner in which information is exchanged in such decision groups can also contribute to the verification of a starting hypothesis and to the relative neglect of alternative hypotheses.

Research by Stasser and colleagues (Stasser & Titus, 1985) on the so-called shared information effect suggests an intriguing explanation for the tendency of decision groups to affirm the starting hypothesis. Let us subdivide the total information distributed among all group members into two components, (1) starting information shared by all group members, and (2) additional, unshared information acquired by individual specialists, according to the division of labour. Stasser and colleages have demonstrated a regular tendency to attend to and weight shared information more strongly than unshared information, presumably because shared information raises a sense of validity and consensus. However, this means that the starting hypothesis—or status quo that exists before individuals can add new information—is overweighted relative to independent other sources of information that could potentially lead to alternative decisions. Again, the shared information effect is certainly not a sign of carelessness or irrationality; it is a side effect of a well-motivated strategy in group decision, namely to cross-validate information and to trust (only) in agreed-upon information. However, one side effect of this strategy is a conservative bias towards the starting hypothesis and a reluctance to accept alternative hypotheses that might arise from unshared new information.

Chapter summary

(1) Environmental information provides the input for social-cognitive processes. Before we can understand cognitive processes, we first of all have to understand the contents and distribution of stimuli in the environment.

(2) Individuals are not passively exposed to the stimulus environment. Rather, their interaction with the environment is characterized by active hypothesis testing processes.

(3) Stimulus-data may be self-selected, they may be self-produced, or they may exist independently of the individual's behaviour.

(4) Research has discovered various reasons why the outcome of this hypothesis-testing process tends to be confirmatory. Very

often, positive evidence is likely to be found for whatever hypothesis is being tested.

(5) This pervasive confirmation bias, which is evident at virtually all stages of cognitive functioning, need not always originate in cognitive or affective distortions. At least sometimes, completely normal unbiased processes also lead to artificial verification of social hypotheses.

Discussion questions

(1) Think of several examples of how the information that the social environment provides about in-groups and out-groups can contribute to inter-group biases.

(2) How can the wording and style of survey or interview questions influence their outcome? Does the pervasive phenomenon of confirmative hypothesis testing also hold for survey research?

(3) Clarify the distinction between linguistic intergroup bias (LIB) and linguistic expectancy bias (LEB).

(4) Try to generate possible explanations for the shared-information effect, that is, for the enhanced weight given in group decision to information that is shared by group members rather than available only to individual members.

(5) How can stereotypes be maintained in spite of disconfirming data?

(6) What conditions facilitate the occurrence of constructive memory illusions?

Recommendations for further reading

Fiedler, K., & Walther, E. (2003). *Stereotypes as inductive hypothesis testing.* Hove, UK: Psychology Press.

Leyens, J.-P., Dardenne, B., Yzerbyt, V., Scaillet, N., & Snyder, M. (1999). Confirmation and disconfirmation: Their social advantages. In W. Stroebe & M. Hewstone (Eds.), *European review of social psychology* (Vol. 10, pp. 199–230). Chichester, UK: Wiley.

Snyder, M. (1984). When belief creates reality. In L. Berkowitz (Ed.), *Advances in experimental social psychology* (Vol. 18, pp. 247–305). New York: Academic Press.

Beyond cold information processing: The interplay of affect and cognition

7

Introduction

In the previous chapters we have discussed a wide spectrum of aspects that are involved in individuals' construction of their social reality. We have learned about encoding, retrieval, and judgmental processes and how they relate to each other. At this point one might wonder whether, with all the emphasis on cognitive aspects, there is a place for individuals' feelings, for their affective states. After all, most of us have had the experience that the world appears quite differently depending on how we feel. For example, we would perceive a party situation (as outlined at the beginning in Chapter 1) differently depending on whether we approach the situation in a happy, a sad, or an angry mood.

The idea that our social judgments and behaviours are influenced by how we feel in a particular situation is not new at all. In this respect, scientific interest has manifested itself in a long tradition of philosophical speculation (e.g., Descartes, 1649/1961) and psychological thinking (e.g., Freud, 1940; James, 1890). In most of these traditional positions, it is argued that affect reduces individuals' ability to think rationally about the social world and that affective states thus impair individuals' perception of their social environment (see Forgas, 2000a, for an overview). The more recent research suggests that affect is not necessarily creating irrationalities, but that in most cases, individuals' affective state provides a very useful source for the regulation of cognitive processes and for the interpretation of the social situation.

At first glance it may appear as if affective influences can hardly be conceptualized within social cognition research. The strong focus on information processing seems to portray the human being as a cold and emotionless information-processing machine. Indeed, in particular with the advent of the information-processing paradigm, emotional processes seemed to fall outside the main focus of researchers. This situation changed very quickly, however, and social psychologists' interest in emotional processes was soon revived. Over the last two decades, research within the social cognition paradigm has accumulated a large body of empirical and theoretical contributions, providing enormous evidence that affective states may influence cognitive processes in virtually every domain of social psychology (for reviews see Bless, 2001; Clore et al., 1994; Forgas, 2000b; Martin & Clore, 2001).

In the remainder of this chapter we will discuss some of the social cognition research on the interplay of affect and cognition. Given the scope of this chapter we thereby have two restrictions. The first restriction pertains to the direction of the affect and cognition relation. We focus primarily on how affective states influence cognitive processes; for example, how being in a particular mood influences the amount of stereotyping (Bodenhausen, Kramer, & Süsser, 1994a). We thus do not discuss the reversed direction, that is, how different cognitive processes elicit different affective states (see Clore et al., 1994). Second, reflecting the focus of research within the social cognition paradigm, we concentrate mostly on moods, that is, on affective states of minor intensity. In contrast to more intense emotions, moods are more diffuse, and they usually do not attract the individual's attention. Exactly these features render moods so interesting for social cognition researchers. Moods do not interrupt individuals' ongoing activities—they act more in the background of other activities (Morris, 1989). For example, we may be in a happy mood, but still continue all our daily activities. Due to this "background character", the consequences of moods are particularly evident in a wide spectrum of processes. We will discuss these consequences with respect to how mood influences individuals' memory, their social judgments, and their style of information processing.

Mood and memory

In Chapter 3 we discussed how the accessibility of concepts strongly influences encoding processes, and in Chapters 4 and 5 it became clear that accessibility of information has a pronounced impact on social judgments. One central assumption of the affect and cognition research holds that the accessibility of information stored in memory is influenced by individuals' affective states, that is, that affective states influence the nature of the information that comes to mind. An example for mood-dependent accessibility of information is reported by Bower (1981). He found that when asked about events in their kindergarten time, individuals recalled more positive than negative events when they were in a happy mood at the time of retrieval, whereas they recalled more negative than positive events when they were in a sad mood at the time of retrieval (see Figure 7.1).

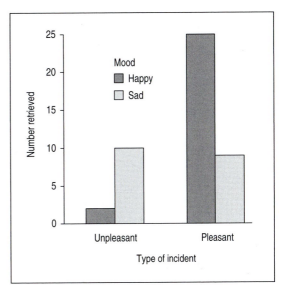

Figure 7.1.

Mood influences individuals' memory. Number of retrieved incidents as a function of retrieval mood and valence of incident (data from Bower, 1981).

The findings obtained in the "kindergarten study" thus support the notion that when we are in a happy mood, we are more likely to recall positive rather than negative events of our past. The assumption that affective states influence the accessibility of information was conceptualized in Gordon Bower's associative network model of human memory (1981). The general logic of this model is derived from prior associative network models (for example, J. R. Anderson & Bower, 1973). Within associative network models memory is conceptualized as a network of nodes each representing a particular concept. The nodes are linked to other nodes and once a concept is activated, it can activate other associated nodes (for a more detailed discussion see Chapter 3). Bower's model holds that affective states function as central nodes in such an associative network. As can be seen in Figure 7.2, these affective nodes are linked to related ideas and events of correspondent valence. In addition, the nodes are also linked to autonomic activity as well as to the muscular and expressive pattern that usually accompanies a particular affective state. When new material is learned, it is associated and linked with the nodes that are active at the time of learning (*encoding*). For example, when you encounter a new acquaintance in a happy mood, this encounter will be associated with that happy mood. When you encounter the new acquaintance in a sad mood, this encounter will be associated with sad mood. Conversely, when an affective node is activated, the

Figure 7.2.

Associative Network
Model (after Bower,
1981).

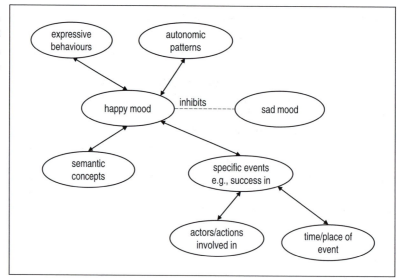

concepts connected to it will receive activation and are more likely to come to mind. As a consequence, being in a happy mood will increase the chance that you remember the encounter with the new acquaintance when you were in a happy mood during the initial encounter.

Two central hypotheses were derived from Bower's model. First, the *state-dependency hypothesis* holds that recall is improved when individuals are in the same affective state at encoding and retrieval. For example, participants were more likely to recall more positive and less negative experiences from their time in kindergarten when they were in a happy rather than in a sad mood (see Figure 7.1). Note that this hypothesis is not restricted to information that is valenced, i.e., positive or negative information. When studying affectively neutral words (e.g., paper, window, etc.), they are more likely to be recalled when the affective state at encoding matches the affective state at retrieval. Second, the *mood-congruent recall hypothesis* holds that material is more likely to be recalled if its affective tone matches the individuals' affective state at the time of retrieval. For example, individuals in a positive mood are more likely to recall words with a positive connotation, such as friendly, nice, beautiful, whereas individuals in a negative mood are more likely to recall words with a negative connotation (Bower, 1981). Note that the state-dependency hypothesis focuses on a match of affective states at encoding and retrieval whereas the mood-congruency hypothesis focuses on the match of affective state at retrieval and the valence of the information.

Initially, the two hypotheses received considerable support (see Bower, 1981). However, subsequent research revealed that effects of mood-dependent memory were less reliable than was initially assumed (see Clore et al., 1994; Eich & Macaulay, 2000). First, it has been found that mood congruency effects are less likely if the stimulus material is highly structured. Presumably the structure, that is the strong association within the material, has such a strong effect that the impact of mood on accessibility is no longer detectable. Imagine, for example, that two lists of words are to be memorized. One list comprises the word "cat" and is learned in a happy mood, whereas the second list is learned in a sad mood and comprises the word "dog." According to the state-dependency hypothesis, "cat" should be more likely to be recalled in a happy mood, and "dog" should be more likely to be recalled in a sad mood. However, because there is a strong associative link between "cat" and "dog," the two words are likely to be recalled together, although they were learned in different affective states. A second interesting observation revealed an asymmetrical pattern of mood congruent recall. On the one hand, happy moods facilitate the recall of happy memories and inhibit the recall of sad memories. On the other hand, however, sad moods may inhibit the recall of happy memories but are less likely to increase the recall of sad memories. Such a pattern is reflected in the results of the kindergarten study (see Figure 7.1). You can see that happy individuals recalled more positive rather than negative events, but that sad individuals recalled an about equal number of positive and negative events. How can this be explained? One account holds that individuals in negative affective states may be motivated to "repair" their mood by attempting "to stop the process of thinking about negative material that might be cued by sadness" (Isen, 1987, p. 217). Research by Alice Isen supports this assumption and suggests that sad individuals' controlled processes (i.e., their attempts to think of positive rather than negative information) may override the automatic impact of sad moods on the accessibility of sad material. Again, we see an interplay of automatic and controlled processes (see Theme 4 of Chapter 2).

Mood and evaluative judgments

Just as common sense suggests, individuals have been found to form more positive judgments when they are in a positive mood and more negative judgments when they are in a negative mood. This tendency for individuals' evaluative judgments to be congruent with their mood state has been reported independent of what the judgmental target pertains to: other persons, consumer products, the quality of life, performance appraisals, and so on (cf. Clore et al., 1994; Forgas, 1992a, 1995a; Schwarz & Clore, 1996).

How can we explain mood-congruent judgments? One explanation rests on Bower's (1981) associative network model, discussed above. It is argued that individuals form their judgments on the basis of the information they recall (see Chapter 5). Due to mood-congruent recall, happy individuals selectively recall positive information and, in turn, their judgments will be more favourable than judgments formed by sad individuals (see Bower, 1991; Forgas, 1992a, 1995a). This logic seems straightforward, and mood-congruent judgments have therefore often been treated as evidence for mood-congruent recall.

A second explanation for mood-congruent judgments was offered by Schwarz and Clore (1983, 1996). Schwarz and Clore question the assumption that mood-congruent judgments are mediated by mood-congruent recall. In proposing the "How-do-I-feel-about-it?" heuristic these authors have suggested that affective states may themselves serve as relevant information in making a judgment. According to this mood-as-information assumption, individuals may simplify complex judgmental tasks by applying a judgmental heuristic (see Chapter 4), specifically by asking themselves, "How do I feel about it?" By doing so, individuals treat their current affective state as their affective reaction to the target as a basis for judgment. For example, when asked to evaluate another person, individuals may not engage in an effortful recall of all relevant information but short cut the processes by asking themselves "How do I feel about this person?" If individuals feel happy they are more likely to evaluate the person positively than if they feel sad. Note that in most cases this seems an adequate strategy. After all, a positive stimulus is more likely to elicit a positive mood than a negative stimulus, and vice versa. For example, it is often quite reasonable to conclude that if we feel happy in the presence of a particular person that this must be a nice person. However, due to the unfocused character of mood states, it is often difficult for individuals to determine the cause of their current feelings and to distinguish between their affective reaction to the object of judgment and their pre-existing mood state. For example, without additional processing, individuals may not be able to differentiate whether their happy mood results from a movie they have just seen, or from the person they encountered when they left the movie theatre. According to this logic, individuals may sometimes misread their pre-existing feelings (here from the happy movie) as a reaction to the target (here to the person they encountered), which results in more favourable evaluations under happy than under sad moods.

Obviously, the mood-as-information approach and the mood-congruent recall hypothesis can both account for the observation of mood-congruent judgments in general. Perhaps most central in the debate over the two approaches, the mood-as-information hypothesis holds that individuals will only use their affective state as a basis of judgment if its informational value has not been called into question. In line with this prediction, the impact of mood on judgment was found to be eliminated if individuals attributed their moods (either correctly or incorrectly) to a source that rendered them irrelevant to the judgment at hand. Related to the above example, when individuals assume that their current mood results from the movie they have just seen and are aware of this influence, their mood is unlikely to influence their judgments of the persons they encounter outside the movie theater. It is argued that such an elimination of mood effects on judgments is unlikely according to the assumption that mood-congruent judgments result from the increased accessibility of mood-congruent information (Schwarz & Clore, 1983; see Box 7.1).

The finding that mood effects were eliminated when individuals did not attribute their mood to the judgmental target is in line with other theorizing that we have discussed in previous chapters (in particular Chapters 4 and 5). Similar to individuals not relying on their mood, individuals did not rely on other feelings, such as feelings of familiarity (Jacoby et al., 1989), or on the ease of retrieval (Schwarz et al., 1991a) when they perceived the feeling as unrelated to the judgmental target. This aspect again emphasizes that it is most often not the affective state per se, but individuals' interpretations of it that influences further processes (see also Chapters 4 and 5). Evidence for the notion that individuals are very flexible in the use of their affective state as a source of information is reported by Martin and colleagues (for an overview see Martin, 2001). This research suggests that experiencing a happy (or sad) mood may not convey the same evaluative implication in every context, but that the implication depends on the configuration of the context. For example, imagine recipients are informed that a particular movie was supposed to make the audience feel sad. In this situation, individuals are more likely to report positive assessments of the movie when they

BOX 7.1.

The "How-do-I-feel-about-it?" heuristic

Schwarz and Clore (1983) suggested that instead of undertaking elaborate analyses of judgmental objects, individuals should ask themselves "How do I feel about it?" and use this feeling as the basis of a judgment. A classic experiment conducted by Schwarz and Clore (1983, Exp. 2) exemplifies the effectiveness of this heuristic. Participants in this study were interviewed on the telephone on either a sunny or a rainy day. Participants were asked for their current mood and assessed their life satisfaction. Not surprisingly, participants were happier on a sunny than on a rainy day. Moreover, they reported themselves to be more satisfied with their life in general on a sunny rather than on a rainy day (see left part of figure). Note that this effect could be mediated by the fact that persons in a good mood remember more positive memory content, and persons in a bad mood more negative content (Bower, 1981), rather than individuals' reliance on the "How-do-I-feel-about-it?" heuristic. In order to exclude this possibility, Schwarz and Clore (1983) introduced additional conditions in which the informational value of the mood was manipulated. Some of the participants were made aware of the fact that the current weather may influence their mood. Note that this manipulation should not influence the activation of mood-congruent material in memory. In contrast, however, directing individuals' attention to the weather as a cause of their mood reduces the informational value for judgments about satisfaction with one's life in general. In other words: Mood is no longer representative for the judgmental object and is therefore no longer used (see section on representativeness in Chapter 5). Consequently, mood effects on judgments of life satisfaction should be reduced when these judgments are based on a "How-do-I-feel-about-it?" heuristic. As can be seen in the right part of the figure, the results support this prediction.

Reported satisfaction with life in general as a function of the weather and participants' attention (after Schwarz & Clore, 1983).

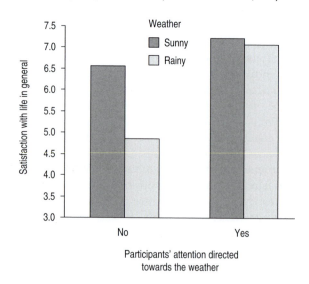

feel sad rather than happy (note, however, that again individuals rely on their affective state as an input for their judgment).

Whereas the results from misattribution studies (see Box 7.1) support the mood-as-information position, there is also evidence in support of the notion that mood-congruent judgments are mediated by mood-congruent recall (Forgas, 1992b, 1995b). In this respect it was found that the more individuals think about a judgment (that is, the more information they retrieve from memory), the more their judgment will reflect their affective state. In other words, according to these findings, mood-congruent judgments become more likely as the amount of processing increases (for overviews see Forgas, 1992a, 1995a).

At the moment the available evidence suggests that mood-congruent judgments may be caused by two different processes. Mood may influence evaluative judgments either directly by serving as a basis of judgment, that is, via a "How-do-I-feel-about-it?" heuristic, or indirectly by influencing what information comes to mind, that is, via mood-congruent recall. Further research will need to investigate the conditions that elicit one process or the other (in this respect see Forgas, 2001; also Bless, 2001, for a more extended discussion of the two accounts).

Mood and processing style

Above we have discussed how affective states may influence individuals' memory and evaluative judgments. In both cases, the primary focus has been on the congruency between the individuals' affective state on the one hand, and the material retrieved from memory or the evaluative judgment on the other. There is, however, a perhaps more intriguing aspect, which suggests that the impact of affective states may extend far beyond this congruency aspect. Affective states may not only influence *what* information is processed, but also *how* it is processed. Indeed, a broad spectrum of research findings has consistently demonstrated that even rather subtle changes in affective states may influence performance in a wide variety of cognitive tasks.

In the previous chapters, we have discussed various aspects related to different styles of information processing. One central aspect pertains to the degree to which individuals' processing is guided by their prior knowledge structures. In the case of a top-down processing, individuals' processing is very strongly based on prior knowledge structures, for example in the form of stereotypes, scripts, and heuristics. In the case of a bottom-up processing, prior knowledge has less impact and individuals' processes are more affected by the data at hand. The general pattern of findings suggests that affective states moderate individuals' reliance on prior knowledge structures. Specifically, happy individuals seem more likely to rely on stereotypes and heuristic processing strategies than sad individuals (for overviews see Bless, 2001; Clore et al., 1994; Isen, 1987). In the remainder of this section we will first discuss major findings on how mood influences cognitive processes in (1) person perception and (2) attitude change, and (3) how mood influences the use of other heuristics. We will then (4) discuss potential explanations for these findings.

Mood and person perception

As we have seen in the previous chapters, individuals may form judgments about other persons via different processing strategies (cf. Fiske & Neuberg, 1990). On the one hand, individuals may extensively rely on their prior knowledge, for example in the form of a stereotype about the social group the target person is assigned to. By assigning a person to the social group of librarians, for example, individuals' prior knowledge may imply that the person is more likely to be introverted than extraverted. On the other hand, individuals may form a judgment by attending more to the individuating information of the specific target, in which case existing stereotypes are less likely to influence judgments. A number of studies have explored whether and how individuals' affective state impacts the different strategies (Bless, Schwarz, & Wieland, 1996c; Bodenhausen et al., 1994a; Bodenhausen, Sheppard, & Kramer, 1994b; Edwards & Weary, 1993; Krauth-Gruber & Ric, 2000). For example, Bodenhausen and colleagues presented participants with a description of a student misconduct. Participants in a happy (but not sad or neutral) mood judged the offender more guilty when he was identified as a member of a group that is stereotypically associated with the described offence—reflecting a more pronounced impact of the stereotype under happy mood (see Box 7.2 for a more detailed description of the study).

The counterintuitive finding that happy moods do not necessarily result in more positive, but often in more stereotypic, judgments is also reflected in research addressing the perception of in-groups (perceiver and judgmental target belong to the same group) versus out-groups (perceiver and judgmental target belong to different

BOX 7.2.

More stereotyping under happy mood?

Bodenhausen, Kramer, and Süsser (1994a) investigated the assumption that a happy mood would increase individuals' reliance on stereotypes in person perception. The researchers experimentally induced either a happy or a neutral mood and provided participants with a description of a student misconduct. The description was held constant, except for the name of the alleged offender. In one condition, the offender had a hispanic name (Roberto Gonzales), presumably triggering the corresponding stereotype that is associated with aggressiveness. In another condition, no particular stereotype could be associated with the offender's name (Robert Garner). Participants were asked to rate the offender's guilt in the described incident. Because the descriptions were identical except for the names, differences in perceived guilt can be attributed to participants' reliance on their stereotype. As can be seen in the figure, the offender's name influenced participants in a happy mood, who judged the offender more guilty when he was identified as a member of a group that is stereotypically associated with the described offence, whereas no impact of the name was observed for neutral-mood participants. These findings reflect a more pronounced impact of the stereotype under happy mood.

Happy participants attributed more guilt to the offender when he was a member of a group that is stereotypically associated with aggression than when no stereotype was applicable. This effect was not observed for individuals in nonmanipulated neutral moods (after Bodenhausen et al., 1995).

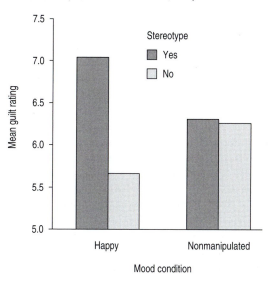

groups). Similarly, suggesting an increased impact of the social category on participants in a happy mood, Forgas and Fiedler (1996) report that happy individuals were more likely to discriminate against the out-group, unless the situation implied a high relevance of the group membership information. In line with these findings, Abele and colleagues (Abele, Gendolla, & Petzold, 1998; see also Abele 2000); found that when participants evaluated a target, the targets' group membership (in-group versus out-group) received more weight when participants were in a happy rather than an average mood. Moreover, inducing a positive mood during inter-group contact resulted in less favourable evaluations of the out-group when the groups were in immediate competition or had a history of prior conflict (Dovidio, Gaertner, & Loux, 2000).

At first glance, these findings on the negative impact of positive affective states seem contrary to research suggesting that negative affective states trigger stereotyping and out-group discrimination (for example the classic scapegoat theory; see Bless, Schwarz, & Kemmel-meier, 1996b, for an overview). The potential solution presumably rests on whether individuals perceive their negative affect as a result of the target person ("integral affect," see Bodenhausen, 1993), in which case negative affect will cause more negative judgments, or whether individuals perceive their negative affect as a result of the current situation in general ("incidental affect," Bodenhausen, 1993). In the latter case negative affect will cause less reliance on stereotypes; depending on the valence of the stereotype, either positive or negative evaluations will become more likely.

Mood and persuasion

Similar to judgments about other persons, attitude judgments following a persuasive communication may reflect two different processing strategies (Eagly & Chaiken, 1993; Petty & Cacioppo, 1986; see the module on *Attitudes and Attitude Change* by Bohner & Wänke, 2002). On the one hand, individuals may elaborate on the presented arguments of a persuasive message. In this case, strong arguments should lead to more yielding to the communication's intention than weak arguments. Alternatively, individuals may base their judgments on peripheral cues, for example the communicator's attractiveness. In this case, argument quality should play a minor role. Researchers have exposed participants in different affective states to either weak or strong arguments. In general, participants in sad moods reported more favourable attitudes toward the advocated position when they were confronted with strong rather than with weak arguments. In contrast, happy participants were not affected by argument quality (e.g., Bless, Bohner, Schwarz, & Strack, 1990; Mackie & Worth, 1989); see Box 7.3 for an example of those studies. These findings were complemented by the observation that attitudes of participants in happy but not neutral moods reflect the presence of peripheral cues (e.g., Mackie & Worth, 1989; see also Bohner, Crow, Erb, & Schwarz, 1992, for an extension of these findings from attitudinal judgments to behaviour).

If we equate the reliance on stereotypes with the reliance on peripheral cues, and reliance on the presented arguments with the reliance on individuating information, these findings converge with those obtained in the person perception domain. In both cases, individuals in a happy mood are more likely to rely on heuristics or stereotypes, while individuals in a sad mood are more likely to attend to the specific information provided in the specific situation.

Mood and other heuristics

The conclusion that happy individuals are more likely to rely on heuristic processing strategies is not restricted to domains of person perception and persuasion. For example, Isen and colleagues report that happy moods increase the likelihood that individuals rely on an availability heuristic (Tversky & Kahneman, 1973) when making frequency judgments (Isen, Means, Patrick, & Nowicki, 1982). In a related vein, happy moods have been found to increase the reliance on other forms of general knowledge structures. For example, when encoding a sequence of events that characterize typical activities, happy individuals are more likely than sad individuals to rely on pre-existing scripts. When confronted with a recognition test, happy individuals more readily recognize information consistent with script as previously presented, resulting in more hits for presented items and more intrusion errors for nonpresented items (Bless et al., 1996). This recall pattern suggests that happy individuals were more likely than sad individuals to rely on their prior knowledge in form of a pre-existing script when encoding the new information.

Explaining mood effects on style of information processing

The reported research on the impact of mood on processes involved in person perception and persuasion suggests that rather minor

BOX 7.3.

More or less persuasion: A function of recipients' mood?

A number of studies have investigated how recipients in different affective states react toward persuasive messages, that is toward attempts to change their attitudes. For example, Bless, Mackie, and Schwarz (1992) asked participants to provide a detailed description of either a positive or a negative life-event. As expected, working on this task elicited either a positive or a negative mood, respectively. After this task, participants listened to a tape-recorded message in which an increase in student fees was announced. Depending on the experimental condition, the message comprised arguments that were pre-tested to be either strong or weak. Subsequently, participants reported their attitudes toward the increase. As can be seen in the figure, participants in a sad mood were more persuaded by strong than by weak arguments, whereas message quality did not influence participants in a happy mood. Obviously, when forming their attitude judgments, sad but not happy individuals took into account the information provided by the message.

Note that, similar to other research addressing this topic, there was no main effect of mood. That is, it was not the case that the persuasive message was more effective for happy than for sad participants. The reported attitudes reflected an interaction of mood and message quality. This implies that when communicators have weak arguments they can increase their chances to change recipients' attitudes when they improve their recipients' mood—this strategy can often be observed in advertising strategies. The findings, however, also imply that when communicators have strong arguments for their case, they should refrain from further increasing their recipients' mood, because then recipients may not take the strong arguments into account.

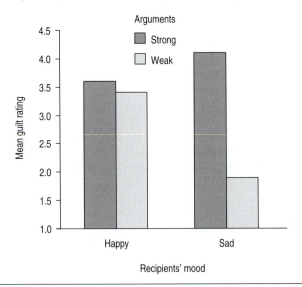

Sad recipients were more strongly influenced by a message comprising strong rather than weak arguments. In contrast, happy recipients were equally persuaded by strong and weak arguments (data from Bless, Mackie, & Schwarz, 1992).

changes of individuals' affective states can have a pronounced impact on how social information is processed. How can we account for these findings? The offered explanations emphasize different aspects, such as processing capacity, processing motivation, mood management, or a general reliance on heuristics under happy moods.

First, it has been suggested that individuals in a happy mood may have fewer cognitive resources than individuals in a neutral mood (Mackie & Worth, 1989). This line of reasoning holds that individuals usually have more positive than negative material stored in memory. As a consequence, more material is potentially activated in memory if individuals are in a happy rather than a sad mood (see considerations on mood-dependent memory outlined above). Due to this activation, happy individuals have fewer resources available for other tasks. As a consequence, happy individuals would be more likely to rely on less taxing strategies, that is, on top-down or heuristic processing. In line with this line of reasoning it has been found that providing extra processing time, that is, reducing the processing load, eliminated the differences between happy and sad mood participants (Mackie & Worth, 1989).

Second, it has been argued that happy moods may reduce individuals' processing motivation. The reduced processing motivation in turn increases the likelihood that happy individuals rely on their prior knowledge structure in the form of stereotypes or heuristics. Different assumptions have been made about why being happy should reduce processing motivation. Focusing on mood management, it has been argued that individuals are motivated to maintain positive affective states and to eliminate negative affective states (Isen, 1987; Wegener & Petty, 1994). Assuming that strenuous cognitive processes interfere with the goal of maintaining positive mood states, researchers argue that individuals in happy moods are less motivated to invest cognitive effort than sad individuals—and in turn they rely on heuristic processing strategies.

A third approach emphasizes the *informative function of affective states*. It is proposed that the affective state may inform the individual about the nature of the current situation (Schwarz, 1990; Schwarz & Clore, 1996). Not surprisingly, individuals usually feel good in situations that are characterized by positive outcomes and/or in situations that do not threaten their current goals. In contrast, individuals usually feel bad in situations that threaten their current goals because of the presence of negative outcomes or the lack of positive outcomes. If so, individuals may consult their affect as a usually valid and quick indicator as to the nature of the current psychological situation. Feeling good would imply that the situation poses no problem, while feeling bad would imply that the current situation is problematic. It is now assumed that individuals in a bad mood are more motivated to engage in detail-orientated systematic processing strategies, which are typically adaptive in handling problematic situations. In contrast, individuals in a good mood may see little reason to spontaneously engage in strenuous processing strategies, unless this is called for by other goals (see Schwarz, 1990). As a consequence, happy individuals will rely more strongly on top-down or heuristic processing whereas sad individuals will attend more to the specifics of the situation and a bottom-up processing. In line with this line of reasoning it has been found that increasing participants' processing motivation, for example by telling them that they would later need to justify their judgments, eliminated the differences between happy and sad mood participants (e.g., Bodenhausen et al., 1994a; see also Bless et al., 1990).

Fourth, it has been suggested that the observed processing differences between happy and sad individuals are not mediated by differences in either processing motivation or processing capacity. Again it is argued that happy moods signal an unproblematic situation. However, this does not imply (or not only) a reduced processing motivation as described above but it may directly imply that it is all right to rely on prior knowledge when constructing social reality. Thus happy individuals may rely on their prior knowledge but may not lack cognitive resources or processing motivation, as implied by the other approaches (Bless et al., 1996a; see Fiedler, 2000, for a similar position). In a study supporting this assumption (Bless et al., 1996a), participants listened to a tape-recorded story about a scripted activity. When later asked to recall the provided information, happy participants committed more intrusion errors than sad participants, that is, they recalled script-consistent information that was not actually presented. This suggests that happy participants relied more strongly on top-down processing than sad participants. In this study, participants simultaneously worked on a second task, a concentration test, while they were listening to the scripted information. The results of this test showed that happy participants outperformed sad participants on this secondary task. The combination of the results of the recall test and the concentration test suggests that, by relying on top-down processing, happy participants spared resources they could then allocate to the secondary task. The improved performance on the secondary task argues against the notion that happy moods reduce processing capacity or motivation.

In combination, the various results suggest that the differential reliance on heuristic processing strategies is a rather robust finding. While the effect is widely accepted and supported by evidence from different domains (see examples from person perception and persuasion described above), the exact mechanisms underlying these differences are still debated. Researchers have provided evidence for each of the outlined theoretical positions (note that the different positions make very similar predictions for a wide spectrum of phenomena). Future research will need to determine the conditions under which the different mechanisms may mediate the impact of mood on individuals' construction of social reality.

Let us return to the starting question of this chapter: With all the emphasis on cognitive aspects in social cognition research, is there a place for individuals' feelings? Although the reported evidence reflects only a small selection of research from the affect and cognition domain (see recommendations for further reading for a wider coverage) it has become obvious that many of our social judgments and behaviours are profoundly influenced by our affective feelings. Social cognition research emphasizes the important role of affective states and provides models on how affective states influence social thinking. Most importantly, much of the available current research suggests that affect is not necessarily creating irrationalities, but that in most cases individuals' affective state provides a very useful source for the regulation of cognitive processes and for the interpretation of the social situation. Social cognition research is thus far away from conceptualizing the human being as a cold and emotionless information-processing machine. On the contrary, affective feelings, either as an antecedent or as a consequence of cognitive processes, are at the very heart of social cognition.

Chapter summary

(1) The impact of affective states on cognitive processes is a widely acknowledged phenomenon and research within the social cognition paradigm has accumulated substantive evidence in support of affective influences on cognitive processes. In contrast to the notion that affective states reduce individuals' cognitive abilities, this research suggests that affective states play an important adaptive role and support individuals in their construction of social reality. Affective states have been

demonstrated to influence a wide spectrum of cognitive processes, among them influences on memory, on evaluative judgments, and on the style of information processing.

(2) Affective states may automatically influence the accessibility of information stored in memory. Information is more likely to be recalled when it is congruent with the current affective state (mood-congruent recall hypothesis) or when it was initially stored in a similar affective state (state-dependency hypothesis). This impact of affective states on memory is less likely with highly structured rather than with unstructured material. Individuals may be motivated to repair their negative affective states. They may do this by retrieving positive rather than negative information from memory.

(3) The finding that evaluative judgments are often congruent with individuals' current affective state is very robust and has been observed in a wide spectrum of domains. On the one hand, it has been explained by the increased accessibility of mood-congruent material. On the other hand, it has been suggested that individuals use their affective state itself as information and employ a "How-do-I-feel-about-it?" heuristic.

(4) Subtle differences in individuals' affective state have been demonstrated to influence their style of information processing. Happy individuals seem more likely to rely on heuristics and general knowledge structures than sad individuals. The different explanations discuss whether and how these differences are mediated by individuals' processing capacity, processing motivation, or reliance on general knowledge structures.

Discussion questions

(1) What is the difference between the state-dependency and the mood-congruent recall hypothesis? Can you think of examples where it is difficult to distinguish the two theoretical mechanisms?

(2) Discuss the two explanations for mood-congruent judgments. Think of everyday examples and consider the implications of mood-congruent judgments.

(3) Consider the automatic activation of mood-congruent material in memory. What would happen if we were not able to counteract this automatic activation, in particular when we are in a sad, depressed mood?

(4) What impact does mood have on individuals' reliance on stereotypes? Discuss the findings obtained by Bodenhausen and colleagues.

(5) What explanations can account for individuals' reliance on heuristics and general knowledge structures as a function of their affective state? What evidence is reported in support of each position?

(6) In supermarkets, many attempts are made to put shoppers in a better mood (e.g., music, small gifts, etc.) Discuss why this might be an effective strategy. Under which circumstances would this strategy be less effective?

Recommendations for further reading

Clore, G. L., Schwarz, N., & Conway, M. (1994). Cognitive causes and consequences of emotion. In R. S. Wyer & T. K. Srull (Eds.), *Handbook of social cognition* (Vol. 1, 2nd ed., pp. 323–417). Hillsdale, NJ: Lawrence Erlbaum Associates Inc.

This chapter provides an overview on the interplay of affect and cognition. It also incorporates how different affective states result from different cognitive processes.

Forgas, J. P. (1995a). Mood and judgment: The affect infusion model (AIM). *Psychological Bulletin, 117*, 39–66.

This paper provides an overview on research supporting the idea that mood-congruent judgments are mediated by mood-congruent recall, and that this relation depends on individuals' processing mode.

Schwarz, N., & Clore, G. L. (1996). Feelings and phenomenal experiences. In E. T. Higgins & A. W. Kruglanski (Eds.), *Social psychology: A handbook of basic principles* (pp. 433–465). New York: Guilford Press.

This chapter provides an overview of a wide spectrum of research findings, thereby emphasizing the informative function of affective states. Moreover it also captures so-called "no-affective" feelings, for example, ease of retrieval or feeling of familiarity.

Concluding remarks 8

The previous chapters have made clear that in order to understand how individuals behave in the social world we need to understand how individuals *think* about the social world. We need to understand how individuals transfer the "objective" situation into their subjective reality, in other words, how they construct social reality. Social cognition research focuses exactly on these internal processes. In borrowing concepts from cognitive psychology and applying them to social phenomena, social cognition research deals with the psychological processes that are involved when individuals think about the social world.

The previous chapters have provided an introduction to the key concepts, the basic assumptions, and the major findings of social cognition research. We discussed how social information is encoded, how the information is stored and retrieved from memory, how social knowledge is structured and represented, and what processes are involved when individuals form judgments and make decisions. Instead of exhaustively covering existing research findings, we chose to focus on the basic concepts and on the broader picture of the social cognition framework, which we hope will make it easier to grasp the core ideas. This selectiveness is in large parts covered by other textbooks in this series.

Despite the selectiveness of this introductory overview, it should be apparent from the previous chapters that over the last two to three decades, social cognition research has been very successful and has exerted a strong impact on numerous areas inside and outside social psychology. Within the broader discipline of social psychology, social cognition research has provided important contributions for virtually every field in social psychology, such as attitudes, perception of persons and groups, aggression, helping behaviour, or interpersonal attraction (for an overview, see Higgins & Kruglanski, 1996). Nowadays almost any publication in social psychology is faced with the request not only to demonstrate the phenomenon, but also to investigate the underlying cognitive mechanisms. The emphasis on processes has also made it possible for research findings in social cognition to be rapidly adopted by areas outside social psychology, for example clinical psychology (e.g., Abramson, 1988), consumer psychology (e.g., Kardes, 1999), survey methodology (e.g., Sudman, Bradburn, & Schwarz, 1996), or health psychology (e.g., Stroebe, 2000).

While social cognition can thus be described as a very successful enterprise, it also has to face a number of challenges. Without going into too much detail, we want to address two such challenges that appear extremely important to us. First, in most social cognition research individuals are quasi "assigned" to social situations, and they are *provided* with information. Thereby it is often neglected that in reality individuals themselves determine which situation they enter, and they often select information actively rather than being passively provided with it. While this may not be a crucial aspect for many research questions, it becomes particularly important when we assume that this research situation influences and changes the psychological processes to be investigated (for a discussion see also Schwarz, 2000). Different processes (with different consequences) may thus be going on when individuals are provided with a description about a person, or when they actively infer the content of such a description themselves. We believe that future social cognition research will benefit from emphasizing and investigating how individuals themselves shape and influence their social situation—and how this activity influences cognitive processes.

Second, after taking a look at the accumulated research in social cognition one may conclude that it can mainly be specified as "semantic" social cognition. Research participants are provided with verbal descriptions of social situations (persons, groups, attitude objects, etc.); then, not only is the "input" given semantically, in many cases the "output," that is, participants' responses, are also strongly confined to words and semantic meanings. They give their responses on scales with verbal endpoints, they have to recall semantic information from memory, etc. In everyday life, many aspects of social life are not—or at least are less directly—linked to semantics. It is probably not the same whether (a) a person is semantically labelled as "Chinese" or whether (b) we see a person who is—among many other aspects—Chinese. If, however, the two situations differ in the cognitive processes (for evidence in this respect see, for example, Gilbert & Hixon, 1991) they elicit, then research that focuses primarily on semantic information provides only part of the picture. At the moment, we do not really know how profound such differences are, but it is surely an important challenge for social cognition research to investigate this issue.

We believe that social cognition will face the various challenges and will continue to influence social psychology profoundly. The exact nature of its future influence is difficult to predict. Independent of the various possible future directions of social cognition, we hope that this book has elicited interest in this highly fascinating field and encouraged readers to pursue it in greater depth.

Glossary

accessibility: The ease and speed with which information stored in memory is found and retrieved.

accountability: Requirement for research participants to justify a generated judgment to others; used to foster systematic (as opposed to heuristic) information processing.

acquiescence bias: Tendency to provide more yes than no responses in interviews and survey research.

activation: Transfer of information from inactive long-term memory to active working memory.

anchoring: An assimilation of a judgment toward a numeric value that has previously been considered.

applicability: Whether a concept can potentially be used to give meaning to a specific stimulus. Whether or not the concept is actually used also depends on the concept's accessibility.

assimilation effect: Judgments of a stimulus are biased towards the position of a context stimulus on the judgment scale.

attention: Processes that enable individuals to selectively attend to the (social) environment.

attribution theory: Deals with the processes that are involved when individuals try to explain behaviour or events.

attribution: Individuals' inferences about the cause of behaviours or events.

automatic processes: Cognitive processes that are initiated and run without controlled processes, requiring no or very few attentional resources.

availability: Judgmental heuristic for judging the frequency or probability of events on the basis of the ease with which relevant memories come to mind.

base rate: Frequency of a characteristic in a relevant population or sample.

bottom-up processing: Information processing that is driven by new stimulus input rather than by abstract knowledge structures in memory; see also top-down processing.

category: Elementary knowledge structure. Class of functionally similar objects sharing one or more features.

cognitive miser: Metaphor for the assumption that individuals try to avoid elaborative and extensive information processing and often rely on simplifying short cuts and heuristics.

concept-driven processing: See top-down processing.

conjunction fallacy: Overestimating the likelihood of a joint occurrence of several characteristics on the basis of similarity.

consistency theories: Hold that individuals experience an aversive state when they perceive that they hold inconsistent beliefs about the social world. Because individuals try to avoid or eliminate this aversive state, they process information in a biased fashion so that perceived inconsistencies are reduced.

constructive memory: Self-generated, imagined, or inferred information is erroneously remembered as if it had been actually experienced.

context dependency: The notion that social judgments (and the underlying processes) are highly dependent on the situational context in which they are formed. For example, a person may be judged more positively in one situation than in another simply because different standards of comparisons are accessible and applied.

contrast effect: Judgments of a stimulus are biased in the direction opposite to the position of a context stimulus on the judgment scale.

controlled processes: Cognitive processes that are consciously initiated by the individual, usually requiring substantial cognitive resources.

data-driven processing: See bottom-up processing.

encoding: Comprises various processes that are involved when an external stimulus is transformed into an internal representation so that it can be retained by the cognitive system. This requires that the external stimulus is given some meaning by relating the new stimulus to prior knowledge.

episodic memory: Memory of experienced events that are tied to particular times and places.

illusory correlations: Observers believe they have seen a correlation in a series of stimulus events, although the actually presented correlation has been absent or clearly lower.

Implicit Association Test (IAT): Computerized procedure for measuring association tendencies related to attitudes and prejudice, based on the sorting speed for attitude objects and relevant attributes.

incidental affect: Affective state that is perceived as independent of the judgmental target.

integral affect: Affective state that is perceived as a result of the judgmental target.

judgmental heuristic: Rules of thumb that allow quick and economic judgments even under high uncertainty.

linguistic inter-group bias: The tendency to describe positive in-group behaviour and negative out-group behaviour in more abstract linguistic terms than negative in-group and positive out-group behaviour.

metacognition: Cognitive processes that involve knowledge about knowledge or processes; for example, knowing that we do not know the answer to a specific question.

mood as information: The notion that affective states may themselves serve as relevant information in making a judgment.

mood-congruent judgment: The tendency to provide more positive judgments in positive rather than negative affective states.

mood-congruent recall: The tendency to recall information that is congruent with one's affective states, for example recalling positive events in happy moods and negative events in sad moods.

mood management: The notion that individuals are motivated to maintain positive affective states and to eliminate negative affective states and consequently engage in cognitive processes that allow them to attain these goals; for example to intentionally think of positive events when in a sad mood.

network models: Conceptualizations of human memory that assume a system of nodes and connections.

positive testing: Selective information search for those events or behaviours that are stated in the hypothesis under focus.

priming effect: The finding that a schema is more accessible and hence more likely to be activated when it has recently been presented or used in the past.

representativeness: Representativeness heuristic for judging category membership on the basis of various aspects of similarity.

retrieval: Processes that are involved when individuals retrieve information from long-term memory into working memory.

salience: The distinctiveness of a stimulus relative to the context reflected in its ability to attract attention (for example, a male in a group of females; a group of people of whom one is in the spotlight).

schema: Knowledge structure linked to adaptive function. Once a schema is activated by specific events, specific reactions are triggered.

script: Temporally organized behavioural routine.

self-fulfilling prophecy: An expectancy-based illusion in social hypothesis testing. Subject persons treat object persons in such a fashion that object persons eventually verify their original (often unjustified) expectations.

self-reference effect: Memory advantage for stimuli that have been encoded or judged in relation to the self.

shared-information effect: In-group decision making, information shared by different group members is more likely to be considered, and is given more weight, than unshared information that is exclusively available to individual members.

state-dependency: Describes the general finding that memory performance is enhanced if individuals are in the same psychological state (e.g., the same mood) at both the time of encoding and the time of retrieval.

stereotype: Category-like knowledge structure associated with a social group. Judgment of persons on the basis of characteristics of their social group.

subliminal: On a subconscious level; out of awareness.

top-down processing: Information processing that is driven by general, superordinate knowledge structures in memory (e.g., schema, stereotype) that influences the perception of new stimuli; see also bottom-up processing.

truncated search process: When searching in memory for applicable information (e.g., for encoding, or for computing a judgment), individuals are unlikely to search for all potentially relevant information but instead truncate the search processes. Due to this truncation, information that has a higher accessibility is more influential.

working memory: The part of our memory system that is currently activated; it has little processing capacity. In order to enter into long-term memory, information has to pass through working memory. Conversely, information from long-term memory needs to enter working memory in order to affect ongoing processes, judgments, and behaviours.

References

Abele, A. (2000) The experience of a positive mood and its impact on inter-group differentiation and stereotyping. In H. Bless & J. P. Forgas (Eds.), *The message within: The role of subjective experience in social cognition and behavior* (pp. 322–339). Philadelphia, PA: Psychology Press.

Abele, A., Gendolla, G. H. E., & Petzold, P. (1998). Positive mood and in-group–out-group differentiation in a minimal group setting. *Personality and Social Psychology Bulletin, 24*, 1343–1357.

Abelson, R. P., Aronson, E., McGuire, W. J., Newcomb, T. M., Rosenberg, M. J., & Tannenbaum, P. H. (Eds.) (1968). *Theories of cognitive consistency: A sourcebook.* Chicago: Rand McNally.

Abramson, L. Y. (Ed.) (1988). *Social cognition and clinical psychology: A synthesis.* New York: Guilford Press.

Ajzen, I., & Fishbein, M. (1980). *Understanding attitudes and predicting social behavior.* Englewood Cliffs, NJ: Prentice Hall.

Anderson, J. R., & Bower, G. H. (1973). *Human associative memory.* Washington, DC: Winston.

Anderson, N. H. (1981). *The foundations of information integration theory.* New York: Academic Press.

Ash, S. E. (1946). Forming impressions of personality. *Journal of Abnormal and Social Psychology, 41*, 258–290.

Bargh, J. A. (1994). The four horsemen of automaticity. In R. S. Wyer & T. K. Srull (Eds.), *Handbook of social cognition* (pp. 1–40). Hillsdale, NJ: Lawrence Erlbaum Associates Inc.

Bargh, J. A. (1999). The cognitive monster: The case against the controllability of automatic stereotype effects. In S. Chaiken & Y. Trope (Eds.), *Dual process theories in social psychology* (pp. 361–382). New York: Guilford Press.

Bargh, J. A., Chen, M., & Burrows, L. (1996). Automaticity of social behavior: Direct effects of trait construct and stereotype activation on action. *Journal of Personality and Social Psychology, 71*, 230–244.

Bargh, J. A., & Pietromonaco, P. (1982). Automatic information processing and social perception: The influence of trait information presented outside of conscious awareness on impression formation. *Journal of Personality and Social Psychology, 43*, 437–449.

Bar-Hillel, M., & Neter, E. (1993). How alike is it versus how likely is it: A disjunction fallacy in probability judgments. *Journal of Personality and Social Psychology, 65*, 1119–1131.

Barsalou, L. W. (1985). Ideals, central tendency, and frequency of instantiation as determinants of graded structure in categories. *Journal of Experimental Psychology: Learning, Memory, and Cognition, 11*, 629–654.

Bar-Tal, D., & Kruglanski, A. W. (Eds.) (1988). *The social psychology of knowledge.*

Cambridge: Cambridge University Press.

Bartlett, F. C. (1932). *Remembering: A study in experimental and social psychology.* Cambridge: Cambridge University Press.

Bem, D. J. (1967). Self-perception: An alternative interpretation of cognitive dissonance phenomena. *Psychological Review, 74*, 183–200.

Berry, D. S., & Zebrowitz-McArthur, L. (1988). What's in a face? Facial maturity and the attribution of legal responsibility. *Personality and Social Psychology Bulletin, 14*, 23–33.

Berscheid, E., Graziano, W., & Monson, T. (1976). Outcome dependency: Attention, attribution, and attraction. *Journal of Personality and Social Psychology, 34*, 978–989.

Betsch, T., & Fiedler, K. (1999). Understanding conjunction effects in probability judgments: The role of implicit mental models. *European Journal of Social Psychology, 29*, 75–93.

Blair, I. V., & Banaji, M. R. (1996). Automatic and controlled processes in stereotype priming. *Journal of Personality and Social Psychology, 70*, 1142–1163.

Bless, H. (2001). The consequences of mood on the processing of social information. In A. Tesser & N. Schwarz (Eds.), *Blackwell handbook in social psychology* (pp. 391–412). Oxford: Blackwell Publishers.

Bless, H., Bohner, G., Schwarz, N., & Strack, F. (1990). Mood and persuasion: A cognitive response analysis. *Personality and Social Psychology Bulletin, 16*, 331–345.

Bless, H., Clore, G. L, Schwarz, N., Golisano, V., Rabe, C., & Wölk, M. (1996a). Mood and the use of scripts: Does happy mood make people really mindless? *Journal of Personality and Social Psychology, 63*, 585–595.

Bless, H., & Forgas, J. P. (Eds.) (2000). *The message within: The role of subjective*

experience in social cognition and behavior. Philadelphia, PA: Psychology Press.

Bless, H., Mackie, D. M., & Schwarz, N. (1992). Mood effects on encoding and judgmental processes in persuasion. *Journal of Personality and Social Psychology, 63*, 585–595.

Bless, H., & Schwarz, N. (1998). Context effects in political judgment: Assimilation and contrast as a function of categorization processes. *European Journal of Social Psychology, 28*, 159–172.

Bless, H., Schwarz, N., Bodenhausen, G. V., & Thiel, L. (2001). Personalized versus generalized benefits of stereotype disconfirmation: Tradeoffs in the evaluation of atypical exemplars and their social groups. *Journal of Experimental Social Psychology, 37*, 386–397.

Bless, H., Schwarz, N., & Kemmelmeier, M. (1996b). Mood and stereotyping: Affective states and the use of general knowledge structures. In W. Stroebe & M. Hewstone (Eds.), *European review of social psychology* (Vol. 7, pp. 63–93). New York: Wiley.

Bless, H., Schwarz, N., & Wieland, R. (1996c). Mood and stereotyping: The impact of category and individuating information. *European Journal of Social Psychology, 26*, 935–959.

Bless, H., & Strack, F. (1998). Social influence on memory: Evidence and speculations. In V. Yzerbyt, G. Lories, & B. Dardenne (Eds.), *Metacognition: cognitive and social dimensions* (pp. 90–106). Thousand Oaks, CA: Sage.

Bless, H., Strack, F., & Schwarz, N. (1993). The informative functions of research procedures: Bias and the logic of conversation. *European Journal of Social Psychology, 23*, 149–165.

Bless, H., & Wänke, M. (2000). Can the same information be typical and atypical? How perceived typicality moderates assimilation and contrast in evaluative judgments. *Personality and Social Psychology Bulletin, 26*, 306–314.

Block, R. A., & Harper, D. R. (1991). Overconfidence in estimation: Testing the anchoring-and-adjustment hypothesis. *Organizational Behavior and Human Decision Processes, 49*, 188–207.

Bodenhausen, G. V. (1993). Emotions, arousal, and stereotype-based discrimination: A heuristic model of affect and stereotyping. In D. M. Mackie & D. L. Hamilton (Eds.), *Affect, cognition, and stereotyping: Interactive processes in group perception* (pp. 13–35). San Diego, CA: Academic Press.

Bodenhausen, G. V., Kramer, G. P., & Süsser, K. (1994). Happiness and stereotypic thinking in social judgment. *Journal of Personality and Social Psychology, 66*, 621–632.

Bodenhausen, G. V., & Lichtenstein, M. (1987). Social stereotypes and information-processing strategies: The impact of task complexity. *Journal of Personality and Social Psychology, 52*, 871–880.

Bodenhausen, G. V., Macrae, C. N., & Sherman, J. S. (1999). On the dialectics of discrimination: Dual processes in social stereotyping. In S. Chaiken & Y. Trope (Eds.), *Dual-process theories in social psychology* (pp. 271–290). New York: Guilford Press.

Bodenhausen, G. V., Schwarz, N., Bless, H., & Wänke, M. (1995). Effects of atypical exemplars on racial beliefs: Enlightened racism or generalized appraisal? *Journal of Experimental Social Psychology, 31*, 48–63.

Bodenhausen, G. V., Sheppard, L. A., & Kramer, G. P. (1994b). Negative affect and social judgment: The differential impact of anger and sadness. *European Journal of Social Psychology, 24*, 45–62.

Bohner, G., Crow, K., Erb, H.-P., & Schwarz, N. (1992). Affect and persuasion: Mood effects on the processing of message content and context cues. *European Journal of Social Psychology, 22*, 511–530.

Bohner, G., Moskowitz, G., & Chaiken, S. (1995). The interplay of heuristic and systematic processing of social information. In W. Stroebe & M. Hewstone (Eds.), *European review of social psychology* (Vol. 6). Chichester, UK: Wiley.

Bohner, G., & Wänke, M. (2002). *Attitudes and attitude change.* [Social psychology: A modular course.] New York: Psychology Press.

Bohner, G., Weisbrod, C., Raymond, P., Barzvi, A., & Schwarz, N. (1993). Salience of rape affects self-esteem: The moderating role of gender and rape myth acceptance. *European Journal of Social Psychology, 23*, 561–579.

Boring, E. G. (1930). A new ambiguous figure. *American Journal of Psychology, 42*, 444–445.

Bower, G. H. (1981). Mood and memory. *American Psychologist, 36*, 129–148.

Bower, G. H. (1991). Mood congruity of social judgments. In J. P. Forgas (Ed.), *Emotion and social judgment* (pp. 31–53). Oxford: Pergamon Press.

Brewer, M. B. (1988). A dual model of impression formation. In T. K. Srull & R. S. Wyer, Jr (Eds.), *A dual model of impression formation: Advances in social cognition* (Vol. 1, pp. 1–35). Hillsdale, NJ: Lawrence Erlbaum Associates Inc.

Broadbent, D. E. (1958). *Perception and communication.* New York: Pergamon.

Brown, R., & Fish, D. (1983). The psychological causality implicit in language. *Cognition, 14*, 233–274.

Bruner, J. S. (1957a). Going beyond the information given. In J. S. Bruner, E. Brunswik, L. Festinger, F. Heider, K. F. Muenzinger, C. E. Osgood, & D. Rapaport, (Eds.), *Contemporary approaches to cognition* (pp. 41–69). Cambridge, MA: Harvard University Press.

Bruner, J. S. (1957b). On perceptual

readiness. *Psychological Review, 64,* 123–152.

Cacioppo, J. T., & Petty, R. E. (1982) The need for cognition. *Journal of Personality and Social Psychology, 42,* 116–131.

Cantor, N. E., & Michel, W. (1977). Traits as prototypes: Effects on recognition memory. *Journal of Personality and Social Psychology, 35,* 38–48.

Carlston, D. E. (1980). The recall and use of traits and events in social inference processes. *Journal of Experimental Social Psychology, 16,* 303–328.

Cervone, D., & Peake, P. K. (1986). Anchoring, efficacy, and action: The influence of judgmental heuristics on self-efficacy judgment and behavior. *Journal of Personality and Social Psychology, 50,* 492–501.

Chaiken, S. (1987). The heuristic model of persuasion. In M. P. Zanna, J. M. Olson, & C .P. Herman (Eds.), *Social influence: The Ontario symposium* (Vol. 5, pp. 3–39). Hillsdale, NJ: Lawrence Erlbaum Associates Inc.

Chaiken, S., & Trope, Y. (1999). *Dual-process theories in social psychology.* New York: Guilford Press.

Chapman, G. B., & Bornstein, B. H. (1996). The more you ask for, the more you get: Anchoring in personal injury verdicts. *Applied Cognitive Psychology, 10,* 519–540.

Chen, S., & Chaiken, S. (1999). The heuristic-systematic model in its broader context. In S. Chaiken & Y. Trope (Eds.), *Dual-process theories in social psychology* (pp. 73–96). New York: Guilford Press.

Clark, H. H., & Haviland, S. E. (1977). Comprehension and the given-new contract. In R. O. Freedle (Ed.), *Discourse production and comprehension* (pp. 1–40). Hillsdale, NJ: Lawrence Erlbaum Associates Inc.

Clore, G. L. (1992). Cognitive phenomenology: Feelings and the construction of judgment. In L. L.

Martin & A. Tesser (Eds.), *The construction of social judgment* (pp. 133–163). Hillsdale, NJ: Lawrence Erlbaum Associates Inc.

Clore, G. L., & Parrott, W. G. (1991). Moods and their vicissitudes: Thoughts and feelings as information. In J. P. Forgas (Ed.), *Emotion and social judgments. International series in experimental social psychology* (pp. 107–123). Oxford: Pergamon.

Clore, G. L., Schwarz, N., & Conway, M. (1994). Cognitive causes and consequences of emotion. In R. S. Wyer & T. K. Srull (Eds.), *Handbook of social cognition* (Vol. 1, 2nd ed., pp. 323–417). Hillsdale, NJ: Lawrence Erlbaum Associates Inc.

Cosmides, L. (1989). The logic of social exchange: Has natural selection shaped how humans reason? Studies with the Wason selection task. *Cognition, 31,* 187–276.

Cosmides, L., & Tooby, J. (1996). Are humans good intuitive staticians after all? Rethinking some conclusions from the literature on judgment under uncertainty. *Cognition, 58,* 1–73.

Craik, F. I. M., & Lockhart, R. S. (1972). Levels of processing: A framework for memory research. *Journal of Verbal Learning and Verbal Behavior, 11,* 671–684.

Darley, J. M., & Gross, P. H. (1983). A hypothesis-confirming bias in labeling effects. *Journal of Personality and Social Psychology, 44,* 20–33.

Davies, M. F. (1997a). Belief persistence after evidential discrediting: The impact of generated versus provided explanations on the likelihood of discredited outcomes. *Journal of Experimental Social Psychology, 33,* 561–578.

Davies, M. F. (1997b). Positive test strategies and confirmatory retrieval processes in the evaluation of personality feedback. *Journal of*

Personality and Social Psychology, 73, 574–583.

Descartes, R. (1961). *Passions of the soul: Essential works of Descartes* (L. Blair, trans.). New York: Bantam Books. (Original work published 1649)

DeSoto, C. B. (1960). Learning a social structure. *Journal of Abnormal and Social Psychology, 60,* 417–421.

Devine, P. G. (1989). Stereotypes and prejudice: Their automatic and controlled components. *Journal of Personality and Social Psychology, 56,* 5–18.

Dijksterhuis, A., Spears, R., Postmes, T., Stapel, D. A., Koomen, W., van Knippenberg, A., & Scheepers, D. (1998). Seeing one thing and doing another: Contrast effects in automatic behavior. *Journal of Personality and Social Psychology, 75,* 862–871.

Dijksterhuis, A., & van Knippenberg, A. (1995). Timing of schema activation and memory. Inhibited access to inconsistent information. *European Journal of Social Psychology, 12,* 383–390.

Dijksterhuis, A., & van Knippenberg, A. (1998). The relation between perception and behavior, or how to win a game of Trivial Pursuit. *Journal of Personality and Social Psychology, 74,* 865–877.

Dougherty, M. R. P., Gettys, C. F., & Ogden, E. E. (1999). MINERVA-DM: A memory processes model for judgments of likelihood. *Psychological Review, 106,* 180–209.

Dovidio, J. F., Evans, N., & Tyler, R. B. (1986). Racial stereotypes: The contents of their cognitive representations. *Journal of Experimental Social Psychology, 22,* 22–37.

Dovidio, J. F., Gaertner, S. L., & Loux, S. (2000). Subjective experiences and inter-group relations: The role of positive affect. In H. Bless & J. P. Forgas (Eds.), *The message within: The role of subjective experience in social cognition and behavior*

(pp. 340–371). Philadelphia, PA: Psychology Press.

Dulany, D. E., & Hilton, D. J. (1991). Conversational implicature, conscious representation, and the conjunction fallacy. *Social Cognition, 9,* 85–110.

Eagly, A. H., & Chaiken, S. (1993). *The psychology of attitudes.* Fort Worth, TX: Harcourt, Brace, Jovanovich College Publishers.

Edwards, J. A., & Weary, G. (1993). Depression and the impression-formation continuum: Piecemeal processing despite the availability of category information. *Journal of Personality and Social Psychology, 64,* 636–645.

Eich, E., & Macaulay, D. (2000). Cognitive and clinical perspectives on mood-dependent memory. In J. P. Forgas, (Ed.), *Feeling and thinking: The role of affect in social cognition.* New York: Cambridge University Press.

Englich, B., & Mussweiler, T. (2001). Sentencing under uncertainty: Anchoring effects in the courtroom. *Journal of Applied Social Psychology, 31,* 1535–1551.

Epstein, S., Donovan, S., & Denes-Raj, V. (1999). The missing link in the paradox of the linda conjunction problem: Beyond knowing and thinking of the conjunction rule, the intrinsic appeal of heuristic processing. *Personality and Social Psychology Bulletin, 25,* 204–214.

Erber, R., & Fiske, S. T. (1984). Outcome dependency and attention to inconsistent information. *Journal of Personality and Social Psychology, 47,* 709–726.

Falk, R., & Konold, C. (1997). Making sense of randomness: Implicit encoding as a basis for judgment. *Psychological Review, 104,* 301–318.

Fazio, R. H., Jackson, J. R., Dunton, B. C., & Williams, C. J. (1995). Variability in automatic activation as an unobtrusive measure of racial attitudes: A bona fide pipeline? *Journal of Personality and Social Psychology, 69*, 1013–1027.

Fazio, R. H., & Towles-Schwen, T. (1999). The mode model of attitude-behavior processes. In S. Chaiken & Y. Trope (Eds.), *Dual process theories in social psychology* (pp. 361–382). New York: Guilford Press.

Festinger, L. (1954). A theory of social comparison processes. *Human Relations, 7*, 117–140.

Festinger, L. (1957). *A theory of cognitive dissonance.* Stanford, CT: Stanford University Press.

Fiedler, K. (1988). The dependence of the conjunction fallacy on subtle linguistic factors. *Psychological Research, 50*, 123–129.

Fiedler, K. (1996). Explaining and simulating judgment biases as an aggregation phenomenon in probabilistic, multiple-cue environments. *Psychological Review, 103*, 193–214.

Fiedler, K. (2000). Explaining major findings and their boundary conditions in terms of mood dependent assimilation and accommodation. In L. L. Martin & G. L. Clore (Eds.), *Mood and social cognition: Contrasting theories.* Mahwah, NJ: Lawrence Erlbaum Associates Inc.

Fiedler, K., Armbruster, T., Nickel, S., Walther, E., & Asbeck, J. (1996). Constructive biases in social judgment: Experiments on the self-verification of question contents. *Journal of Personality and Social Psychology, 71*, 861–873.

Fiedler, K., & Schenck, W. (2001). Spontaneous inferences from pictorially presented behaviors. *Personality and Social Psychology Bulletin, 27*, 1533–1546.

Fiedler, K., & Walther, E. (2003). *Stereotypes as inductive hypothesis testing.* Hove, UK: Psychology Press.

Fiedler, K., Walther, E., & Nickel, S. (1999). The autoverification of social hypothesis. Stereotyping and the power

of sample size. *Journal of Personality and Social Psychology, 77*, 5–18.

Fischhoff, B. (1975). Hindsight foresight: The effect of outcome knowledge on judgment under uncertainty. *Journal of Experimental Psychology, 89*, 288–299.

Fishbein, M., & Ajzen, I. (1974). Attitudes toward objects as predictors of single and multiple behavioral criteria. *Psychological Review, 81*, 59–74.

Fiske, S. T., & Neuberg, S. L. (1990). A continuum of impression formation from category-based to individuating processing: Influences of information and motivation on attention and interpretation. In M. P. Zanna (Ed.), *Advances in experimental social psychology* (Vol. 23, pp. 1–74). Orlando, FL: Academic Press.

Fiske, S. T., & Taylor, S. E. (1991). *Social cognition* (2nd ed.). New York: McGraw-Hill.

Fiske, S. T., Kenny, D. A., & Taylor, S. E. (1982). Structural models for the mediation of salience effects on attribution. *Journal of Experimental Social Psychology, 18*, 105–127.

Florack, A., Scarabis, M., & Bless, H. (2001). When do associations matter?: The use of automatic associations towards ethnic groups in person judgments. *Journal of Experimental Social Psychology, 37*, 518–524.

Forgas, J. P. (1992a). Affect in social judgments and decisions: A multi-process model. In M. P. Zanna (Ed.), *Advances in experimental social psychology* (Vol. 25, pp. 227–275). San Diego, CA: Academic Press.

Forgas, J. P. (1992b). On mood and peculiar people: Affect and person typicality in impression formation. *Journal of Personality and Social Psychology, 62*, 863–875.

Forgas, J. P. (1995a). Mood and judgment: The affect infusion model (AIM). *Psychological Bulletin, 117*, 39–66.

Forgas, J. P. (1995b) Strange couples: Mood

effects on judgments and memory about prototypical and atypical targets. *Personality and Social Psychology Bulletin, 21*, 747–765.

Forgas, J. P. (2000a). *Feeling and thinking: The role of affect in social cognition.* New York: Cambridge University Press.

Forgas, J. P. (2000b). Affect and information processing strategies: An interactive relationship. In J. P. Forgas (Ed.), *Feeling and thinking: The role of affect in social cognition.* New York: Cambridge University Press.

Forgas, J. P. (2001). Affect and the "social mind": Affective influences on strategic interpersonal behaviors. In J. P. Forgas & K. D. Williams (Eds.), *The social mind: Cognitive and motivational aspects of interpersonal behavior* (pp. 46–71). New York: Cambridge University Press.

Forgas, J. P., & Bower, G. H. (1987). Mood effects on person perception judgments. *Journal of Personality and Social Psychology, 53*, 53–60.

Forgas, J. P., & Fiedler, K. (1996). Us and them: Mood effects on inter-group discrimination. *Journal of Personality and Social Psychology, 70*, 28–40.

Försterling, F. (2001). *Attribution: An introduction to theories, research and applications.* [Social psychology: A modular course.] Philadelphia, PA: Psychology Press.

Freud, S. (1940–1968). *Gesammelte Werke.* Frankfurt, Germany: Fischer.

Funder, D. C. (1987). Errors and mistakes: Evaluating the accuracy of social judgment. *Psychological Bulletin, 101*, 75–90.

Gavanski, I., & Roskos-Ewoldsen, D. R. (1991). Representativeness and conjoint probability. *Journal of Personality and Social Psychology, 61*, 181–194.

Gigerenzer, G. (1991). How to make cognitive illusions disappear: Beyond "heuristics and biases." In W. Stroebe & M. Hewstone (Eds.), *European review of social psychology* (pp. 83–115). New York: John Wiley & Sons.

Gigerenzer, G. (1996). On narrow norms and vague heuristics: A reply to Kahneman and Tversky. *Psychological Review, 103*, 592–596.

Gigerenzer, G., & Hoffrage, U. (1995). How to improve bayesian reasoning without instruction: Frequency formats. *Psychological Review, 102*, 684–704.

Gigerenzer, G., Hoffrage, U., & Kleinbölting, H. (1991). Probabilistic mental models: A Brunswikian theory of confidence. *Psychological Review, 98*, 506–528.

Gigerenzer, G., & Hug, K. (1991). Domainspecific reasoning: Social contracts, cheating, and perspective change. *Cognition, 43*, 127–171.

Gilbert, D. T., & Hixon, J. G. (1991). The trouble of thinking: Activation and application of stereotypic beliefs. *Journal of Personality and Social Psychology, 60*, 509–517.

Gilbert, D. T., Pelham, B. W., & Krull, D. S. (1988). On cognitive busyness: When person perceivers meet persons perceived. *Journal of Personality and Social Psychology, 54*, 733–740.

Gilovich, T. (1981). Seeing the past in the present: The effect of associations to familiar events on judgments and decisions. *Journal of Personality and Social Psychology, 40*, 797–808.

Gilovich, T., Vallone, R., & Tversky, A. (1985). The hot hand in basketball: On the misperception of random sequences. *Cognitive Psychology, 17*, 295–314.

Gollwitzer, P. M., & Moskowitz, G. B. (1996). Goal effects on action and cognition. In E. T. Higgins & A. W. Kruglanski (Eds.), *Social psychology: A handbook of basic principles* (pp. 361–399). New York: Guilford Press.

Graesser, A. C., Gordon, S. E., & Sawyer, J. D. (1979). Recognition memory for typical and atypical actions in scripted activities: Tests of a script pointer + tag hypothesis. *Journal of Verbal Learning and Verbal Behavior, 18,* 319–332.

Grayson, C. E., & Schwarz, N. (1999). Beliefs influence information processing strategies: Declarative and experiential information in risk assessment. *Social Cognition, 17,* 1–18.

Greening, L., Dollinger, S. J., & Pitz, G. (1996). Adolescents' perceived risk and personal experience with natural disasters: An evaluation of cognitive heuristics. *Acta Psychologica, 91,* 27–38.

Greenwald, A. G., & Banaji, M. R. (1995). Implicit social cognition: Attitudes, self-esteem, and stereotypes. *Psychological Review, 101,* 4–27.

Greenwald, A. G., McGee, D. E., & Schwartz, J. L. K. (1998). Measuring individual differences in implicit cognition: The implicit association test. *Journal of Personality and Social Psychology, 74,* 1464–1480.

Greve, W. (2001). Traps and gaps in action explanation: Theoretical problems of a psychology of human action. *Psychological Review, 108,* 435–451.

Grice, H. P. (1975). Logic and conversation. In P. Cole & J. L. Morgan (Eds.), *Syntax and semantics 3: Speech acts* (pp. 41–58). New York: Academic Press.

Griffin, D., & Buehler, R. (1999). Frequency, probability, and prediction: Easy solutions to cognitive illusions? *Cognitive Psychology, 38,* 48–78.

Hamilton, D. L., & Gifford, R. K. (1976). Illusory correlation in interpersonal perception: A cognitive basis of stereotypic judgments. *Journal of Experimental Social Psychology, 12,* 392–407.

Hamilton, D. L., Katz, L. B., & Leirer, V. O. (1980). Cognitive representation of personality impressions: Organizational processes in the first impression formation. *Journal of Personality and Social Psychology, 39,* 1050–1063.

Hamilton, D. L., & Sherman, J. W. (1994).

Stereotypes. In R. S. Wyer & T. K. Srull (Eds.), *Handbook of social cognition* (Vol. 1, 2nd ed., pp. 1–68). Hillsdale, NJ: Lawrence Erlbaum Associates Inc.

Hamilton, D. L., & Sherman, S. J. (1996). Perceiving persons and groups. *Psychological Review, 103,* 336–355.

Hastie, R., & Kumar, A. (1979). Person memory: Personality traits as organizing principles in memory for behaviors. *Journal of Personality and Social Psychology, 37,* 25–38.

Hastie, R., & Park, B. (1986). The relationship between memory and judgment depends on whether the judgment task is memory-based or on-line. *Psychological Review, 93,* 258–268.

Hawkins, S. A., & Hastie, R. (1990). Hindsight: Biased judgments of past events after the outcomes are known. *Psychological Bulletin, 107,* 311–327.

Heider, F. (1946). Attitudes and cognitive organization. *Journal of Psychology, 21,* 107–112.

Hell, W., Fiedler, K., & Gigerenzer, G. (1993). *Kognitive Täuschungen. Fehl-Leistungen und Mechanismen des Urteilens, Denkens und Erinnerns.* Heidelberg, Germany: Spektrum Akademischer Verlag.

Helmholtz, H. v. (1903). Optisches über Malerei. Umarbeitung von Vorträgen, gehalten in den Jahren 1871–1873. In H. v. Helmholtz (Ed.), *Vorträge und Reden.* Braunschweig, Germany: Vieweg und Sohn.

Herr, P. M. (1986). Consequences of priming: Judgment and behavior. *Journal of Experimental Social Psychology, 51,* 1106–1115.

Herr, P. M., Sherman, S. J., & Fazio, R. H. (1983). On the consequences of priming: Assimilation and contrast effects. *Journal of Experimental Social Psychology, 19,* 323–340.

Hewstone, M. (1994). Revising and change of stereotypic beliefs: In search of the elusive subtyping model. In W. Stroebe

& M. Hewstone (Eds.), *European review of social psychology* (Vol. 5, pp. 69–109). Chichester, UK: Wiley.

Higgins, E. T. (1981). The "communication game": Implications for social cognition and persuasion. In E. T. Higgins, C. P. Herman & M. P. Zanna (Eds.), *Social cognition: The Ontario Symposium* (Vol. 1, pp. 343–392). Hillsdale, NJ: Lawrence Erlbaum Associates Inc.

Higgins, E. T. (1996). Knowledge activation: Accessibility, applicability, and salience. In E. T. Higgins & A. W. Kruglanski (Eds.), *Social psychology: Handbook of basic principles* (pp. 133–168). New York: Guilford Press.

Higgins, E. T. (1997). Biases in social cognition: "Aboutness" as a general principle. In C. McGarty & S. A. Haslam (Eds.), *The message of social psychology* (pp. 182–199). Cambridge, MA: Blackwell.

Higgins, E. T. (1998). The aboutness principle: A pervasive influence on human inference. *Social Cognition, 16,* 173–198.

Higgins, E. T., & A. W. Kruglanski (Eds.), (1996). *Social psychology: Handbook of basic principles.* New York: Guilford Press.

Higgins, E. T., Rholes, W. S., & Jones, C. R. (1977). Category accessibility and impression formation. *Journal of Experimental Social Psychology, 13,* 141–154.

Hilton, D. J. (1995). The social context of reasoning: Conversational inference and rational judgment. *Psychological Bulletin, 118,* 248–271.

Hunt, R. R., & McDaniel, M. A. (1993). The enigma of organization and distinctiveness. *Journal of Memory and Language, 32,* 421–445.

Ichheiser, G. (1949). Misunderstanding in human relations: A study in false social perception. *American Journal of Sociology, 55,* 1–70.

Isen, A. M. (1987). Positive affect, cognitive processes, and social behavior. In L. Berkowitz (Ed.), *Advances in experimental social psychology* (Vol. 20, pp. 203–253). San Diego, CA: Academic Press.

Isen, A. M., Means, B., Patrick, R., & Nowicki, G. (1982). Some factors influencing decision making strategy and risktaking. In M. S. Clark & S. T. Fiske (Eds.), *Affect and cognition: The 17th Annual Carnegie Mellon Symposium on Cognition* (pp. 241–261). Hillsdale, NJ: Lawrence Erlbaum Associates Inc.

Jacoby, L. L., & Dallas, M. (1981). On the relationship between autobiographical memory and perceptual learning. *Journal of Experimental Psychology: General, 110,* 306–340.

Jacoby, L. L., Kelley, C., Brown, J., & Jasechko, J. (1989). Becoming famous overnight: Limits on the ability to avoid unconscious influences of the past. *Journal of Personality and Social Psychology, 56,* 326–338.

Jacoby, L. L., & Woloshyn, V. (1989). Becoming famous without being recognized: Unconscious influences of memory produced by dividing attention. *Journal of Experimental Psychology: General, 118,* 115–125.

Jacowitz, K. E., & Kahneman, D. (1995). Measures of anchoring in estimation tasks. *Personality and Social Psychology Bulletin, 21,* 1161–1166.

James, W. (1890). The principles of psychology. In R. M. Hutchins (Ed.), *The great book of the Western world* (p. 348). Chicago: Encyclopaedia Brittanica, LIII.

Jones, E. E., & Davis, K. E. (1965). From acts to dispositions: The attribution process in person perception. In L. Berkowitz (Ed.), *Advances in experimental social psychology* (Vol. 2, pp. 219–266). New York: Academic Press.

Jones, E. E., & Harris, V. A. (1967). The attribution of attitudes. *Journal of Experimental Social Psychology, 3,* 1–24.

Jones, E. E., & Nisbett, R. E. (1972). The actor and the observer: Divergent perceptions of the causes of behavior. In E. E. Jones, D. E. Kanouse, H. H. Kelley, R. E. Nisbett, S. Valins, & B. Weiner (Eds.), *Attribution: Perceiving the causes of behavior*, Morristown, NJ: General Learning Press.

Judd, C. M., & Park, B. (1988). Outgroup-homogeneity: Judgments of variability at the individual and the group levels. *Journal of Personality and Social Psychology, 54*, 778–788.

Jungermann, H., Pfister, H. R., & Fischer, K. (1998). *Die Psychologie der Entscheidung. Eine Einführung.* Heidelberg, Germany: Spektrum Akademischer Verlag.

Jussim, L. (1991). Social perception and social reality: A reflection-construction model. *Psychological Review, 98*, 54–73.

Kahneman, D., & Miller, D. (1986). Norm theory: Comparing reality to its alternatives. *Psychological Review, 93*, 136–153.

Kahneman, D., & Tversky, A. (1972). Subjective probability: A judgment of representativeness. *Cognitive Psychology, 3*, 430–454.

Kahneman, D., & Tversky, A. (1973). On the psychology of prediction. *Psychological Review, 80*, 237–251.

Kahneman, D., & Tversky, A. (1996). On the reality of cognitive illusions. *Psychological Review, 103*, 582–591.

Kardes, F. R. (1999). *Consumer behavior and managerial decision making.* Reading, MA: Addison-Wesley.

Kelley, C. M., & Jacoby, L. L. (1990). The construction of subjective experience: Memory attributions. *Mind and Language, 5*, 49–68.

Kelley, C. M., & Jacoby, L. L. (1998). Subjective reports and process dissociation: Fluency, knowing, and feeling. *Acta Psychologica, 98*, 127–140.

Kelley, H. H. (1967). Attribution theory in social psychology. In D. Levine (Ed.), *Nebraska Symposium on Motivation* (Vol. 15, pp. 192–241). Lincoln, NE: University of Nebraska Press.

Kelley, H. H. (1972). Attribution in social interaction. In E. E. Jones, D. E. Kanouse, H. H. Kelley, R. E. Nisbett, S. Valins, & B. Weiner (Eds.), *Attribution: Perceiving the causes of behavior* (pp. 151–174). Morristown, NJ: General Learning Press.

Klauer, K. C., Rossnagel, C., & Musch, J. (1997). List-context effects in evaluative priming. *Journal of Experimental Psychology: Learning, Memory and Cognition, 23*, 246–255.

Klayman, J., & Ha, Y.-W. (1987). Confirmation, disconfirmation, and information in hypothesis testing. *Psychological Review, 94*, 211–228.

Klein, S. B., & Loftus, J. (1988). The nature of self-referent encoding: The contribution of elaborative and organizational processes. *Journal of Personality and Social Psychology, 55*, 5–11.

Koehler, J. J. (1996). The base rate fallacy reconsidered: Descriptive, normative, and methodological challenges. *Behavioral and Brain Sciences, 19*, 1–53.

Koffka, K. (1935). *Principles of Gestalt psychology.* New York: Harcourt, Brace, & World.

Krauss, R. M., & Weinheimer, S. (1966). Concurrent feedback, confirmation, and the encoding of referents in verbal communication. *Journal of Personality and Social Psychology, 4*, 343–346.

Krauth-Gruber, S., & Ric, F. (2000). Affect and stereotypic thinking: A test of the mood-and-general-knowledge-model. *Personality and Social Psychology Bulletin, 26*, 1587–1597.

Kruglanski, A. W. (1989a). *Lay epistemics and human knowledge: Cognitive and motivational biases.* New York: Plenum Press.

Kruglanski, A. W. (1989b). The psychology of being "right": On the problem of accuracy in social perception and cognition. *Psychological Bulletin, 106,* 395–409.

Kuiper, N. A., & Rogers, T. B. (1979). Encoding of personal information: Self-other differences. *Journal of Personality and Social Psychology, 37,* 499–514.

Kunda, Z. (1990). The case for motivated reasoning. *Psychological Bulletin, 108,* 480–498.

Kunda, Z. (1999). *Social cognition: Making sense of people.* Cambridge, MA: MIT Press.

Kunda, Z., & Oleson, K. C. (1995). Maintaining stereotypes in the face of disconfirmation: Constructing grounds for subtyping. *Journal of Personality and Social Psychology, 68,* 565–579.

Kunda, Z., & Oleson, K. C. (1997). When exceptions prove the rule: How extremity of deviance determines the impact of deviant examples on stereotypes. *Journal of Personality and Social Psychology, 72,* 965–979.

Kunda, Z., & Thagard, P. (1997). Forming impressions from stereotypes, traits, and behaviors: A parallel-constraint-satisfaction theory. *Psychological Review, 103,* 284–308.

Lambert, A. J., & Wyer, R. S. (1990). Stereotypes and social judgment: The effects of typicality and group heterogeneity. *Journal of Personality and Social Psychology, 59,* 676–691.

Langer, E. J., Fiske, S., & Taylor, S. E. (1976). Stigma, staring, and discomfort: A novel-stimulus hypothesis. *Journal of Experimental Social Psychology, 12,* 451–463.

Lepore, L., & Brown, R. (1997). Category and stereotype activation: Is prejudice inevitable? *Journal of Personality and Social Psychology, 72,* 275–287.

Leyens, J-P., Dardenne, B., Yzerbyt, V., Scaillet, N., & Snyder, M. (1999). Confirmation and disconfirmation: Their social advantages. In W. Stroebe & M. Hewstone (Eds.), *European review of*

social psychology (Vol. 10, pp. 199–230). Chichester, UK: Wiley.

Leyens, J.-P., Yzerbyt, V., & Corneille, O. (1996). The role of applicability in the emergence of the overattribution bias. *Journal of Personality and Social Psychology, 70,* 219–229.

Liberman, A., & Trope, Y. (1999). Social hypothesis testing: Cognitive and motivational mechanisms. In S. Chaiken & Y. Trope (Eds.), *Dual-process theories in social psychology* (pp. 239–270). New York: Guilford Press.

Lichtenstein, S., Slovic, P., Fischhoff, B., Layman, M., & Combs, B. (1978). Judged frequency of lethal events. *Journal of Experimental Psychology: Human Learning and Memory, 4,* 551–578.

Loftus, E. F. (1975). Leading questions and the eyewitness report. *Cognitive Psychology, 7,* 560–572.

Loftus, E. F. (1979). *Eyewitness testimony.* Cambridge, MA: Harvard University Press.

Loftus, E. F., & Palmer, J. C. (1974). Reconstruction of automobile destruction: An example of the interaction between language and memory. *Journal of Verbal Learning and Verbal Behavior, 13,* 585–589.

Lombardi, W. J., Higgins, E. T., & Bargh, J. A. (1987). The role of consciousness in priming effects on categorization: Assimilation and contrast as a function of awareness of the priming task. *Personality and Social Psychology Bulletin, 13,* 411–429.

Luchins, A. S. (1942). Mechanization in problem solving. *Psychological Monographs, 54* (whole No. 248).

Maass, A. (1999). Linguistic inter-group bias: Stereotype perpetuation through language. *Advances in Experimental Social Psychology, 31,* 79–121.

Maass, A., Corvino, P., & Arcuri, L. (1994). Linguistic inter-group bias and the mass media. *Revue de Psychologie Sociale, 1,* 31–43.

Maass, A., Milesi, A., Zabbini, S., & Stahlberg, D. (1995). Linguistic intergroup bias: Differential expectancies or in-group protection? *Journal of Personality and Social Psychology, 68,* 116–126.

Maass, A., Salvi, D., Arcuri, L., & Semin, G. R. (1989). Language use in intergroup contexts: The linguistic intergroup bias. *Journal of Personality and Social Psychology, 57,* 981–993.

Mackie, D. M., & Worth, L. T. (1989). Cognitive deficits and the mediation of positive affect in persuasion. *Journal of Personality and Social Psychology, 57,* 27–40.

MacLeod, C., & Campbell, L. (1992). Memory accessibility and probability judgments: An experimental evaluation of the availability heuristic. *Journal of Personality and Social Psychology, 63,* 890–902.

Macrae, C. N., Bodenhausen, G. V., & Milne, A. B. (1995). The dissection of selection in person perception: Inhibitory processes in social stereotyping. *Journal of Personality and Social Psychology, 69,* 397–407.

Macrae, C. N., Hewstone, M., & Griffiths, R. J. (1993). Processing load and memory for stereotype-based information. *European Journal of Social Psychology, 23,* 77–87.

Madon, S., Jussim, L., & Eccles, J. (1997). In search of the powerful self-fulfilling prophecy. *Journal of Personality and Social Psychology, 72,* 791–809.

Manis, M., Shedler, J., Jonides, J., & Nelson, T. E. (1993). Availability heuristic in judgments of set size and frequency of occurrence. *Journal of Personality and Social Psychology, 65,* 448–457.

Manktelow, K. (1999). *Reasoning and thinking.* [Cognitive psychology: A modular course.] Hove, UK: Psychology Press.

Martin, L. L. (1986). Set/Reset: The use and disuse of concepts in impression formation. *Journal of Personality and Social Psychology, 51,* 493–504.

Martin, L. L. (2001). Moods don't cause effects, people do: A mood as input look at mood effects. In L. L. Martin & G. L. Clore (Eds.), *Mood and social cognition: Contrasting theories.* Mahwah, NJ: Lawrence Erlbaum Associates Inc.

Martin, L. L., & Clore, G. L. (Eds.) (2001). *Mood and social cognition: Contrasting theories.* Mahwah, NJ: Lawrence Erlbaum Associates Inc.

Martin, L. L., Seta, J. J., & Crelia, R. (1990). Assimilation and contrast as a function of people's willingness and ability to expend effort in forming an impression. *Journal of Personality and Social Psychology, 59,* 27–37.

Martin, L. L., Strack, F., & Stapel, D. A. (2001). How the mind moves: Knowledge accessibility and the fine-tuning of the cognitive. In A. Tesser & N. Schwarz (Eds.), *Blackwell handbook of social psychology: Intraindividual processes* (Vol. 1, pp. 236–256). London: Blackwell.

Martin, L. L., & Tesser, A. (1996). Some ruminative thoughts. In R. S. Wyer, Jr (Ed.), *Advances in social cognition* (Vol. 9, pp. 1–47). Mahwah, NJ: Lawrence Erlbaum Associates Inc.

Maurer, K. L., Park, B., & Rothbart, M. (1995). Subtyping versus subgrouping processes in stereotype representation. *Journal of Personality and Social Psychology, 69,* 812–824.

McArthur, L. Z. (1981). What grabs you? The role of attention in impression formation and causal attribution. In E. T. Higgins, C. P. Herman & M. P. Zanna (Eds.), *Social cognition: The Ontario Symposium* (Vol. 1, pp. 201–246). Hillsdale, NJ: Lawrence Erlbaum Associates Inc.

McArthur, L. Z., & Baron, R. (1983). Toward an ecological theory of social perception. *Psychological Bulletin, 90,* 215–238.

McArthur, L. Z., & Ginsberg, E. (1981). Causal attribution to salient stimuli: An investigation of visual fixation mediators. *Personality and Social Psychology Bulletin, 7*, 547–553.

McArthur, L. Z., & Post, D. L. (1977). Figural emphasis and person perception. *Journal of Experimental Social Psychology, 13*, 520–535.

McCloskey, M., & Zaragoza, M. (1985). Misleading post-event information and memory for events: Arguments and evidence against memory impairment hypotheses. *Journal of Experimental Psychology: General, 114*, 1–16.

McGuire, W. J. (1985). Attitudes and attitude change. In G. Lindzey & E. Aronson (Eds.), *The handbook of social psychology* (Vol. 2, 3rd ed., pp. 233–346). New York: Random House.

Meyer, D. E., & Schvaneveldt, R. W. (1971). Facilitation in recognising pairs of words: Evidence of a dependence between retrieval operations. *Journal of Experimental Psychology, 90*, 227–234.

Millar, M. G., & Tesser, A. (1986). Thought-induced attitude change: The effects of schema structure and commitment. *Journal of Personality and Social Psychology, 51*, 259–269.

Morris, W. N. (1989). *Mood: The frame of mind.* New York: Springer.

Murphy, S. T., & Zajonc, R. B. (1993). Affect, cognition, and awareness. *Journal of Personality and Social Psychology, 64*, 723–739.

Mussweiler, T., & Strack, F. (1998). *The use of category and exemplar knowledge in the solution of anchoring tasks.* Manuskript eingereicht zur Veröffentlichung, Germany: Universität Würzburg.

Mussweiler, T., & Strack, F. (1999a). Comparing is believing: A selective accessibility model of judgmental anchoring. In W. Stroebe & M. Hewstone (Eds.), *European review of social psychology* (Vol. 10, pp. 135–167). Chichester, UK: Wiley.

Mussweiler, T., & Strack, F. (1999b). Hypothesis-consistent testing and semantic priming in the anchoring paradigm: A selective accessibility model. *Journal of Experimental Social Psychology, 35*, 136–164.

Mussweiler, T., Strack, F., & Pfeiffer, T. (2000). Overcoming the inevitable anchoring effect: Considering the opposite compensates for selective accessibility. *Personality and Social Psychology Bulletin, 26*, 1142–1150.

Mynatt, C. R., Doherty, M. E., & Tweney, R. D. (1977). Confirmation bias in a simulated research environment: An experimental study of scientific inference. *Quarterly Journal of Experimental Psychology, 29*, 85–95.

Neale, M. A., & Northcraft, G. B. (1991). Behavioral negotiation theory: A framework for conceptualizing dyadic bargaining. In L. L. Cummings & B. M. Staw (Eds.), *Research in organizational behavior* (pp. 147–190). Greenwich, CT: JAI.

Neuberg, S. L., & Fiske, S. T. (1987). Motivational influences on impression formation. Outcome dependency, accuracy-driven attention, and individuating processes. *Journal of Personality and Social Psychology, 53*, 431–444.

Nisbett, R. E., & Ross, L. (1980). *Human inference: Strategies and shortcomings of social judgment.* Englewood Cliffs, NJ: Prentice-Hall.

Nisbett, R. E., & Wilson, T. D. (1977). Telling more than we can know: Verbal reports on mental processes. *Psychological Review, 84*, 231–259.

Northcraft, G. B., & Neale, M. A. (1987). Experts, amateurs, and real estate: An anchoring-and-adjustment perspective on property pricing decisions. *Organizational Behavior and Human Decision Processes, 39*, 84–97.

Oaksford, M., & Chater, N. (1994). A rational analysis of the selection task as optimal data selection. *Psychological Review, 101*, 608–631.

Palmere, M., Benton, S. L., Glover, J. A., & Roning, R. (1983). Elaboration and recall of main ideas in prose. *Journal of Educational Psychology, 75*, 898–907.

Park, B., Judd, C. N., & Ryan, C. S. (1991). Social categorization and the representation of variability information. *European Review of Social Psychology, 2*, 211–245.

Petty, R. E., & Cacioppo, J. T. (1981). *Attitudes and persuasion: Classic and contemporary approaches.* Dubuque, IA: William C. Brown.

Petty, R. E., & Cacioppo, J. T. (1986). *Communication and persuasion: Central and peripheral routes to attitude change.* New York: Springer-Verlag.

Petty, R. E., & Cacioppo, J. T. (1996). *Attitudes and persuasion: Classic and contemporary approaches.* Boulder, CO: Westview Press.

Petty, R. E., & Wegener, D. T. (1993). Flexible correction processes in social judgment: Correcting for context-induced contrast. *Journal of Experimental Social Psychology, 29*, 137–165.

Petty, R. E., & Wegener, D. T. (1999). The elaboration likelihood model: Current status and controversies. In S. Chaiken & Y. Trope (Eds.), *Dual-process theories in social psychology* (pp. 41–72). New York: Guilford Press.

Philippot, P., Schwarz, N., Carrera, P., De Vries, N., & Van Yperen, N. W. (1991). Differential effects of priming at the encoding and the judgment stage. *European Journal of Social Psychology, 21*, 293–302.

Pohl, R. F. (1992). Der Rückschau-Fehler: Systematische Verfälschung der Erinnerung bei Experten und Novizen. *Kognitionswissenschaft, 3*, 38–44.

Pryor, J. B., & Kriss, N. (1977). The cognitive dynamics of salience in the attribution process. *Journal of Personality and Social Psychology, 35*, 49–55.

Pyszczynski, T., & Greenberg, J. (1987). Towards an integration of cognitive and motivational perspectives on social inference: A biased hypothesis-testing model. In L. Berkowitz (Ed.), *Advances in experimental social psychology* (Vol. 20, pp. 297–340). New York: Academic Press.

Quattrone, G. A. (1982). Overattribution and unit formation: When behavior engulfs the person. *Journal of Personality and Social Psychology, 42*, 593–607.

Ray, W. S. (1983). Cognitive accessibility and causal attributions. *Personality and Social Psychology Bulletin, 8*, 719–727.

Rholes, W. S., & Pryor, J .B. (1982). Cognitive accessibility and causal attributions. *Personality and Social Psychology Bulletin, 8*, 719–727.

Ritov, I. (1996). Anchoring in simulated competitive market negotiation. *Organizational Behavior and Human Decision Processes, 67*, 16–25.

Roediger, H. L., & McDermott, K. B. (1995). Creating false memories: Remembering words not presented in lists. *Journal of Experimental Psychology: Learning, Memory, and Cognition, 21*, 803–814.

Roese, N. J., & Olson, J. M. (1995). *What might have been: The social psychology of counterfactual thinking.* Mahwah, NJ: Lawrence Erlbaum Associates Inc.

Rosch, E., Mervis, C. B., Graw, W., Johnson, D., & Boyes-Braem, P. (1976). Basic objects in natural categories. *Cognitive Psychology, 8*, 382–439.

Rosenthal, R. (1966). *Experimenter effects in behavioral research.* New York: Appleton-Century Crofts.

Rosenthal, R. (1991). Teacher expectancy effects: A brief update 25 years after the Pygmalion experiment. *Journal of Research in Education, 1*, 3–12.

Rosenthal, R., & Jacobson, L. (1968). *Pygmalion in the classroom.* New York: Holt, Rinehart & Winston.

Ross, L. (1977). The intuitive psychologist

and his shortcomings: Distortions in the attribution process. In L. Berkowitz (Ed.), *Advances in experimental social psychology* (Vol. 10, pp. 174–221). New York: Academic Press.

Ross, L., Lepper, M., Strack, F., & Steinmetz, J. L. (1977). Social explanation and social expectation: The effects of real and hypothetical explanations upon subjective likelihood. *Journal of Personality and Social Psychology, 35,* 817–829.

Ross, M., & Sicoly, F. (1979). Egocentric biases in availability and attribution. *Journal of Personality and Social Psychology, 37,* 322–336.

Rothbart, M., & Lewis, S. (1988). Inferring category attributes from exemplar attributes: Geometric shapes and social categories. *Journal of Personality and Social Psychology, 55,* 861–872.

Rothman, A. J., & Schwarz, N. (1998). Constructing perceptions of vulnerability: Personal relevance and the use of experiential information in health judgments. *Personality and Social Psychology Bulletin, 24,* 1053–1064.

Rottenstreich, Y., & Tversky, A. (1997). Unpacking, repacking, and anchoring: Advances in support theory. *Psychological Review, 104,* 406–415.

Ruscher, J. B., & Fiske, S. T. (1990). Interpersonal competition can cause indivituating impression formation. *Journal of Personality and Social Psychology, 58,* 832–842.

Schachter, S., & Singer, J. E. (1962). Cognitive, social, and physiological determinants of emotional state. *Psychological Review, 69,* 379–399.

Schaller, M. (1992). Ingroup favoritism and statistical reasoning in social inference: Implications for formation and maintenance of group stereotypes. *Journal of Personality and Social Psychology, 63,* 61–74.

Schwarz, N. (1990). Feelings as information: Informational and motivational functions of affective states. In R. M. Sorrentino & E. T. Higgins, *Handbook of motivation and Cognition: Foundations of social behavior* (Vol. 2, pp. 527–561). New York: Guilford Press.

Schwarz, N. (1994). Judgment in a social context: Biases, shortcomings, and the logic of conversation. In M. Zanna (Ed.), *Advances in experimental social psychology* (Vol. 26, pp. 123–162). New York: Academic Press.

Schwarz, N. (1996). *Cognition and communication: Judgmental biases, research methods, and the logic of conversation.* Mahwah, NJ: Lawrence Erlbaum Associates Inc.

Schwarz, N. (1998). Accessible content and accessibility experiences: The interplay of declarative and experiential information in judgment. *Personality and Social Psychology Review, 2,* 87–99.

Schwarz, N. (2000). Social judgment and attitudes: Warmer, more social, and less conscious. *European Journal of Social Psychology, 30,* 149–176.

Schwarz, N., & Bless, H. (1992a). Constructing reality and its alternatives: An inclusion-exclusion model of assimilation and contrast effects in social judgment. In L. L. Martin & A. Tesser (Eds.), *The construction of social judgment* (pp. 217–245). Hillsdale, NJ: Lawrence Erlbaum Associates Inc.

Schwarz, N., & Bless, H. (1992b). Scandals and the public's trust in politicians. *Personality and Social Psychology Bulletin, 18,* 574–579.

Schwarz, N., Bless, H., Strack, F., Klumpp, G., Rittenauer-Schatka, H., & Simons, A. (1991a). Ease of retrieval as information: Another look at the availability heuristic. *Journal of Personality and Social Psychology, 61,* 195–202.

Schwarz, N., & Clore, G.L. (1983). Mood, misattribution, and judgments of well-being: Informative and directive functions of affective states. *Journal of*

Personality and Social Psychology, 45, 513–523.

Schwarz, N., & Clore, G. L. (1988). How do I feel about it? Informative functions of affective states. In K. Fiedler & J. P. Forgas (Eds.), *Affect, cognition, and social behavior* (pp. 44–62). Toronto: Hogrefe International.

Schwarz, N., & Clore, G. L. (1996). Feelings and phenomenal experiences. In E. T. Higgins & A. W. Kruglanski (Eds.), *Social psychology: A handbook of basic principles* (pp. 433–465). New York: Guilford Press.

Schwarz, N., & Strack, F. (1991). Context effects in attitude surveys: Applying cognitive theory to social research. In W. Stroebe & M. Hewstone (Eds.), *European review of social psychology* (Vol. 2, pp. 31–50). Chichester, UK: Wiley.

Schwarz, N., & Strack, F. (1999). Reports of subjective well-being: Judgmental processes and methodological implications. In D. Kahneman, E. Diener, & N. Schwarz (Eds.), *Foundations of hedonic psychology: Scientific perspectives on enjoyment and suffering* (pp. 61–84). New York: Russell-Sage.

Schwarz, N., Strack, F., Hilton, D., & Naderer, G. (1991b). Base rates, representativeness, and the logic of conversation: The contextual relevance of "irrelevant" information. *Social Cognition, 9,* 67–84.

Schwarz, N., Strack, F., & Mai, H. P. (1991c). Assimilation and contrast effects in part-whole question sequences: A conversational-logic analysis. *Public Opinion Quarterly, 55,* 3–23.

Selfridge, O. G. (1955). Pattern recognition and modern computers. In *Proceedings of the Western Joint Computer Conference.* New York: The American Institute of Electrical Engineers.

Semin, G. R., & De Poot, C. J. (1997). The question-answer paradigm: You might regret not noticing how a question is worded. *Journal of Personality and Social Psychology, 73,* 472–480.

Semin, G. R., & Fiedler, K. (1988). The cognitive functions of linguistic categories in describing persons: Social cognition and language. *Journal of Personality and Social Psychology, 54,* 558–568.

Semin, G. R., Rubini, M., & Fiedler, K. (1995). The answer is in the question: The effect of verb causality on locus of explanation. *Personality and Social Psychology Bulletin, 21,* 834–841.

Semin, G. R., & Strack, F. (1980). The plausibility of the implausible: A critique to Snyder and Swann (1978). *European Journal of Social Psychology, 10,* 379–388.

Shafir, E. B., Smith, E. E., & Osherson, D. N. (1990). Typicality and reasoning fallacies. *Memory and Cognition, 18,* 229–239.

Shavitt, S., & Wänke, M. (2000). Consumer cognition, marketing, and advertising. In A. Tesser & N. Schwarz (Eds.), *Handbook of social psychology* (pp. 569–590). Oxford: Blackwell.

Shiffrin, R. M., & Schneider, W. (1984). Automatic and controlled processing revisited. *Psychological Review, 91,* 269–276.

Siemer, A., & Reisenzein, R. (1998). Effects of mood on evaluative judgments: Influence of reduced processing capacity and mood salience. *Cognition and Emotion, 12,* 783–805.

Simon, H. A. (1957). *Models of man: Social and rational.* New York: Wiley.

Skinner, B. F. (1938). *The behavior of organisms.* New York: Appleton-Century-Crofts.

Skowronski, J., & Carlston, D. E. (1987). Social judgment and social memory: The role of cue diagnosticity in negativity, positivity, and extremity biases. *Journal of Personality and Social Psychology, 52,* 689–699.

Slusher, M. P., & Anderson, C. A. (1987). When reality monitoring fails: The role of imagination in stereotype maintenance. *Journal of Personality and Social Psychology, 52,* 653–662.

Smith, C. A. (1989). Dimensions of appraisal and physiological response in emotion. *Journal of Personality and Social Psychology, 56,* 339–353.

Smith, E. R., & Lerner, M. (1986). The development of automatism of social judgments. *Journal of Personality and Social Psychology, 50,* 246–259.

Snyder, M. (1984). When belief creates reality. In L. Berkowitz (Ed.), *Advances in experimental social psychology* (Vol. 18, pp. 247–305). New York: Academic Press.

Snyder, M., & Swann, W. B. (1978). Hypothesis-testing strategies in social interaction. *Journal of Personality and Social Psychology, 36,* 1202–1212.

Snyder, M., & Uranowitz, S. W. (1978). Reconstructing the past: Some cognitive consequences of person perception. *Journal of Personality and Social Psychology, 36,* 941–950.

Sperber, D., & Wilson, D. (1986). *Relevance. Communication and cognition.* Oxford: Blackwell.

Srull, T. K., & Wyer, R. S. (1980). Category accessibility and social perception: Some implications for the study of person memory and interpersonal judgments. *Journal of Personality and Social Psychology, 38,* 841–856.

Stangor, C., & McMillan, D. (1992). Memory for expectancy-congruent and expectancy-incongruent information: A review of the social and social developmental literatures. *Psychological Bulletin, 111,* 42–61.

Stapel, D. A., Koomen, W., & van der Pligt, J. (1996). The referents of trait inferences: The impact of trait concepts versus actor-trait links on subsequent judgments. *Journal of Personality and Social Psychology, 70,* 437–450.

Stapel, D. A., Reicher, S. D., & Spears, R. (1995). Contextual determinants of strategic choice: Some moderators of the availability heuristic. *European Journal of Social Psychology, 25,* 141–158.

Stasser, G., & Titus, W. (1985). Pooling of unshared information in group decision making: Biased information sampling during discussion. *Journal of Personality and Social Psychology, 48,* 1467–1478.

Stepper, S., & Strack, F. (1993). Proprioceptive determinants of emotional and nonemotional feelings. *Journal of Personality and Social Psychology, 64,* 211–220.

Strack, F. (1988). Social Cognition: Sozialpsychologie innerhalb des Paradigmas der Informations verarbeitung. *Psychologische Rundschau, 39,* 72–82.

Strack, F. (1992). The different routes to social judgments: Experiential vs. informational strategies. In L. L. Martin & A. Tesser (Eds.), *The construction of social judgment* (pp. 249–275). Hillsdale, NJ: Lawrence Erlbaum Associates Inc.

Strack, F. (1994). Response processes in social judgment. In R. S. Wyer & T. K. Srull (Eds.), *Handbook of social cognition* (pp. 287–322). Hillsdale, NJ: Lawrence Erlbaum Associates Inc.

Strack, F., & Bless, H. (1994). Memory for nonoccurrences: Metacognitive and presuppositional strategies. *Journal of Memory and Language, 33,* 203–217.

Strack, F., Erber, R., & Wicklund, R. A. (1982). Effects of salience and time pressure on ratings of social causality. *Journal of Experimental Social Psychology, 18,* 581–594.

Strack, F., & Förster, J. (1998). Self-reflection and recognition: The role of metacognitive knowledge in the attribution of recollective experience. *Review of Personality and Social Psychology, 2,* 111–123.

Strack, F., & Gonzales, M. H. (1993). Wissen und Fühlen: Noetische und experientielle Grundlagen heuristischer Urteilsbildung. In W. Hell, K. Fiedler, & G. Gigerenzer (Eds.), *Kognitive Täuschungen. Fehl-Leistungen und Mechanismen des Urteilens, Denkens und Erinnerns* (pp. 291–315). Heidelberg, Germany: Spektrum Akademischer Verlag.

Strack, F., & Hannover, B. (1996). Awareness of influence as a precondition for implementing correctional goals. In P. Gollwitzer & J. A. Bargh (Eds.), *The psychology of action: Linking cognition and motivation to behavior* (pp. 579–595). New York: Guilford Press.

Strack, F., Martin, L. L., & Schwarz, N. (1988a). Priming and communication: Social determinants of information use in judgments of life satisfaction. *European Journal of Social Psychology, 18,* 429–442.

Strack, F., Martin, L. L., & Stepper, S. (1988b). Inhibiting and facilitating conditions of the human smile: A nonobtrusive test of the facial feedback hypothesis. *Journal of Personality and Social Psychology, 54,* 768–777.

Strack, F., & Mussweiler, T. (1997). Explaining the enigmatic anchoring effect: Mechanisms of selective accessibility. *Journal of Personality and Social Psychology, 73,* 437–446.

Strack, F., & Mussweiler, T. (2001). Resisting influence. Judgmental correction and its goals. In J. P. Forgas & K. D. Williams (Eds.), *Social influence. Direct and indirect processes* (pp. 199–212). Philadelphia, PA: Psychology Press.

Strack, F., & Neumann, R. (2000). Furrowing the brow may undermine perceived fame: The role of facial feedback in judgments of celebrity. *Personality and Social Psychology Bulletin, 26,* 762–768.

Strack, F., Schwarz, N., Bless, H., Kübler, A., & Wänke, M. (1993). Awareness of the influence as a determinant of assimilation vs. contrast. *European Journal of Experimental Social Psychology, 23,* 53–62.

Strack, F., Schwarz, N., & Gschneidinger, E. (1985). Happiness and reminiscing: The role of time perspective, affect, and mode of thinking. *Journal of Personality and Social Psychology, 49,* 1460–1469.

Strack, F., Schwarz, N., & Wänke, M. (1991). Semantic and pragmatic aspects of context effects in social and pychological research. *Social Cognition, 9,* 111–125.

Stroebe, W. (2000). *Social psychology and health.* Buckingham, UK: Open University Press.

Sudman, S. Bradburn, N. M., & Schwarz, N. (1996). *Thinking about anwers: The application of cognitive processes to survey methodology.* San Francisco: Jossey-Bass.

Swann, W. B., Giuliano, T., & Wegner, D. M. (1982). Where leading questions can lead: The power of conjecture in social interaction. *Journal of Personality and Social Psychology, 42,* 1025–1035.

Switzer, F. S., & Sniezek, J. A. (1991). Judgment processes in motivation: Anchoring and adjustment effects on judgment and behavior. *Organizational Behavior and Human Decision Processes, 49,* 208–229.

Tajfel, H. (1969). Cognitive aspects of prejudice. *Journal of Social Issues, 25,* 79–97.

Taylor, S. E., & Fiske, S. T. (1975). Point-of-view and perceptions of causality. *Journal of Personality and Social Psychology, 32,* 439–445.

Taylor, S. E., & Fiske, S. T. (1978). Salience, attention, and attribution: Top of the head phenomena. In L. Berkowitz (Ed.), *Advances in experimental social psychology* (Vol. 11, pp. 249–288). New York: Academic Press.

Tesser, A. (1978). Self-generated attitude change. In L. Berkowitz (Ed.), *Advances in experimental social psychology* (Vol. 11, pp. 289–338). New York: Academic Press.

Tetlock, P. E. (1992). The impact of accountability on judgment and choice: Toward a social contingency model. In M. P. Zanna (Ed.), *Advances in experimental social psychology* (Vol. 25, pp. 331–376). San Diego, CA: Academic Press.

Tetlock, P., Skitka, L., & Boettger, R. (1989). Social and cognitive strategies for coping with accountability: Conformity, complexity, and bolstering. *Journal of Personality and Social Psychology, 57*, 632–640.

Traud, G. R. (2000). Behavioral Finance und der Kurs des Euro. In H. Löchel (Ed.), *Finanzmärkte in Euroland: Funktionsbedingungen und Perspektiven* (pp. 139–153). Frankfurt, Germany: Bankakademie Verlag.

Trope, Y. (1986). Identification and inference processes in dispositional attribution. *Psychological Review, 93*, 239–257.

Trope, Y., & Bassok, M. (1983). Information-gathering strategies in hypothesis testing. *Journal of Personality and Social Psychology, 43*, 22–34.

Trope, Y., Cohen, O., & Maoz, Y. (1988). The perceptual and inferential effects of situational inducements on dispositional attributions. *Journal of Personality and Social Psychology, 55*, 165–177.

Tulving, E. (1983). *Elements of episodic memory*. London: Oxford University Press.

Tversky, A., & Kahneman, D. (1973). Availability: A heuristic for judging frequency and probability. *Cognitive Psychology, 5*, 207–232.

Tversky, A., & Kahneman, D. (1974). Judgment under uncertainty: Heuristics and biases. *Science, 185*, 1124–1131.

Tversky, A., & Kahneman, D. (1983). Extensional versus intensional reasoning: The conjunction fallacy in probability judgment. *Psychological Review, 90*, 293–315.

Tversky, A., & Koehler, D. J. (1994). Support theory: A nonextensional representation of subjective probability. *Psychological Review, 101*, 547–567.

Tversky, B., & Tuchin, M. (1989). A reconciliation of the evidence on eyewitness memory: Comments on McCloskey & Zaragoza (1985). *Journal of Experimental Psychology: General, 118*, 86–91.

Uleman, J. S., & Bargh, J. A. (Eds.) (1989). *Unintended thought*. New York: Guilford Press.

Vallacher, R. R., & Wegner, D. M. (1987). What do people think they're doing? Action identification and human behavior. *Psychological Review, 94*, 3–15.

Wagenaar, W. A., & Keren, G. B. (1988). Chance and luck are not the same. *Journal of Behavioral Decision Making, 1*, 65–75.

Wänke, M., & Bless, H. (2000). The effects of subjective ease of retrieval on attitudinal judgments: The moderating role of processing motivation. In H. Bless & J. P. Forgas (Eds.), *The message within: The role of subjective experience in social cognition and behavior* (pp. 143–161). Philadelphia, PA: Psychology Press.

Wänke, M., Bless, H., & Biller, B. (1996). Subjective experience versus content of information in the construction of attitude judgments. *Personality and Social Psychology Bulletin, 22*, 1105–1113.

Wänke, M., Bless, H., & Igou, E. R. (2001). Next to a star: Paling, shining, or both? Turning inter-exemplar contrast into inter-exemplar assimiliation. *Personality and Social Psychology, 27*, 14–29.

Wänke, M., Bohner, G., & Jurkowitsch, A. (1997). There are many reasons to drive a BMW: Does imagined ease of argument generation influence attitudes? *Journal of Consumer Research, 24*, 170–177.

Wänke, M., Schwarz, N., & Bless, H. (1995). The availability heuristic revisited: experienced ease of retrieval in mundane frequency estimates. *Acta Psychologica, 89*, 83–90.

Wason, P. C. (1966). Reasoning. In B. Foss (Ed.), *New horizons in psychology* (pp. 135–151). London: Penguin.

Watson, J. (1930). *Behaviorism*. New York: Norton.

Weber, R., & Crocker, J. (1983). Cognitive processes in the revision of stereotypic beliefs. *Journal of Personality and Social Psychology, 45*, 961–977.

Wegner, D. M. (1994). Ironic processes of mental control. *Psychological Review, 101*, 34–52.

Wegner, D. M., Wenzlaff, R., Kerker, R. M., & Beattie, A. E. (1981). Incrimination through innuendo: Can media questions become public answers. *Journal of Personality and Social Psychology, 40*, 822–832.

Wegener, D. T., & Petty, R. E. (1994). Mood management across affective states: The hedonic contingency hypothesis. *Journal of Personality and Social Psychology, 66*, 1034–1048.

Wegener, D. T., & Petty, R. E. (1997). The flexible correction model: The role of naïve theories of bias in bias correction. In M. P. Zanna (Ed.), *Advances in experimental social psychology* (Vol. 29, pp. 141–208). Mahwah, NJ: Lawrence Erlbaum Associates Inc.

Weinstein, N. D. (1980). Unrealistic optimism about future life events. *Journal of Personality and Social Psychology, 39*, 806–820.

Wertheimer, M. (1945). *Productive thinking*. New York: Harper.

Whyte, G., & Sebenius, J. K. (1997). The effect of multiple anchors on anchoring in individual and group judgment. *Organizational Behavior and Human Decision Processes, 69*, 75–85.

Wigboldus, D. H. J., Semin, G. R., & Spears, R. (2000). How do we communicate stereotypes? Linguistic bases and inferential consequences. *Journal of Personality and Social Psychology, 78*, 5–18.

Wilson, T. D., Lisle, D. J., & Schooler, J. W. (1993). Introspecting about reasons can reduce post-choice satisfaction. *Personality and Social Psychology Bulletin, 19*, 331–339.

Wilson, T. D., & Brekke, N. (1994). Mental contamination and mental correction: Unwanted influences on judgments and evaluations. *Psychological Bulletin, 116*, 117–142.

Wilson, T. D., Dunn, D. S., & Kraft, D. (1989). Introspection, attitude change, and attitude-behavior consistency: The disruptive effects of explaining why we feel the way we do. In L. Berkowitz (Ed.), *Advances in experimental social psychology* (Vol. 22, pp. 287–343), San Diego, CA: Academic Press.

Wilson, T. D., Houston, C., Etling, K. M., & Brekke, N. (1996). A new look at anchoring effects: Basic anchoring and its antecedents. *Journal of Experimental Psychology: General, 125*, 387–402.

Wyer, R. S., & Srull, T. K. (1989). *Memory and cognition in its social context*. Hillsdale, NJ: Lawrence Erlbaum Associates Inc.

Yates, J. F., & Carlson, B. W. (1986). Conjunction errors: Evidence for multiple judgment procedures, including "signed summation." *Organizational Behavior and Human Decision Processes, 37*, 230–253.

Zajonc, R. B. (1984). On the primacy of affect. *American Psychologist, 39*, 117–123.

Zuckerman, M., Knee, C. R., Hodgins, H. S., & Miyake, K. (1995). Hypothesis confirmation: The joint effect of positive test strategy and acquiescence response set. *Journal of Personality and Social Psychology, 68*, 52–60.

Author index

Abele, A., 190
Abelson, R.P., 3
Abramson, L.Y., 200
Ajzen, I., 48
Anderson, C.A., 147
Anderson, J.R., 181
Anderson, N.H., 45, 121
Arcuri, L., 172–174
Armbruster, T., 169
Aronson, E., 3
Asbeck, J., 169
Ash, S.E., 84

Banaji, M.R., 76, 77, 79
Bargh, J.A., 26, 34, 65, 75, 76, 82, 122–124, 133
Bar-Hillel, M., 97
Baron, R., 33
Barsalou, L.W., 57
Bar-Tal, D.,
Bartlett, F.C., 119, 137
Barzvi, A., 166
Bassok, M., 151
Beattie, A.E., 147
Bem, D.J., 120
Benton, S.L., 35
Berry, D.S., 54
Berscheid, E., 32
Betsch, T., 97
Biller, B., 92, 93
Blair, I.V., 76, 77
Bless, H., 21, 34, 74, 75, 80, 90, 92, 93, 106, 107, 110, 114, 123, 125–127, 129,

131–134, 137–139, 165, 180, 185, 187–192, 194
Block, R.A., 99
Bodenhausen, G.V., 21, 24, 45, 67, 109, 126, 133, 135, 165, 180, 188–190, 194, 197
Boettger, R., 135
Bohner, G., 3, 91, 93, 108, 166, 190, 191, 194
Boring, E.G., 8
Bornstein, B.H., 103
Bower, G.H., 63, 181–184, 186
Boyes-Braem, P., 56
Bradburn, N.M., 200
Brekke, N., 99, 100, 122
Brewer, M.B., 21, 109
Broadbent, D.E., 30
Brown, J., 106, 120, 122–124, 185
Brown, R., 26, 34, 77 79, 156
Bruner, J.S., 9, 12, 32, 36, 119
Buehler, R., 95, 112
Burrows, L., 65, 76

Cacioppo, J.T., 5, 26, 45, 80, 108, 134, 136, 137, 190
Campbell, L., 92
Cantor, N.E., 57
Carlson, B.W., 111

Carlston, D.E., 41, 46
Carrera, P., 126
Cervone, D., 103
Chaiken, S., 26, 45, 48, 105, 108, 114, 116, 190
Chapman, G.B., 103
Chater, N., 151
Chen, M., 65, 76
Chen, S., 105, 108
Clark, H.H., 129, 130
Clore, G.L., 105, 106, 108, 120, 180, 183–186, 188, 191, 193, 194, 197
Cohen, O., 121
Combs, B., 92
Conway, M., 105, 180, 183, 184, 188, 197
Corneille, O., 103
Corvino, P., 174
Cosmides, L., 12, 13, 111, 112
Craik, F.I.M., 35, 139
Crelia, R., 74, 121, 122, 136
Crocker, J., 21, 126, 165
Crow, K., 191

Dalla, M., 106
Dardenne, B., 178
Darley, J.M., 124
Davies, M.F., 93
Davis, K.E., 4, 119
De Poot, C.J., 155
De Vries, N., 126
Denes-Ray, V., 97

Subject index

Abstractness 55, 172–173, 175–176
Accessibility 37–38, 60–61, 101–102, 121, 129–130, 166–168, 180–181, 183
Accountability 135
Acquiescence 153–154, 157, 158
Affective states 179–197
Affective and nonaffective feelings 87
Affective feelings 105, 106, *see also* affect
Amount of processing 11, 25, 27, 32–33, 35, 134, 187
Anchoring 101–102
Anchoring and adjustment 86, 98–99, 102, 117
Anchoring effect 99–103, 113, 115
Anchoring heuristic 111, 115, 172
Applicability 37–38, 60, 102, 127
Assimilation effect 73, 75, 93, 99, 120, 126–127, 133, 136, 141
Associative network 53, 55–56, 58–60, 80–81, 181, 182
Attention 29–36, 40, 42, 71–72
Attribution 4, 43, 93, 119, 185
Automatic processes 20, 26–28, 65, 76, 183
Automaticity 33
Availability 60, 167
  availability heuristic 46–47, 86–89, 92–93, 112–115, 117
  availability influences 89
Awareness 26–28, 34, 75, 106, 122, 125, 133, 137

Balance theory 58
Base rate 95, 110, 112, 132

Behaviourism 6
Bias 59–60, 73–74, 85, 116
Bottom-up processes 20–21, 23–24, 52, 71, 188, 194

Category 36–39, 52–54, 57, 60, 64, 69, 81
Cognitive consistency 57–58
Cognitive map 53, 55
Cognitive miser 5, 14, 113
Communication 47, 109, 128, 172, 174
Communication contract 156
Concept-driven processing 21, *see also* top-down processing
Confirmation 147, 149, 152–154, 156–160, 163
Confirmation bias 146, 148, 151, 163
Conjunction effect 97, 110–112
Conjunction error 97
Consistency seeker 3, 14
Constructive memory 51, 166, 168–170
Contamination 122, 140–141
Context dependency 7, 8, 23
Contrast effect 73–75, 124, 126–127, 133, 136, 141
Controllability 33
Controlled processes 20, 26–28, 65, 76, 183
Conversational norms 132–133, *see also* communication contract
Cooperation principle 128–130, 155
Cooperative communication 154–156, 158, 175
Correction effect 73, 115, 140

Cue 85, 106
  heuristic 87, 89, 104, 116
  peripheral 190–191
  proximal 9

Data-driven processing 21, *see also* bottom-up processing
Decision 19, 43–44, 171
Demand characteristics 169
Diagnosticity 152
Diagnosticity of information 46
Dissonance theory 3

Ease of retrieval 24, 87–92, 106, 114, 125, 134, 185
Egocentric bias 167
Elaboration 69
Elaboration likelihood model (ELM) 108
Encoding 18, 20–21, 23, 35–39, 69, 71, 162–163, 181–182
Exemplar 53, 56–57, 59, 126
Expectancy 30–32, 54, 72, 150, 162–164, 175
  expectancy-consistent information 72
  expectancy-inconsistent information 72

Feelings 66, 104, 135
Feeling of ease of retrieval 106
Feeling of effort 106
Feeling of familiarity 106, 122–123, 185
Feeling of knowing 114
Frequency 38–39, 45, 87–88, 92, 95, 112, 161
Fundamental attribution error 43, 103, 121

Gambler's fallacy 98
Gestalt theory 6, 57
Guessing 169–170

Heuristic systematic model (HSM) 108
Heuristic 24, 45–47, 83–86, 105–106, 108–109, 116–117, 121, 186, 191
  heuristic cues 87, 89, 104, 116
  heuristic stimuli 85
Hindsight bias 103
Hypothesis-testing 100–101, 145, 146, 148, 152, 156–157, 160–161, 163, 166, 172

Ideal type 57
Illusory correlation 160–161

Implicit association test (IAT) 79–80
Impression set 40
Inclusion/exclusion model 74–75, 132
Inference 19
Information search 148–152, 158, 161–163, 172
In-group 57, 173–176, 188, 190, *see also* out-group
Intrusion error 42, 72
Intuitive scientist 86, *see also* lay scientist

Judgment formation 120–121
Judgment strategies 85
Judgment 9, 19–21, 23–24, 33–34, 37, 40, 42–45, 171, 184–185
  memory-based judgment 171–172
  online judgment 171–172
Judgmental distortion 85, 113
Judgmental heuristic 83–86, 104, 113–115
Judgmental scale 85

Knowledge structures 53–55, 60, 67–68, 70, 72

Lay scientist 4, 14, *see also* intuitive scientist
Legal judgments 103
Linguistic category model (LCM) 173
Linguistic intergroup bias (LIB) 172–174, 176

Memory 18–20, 26, 51, 59–60, 181
  memory organization 51
  memory representation 169
  memory retrieval 59
  memory set 40
Mood 63, 105, 114, 179–197, *see also* affective states
Mood-as-information 184–185
Mood-congruency 182–184
Mood-congruent recall 182, 187
Mood-dependent accessibility 181
Motivated search 152
Motivated tactician 5, 15, 113
Motoric feelings 107

Need for cognition 136–137
Nonaffective feelings 106

Optical illusions 83
Out-group 57, 173–174, 176, 188, 190, *see also* in-group

Perception 29, 84, 162–163
Person perception 21, 26, 36, 108–109, 188
Persuasion 108, 190, 192
Positive testing 101, 151, 154
Presupposition 150–151
Priming 38–39, 60–62, 64–66, 75, 77–78, 81, 122–124
  action priming 65–66, 76, 81
  analogy priming 64
  associative priming 65
  evaluative priming 63, 81
  mood priming 63, 81
  procedural priming 66, 81
  semantic priming 63, 81, 100, 102
  valence priming 62
Probability 87, 94–95, 98, 111
Processing capacity 19, 23–26, 29, 39, 45, 57, 109, 114, 134, 193–194
Processing motivation 26, 39, 109, 134, 193–194
Prototype 57, 132

Recall 34–35, 42, 69, 71, 167, 181
Recency 38–39, 45, 120
Regulation of judgments 120
Representativeness 94–96, 111, 123, 125, 133, 142, 186
Representativeness heuristic 86, 94–97, 106, 111, 117, 132
Retrieval 18, 20–21, 23, 35, 37, 39, 40, 42, 47, 51, 59, 162, 182
  retrieval cue 59, 89
  retrieval structure 166, 170
Rules of thumb 24, 83, 85, 117

Salience 30, 31, 33–35
Satisficing 121
Schema 53–54, 56, 60, 71, 81, 119
Script 53–54, 60, 71, 81, 191, 194
Selective accessibility 61, 66, 111

Selective accessibility model (SAM) 100–102, 111
Selective attention 147
Selective recall 171
Selective retrieval 166
Self 11, 68–70, 81
  self knowledge 137
  self-reference 167
  self-reference effect 68–69
Self-fulfilling prophecy 153
Semantic memory 59
Shared information 172
Shared-information effect 176–177
Social contracts 12
Social norms 48
Standard of comparison 75, 133, 141
State-dependency hypothesis 182–183
Stereotype 18, 21, 24, 36–37, 45, 53–54, 56, 63, 76, 78–79, 80–81, 108, 135, 188–189, 191
Stereotype change 126
Stereotype inhibition 67
Stimulus-onset asynchrony (SOA) 62–63, 76–77
Storage 20, 23, 37, 39–41
Subjective experience 105, 117, 125, 142
Subtyping 165–166
Support theory 116

Task understanding 109–110
Theory of probability 96
Top-down processes 20–21, 23–24, 71, 187, 193–194, *see also* concept-driven processing
Truncated search process 39, 45–46, 52, 60
Typicality 125–126, 133

Unrealistic optimism 165

Verification effect 162–163
Verification tendency 147, 150

Wason selection task 12–13
Working memory 21–23